scraptherapy®

THE VERSATILE
Nine Patch

18 fresh designs for a favorite quilt block

Joan Ford

The Taunton Press

Text © 2017 by John Ford

Photographs by Burcu Avsar © 2017; Helen Norman © 2017; photographs by
Scott Phillips © 2017 by The Taunton Press, Inc.

Illustrations © 2017 by The Taunton Press, Inc.

The Taunton Press
Inspiration for hands-on living®

The Taunton Press, Inc., 63 South Main Street, PO Box 5506, Newtown, CT 06470-5506
Email:tp@taunton.com

Editor: Carolyn Mandarano
Technical Editor: April Mohr
Copy Editor: Betty Christiansen
Indexer: Heidi Blough
Jacket/Cover design: Rita Sowins / Sowins Design
Interior and Layout design: Rita Sowins / Sowins Design
Photographers: Burcu Avsar: pp. 30, 31, 36, 38, 205–208, 211 (right), 212, 213;
Helen Norman: pp. iv, 1, 2, 5, 12 (left), 16, 42–44, 54, 62, 66, 70, 80, 92, 100, 110, 126, 134,
140, 148, 158, 162, 176, 185, 192; Scott Phillips: pp. 6, 7, 10, 11, 12 (top and bottom right),
13–15, 18–24, 26–28, 33–35, 37, 38 (right), 41, 53, 68, 77, 91, 108, 109, 144, 157, 160, 189,
210, 211 (left and center)

The following names/manufacturers appearing in *ScrapTherapy*® *The Versatile
Nine Patch* are trademarks: Pigma®, Qtools™, Quiltsmart®, ScrapTherapy®, ZigZapps!™

Library of Congress Cataloging-in-Publication Data

Names: Ford, Joan, 1961- author.
Title: Scraptherapy the versatile nine patch : 18 fresh designs for a
    favorite quilt block / Joan Ford.
Description: Newtown, CT : The Taunton Press, Inc., 2017. | Includes index.
Identifiers: LCCN 2016051530 | ISBN 9781631866753
Subjects: LCSH: Patchwork--Patterns. | Quilting--Patterns. | Nine patch
    quilts.
Classification: LCC TT835 .F6676 2017 | DDC 746.46--dc23
LC record available at https://lccn.loc.gov/2016051530

Printed in the United States of America
10 9 8 7 6 5 4 3 2 1

Every small business hits a bump in the road from time to time. Mine has, several times. And sometimes it takes someone outside of the business to recognize that the problem isn't the business, but rather the person in charge. Shelly Stokes, thanks for prompting me not once, but several times over the years, to move my business—and me—in new, better directions. Quilty hugs to you!

Acknowledgments

Like making a scrappy quilt, writing a book of quilt patterns and instructions can be a fantastic, joyful journey with many twists and turns.

To make a cherished quilt, you start with an idea or pattern, then add fabrics, colors, tools, techniques, and advice from your closest quilty co-conspirators. After hours, weeks, or months of persistent and careful work—and a little bit of backward sewing along with a few late-night sewing sessions—the resulting quilted project is ready to provide comfort, decorate a table, or tote fresh veggies from the market.

Quilting can be a very social or very solitary process, but when you really think about it, even if you're working alone in your quilt studio, the quilt is a collaboration of fabric designs, techniques you've learned from others along the way, and honed skills from quilters who have passed on their talents and experiences. Many hands, hearts, and minds are always in the mix.

Likewise, this book has a whole team of expertise as its foundation. It simply wouldn't exist without the amazing talents at The Taunton Press. About a million (or so it seems) layers of editors with sharp eyes and fine-tuned grammar skills review text, photos, and illustrations. Photographers, stylists, and graphic artists whose skills with color, shape, and computer image graphics are mind-blowing. A sales team that makes sure this book is where you can find it, buy it, and use it.

I extend special thanks to Maria, Rosalind, Lynne, Scott, Helen, John, and all the other behind-the-scenes staff whose names I'll never know but whose talents are very much integrated within these pages. And the hugest whopping heaps of gratitude to Carolyn, my amazing editor, who followed the entire process from concept to the book in your hands with insanely innovative ideas and suggestions as well as the patience of a saint as deadlines approached and were amended to accommodate my sometimes nutty schedule.

To Mattie at Quiltsmart®, who patiently revised several variations of detailed art to make sure the ScrapTherapy® Mini, Middle, and Little Scrap Grid interfacings were just right, hugs and thanks abound.

And of course, the book is nothing if it isn't read and used to make cherished quilty memories from scrappy bits of blissfully hoarded cloth pieces. Thank you for reading, sewing, furling, and quilting.

Contents

Introduction   2

Techniques for Making a 9-Patch

CHAPTER 1
WHAT IS A 9-PATCH?   6

CHAPTER 2
USING THE 9-PATCH INTERFACING   16

CHAPTER 3
THE SEVEN STEPS REVISITED   28

The Projects

Moody Blue   44

Button Collection Pillow   54

Daisy Fresh Runner   62

Fiesta!   69

Pomegranate Rose Table Topper   79

Mix 'n' Match Mug Mats   92

Split the Check   100

Cross-Body Market Sack   110

Bolster Pillow   125

Beetle Mania   133

Citrus Coverlet   140

Elsa's Prayer Quilt   147

Sneaky Peek Project Pouches   162

Argyle Dreams   176

Laptop Sleeve   191

Appendix 1: Quiltmaking Basics   204
Appendix 2: Quilting 101   209
Glossary   214
Resources   217
Metric Equivalents   217
Index   218

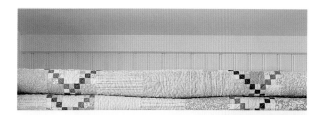

Introduction

As I've stated many times, February 8, 2003, marks my first quilting class. On that day, I'm fairly certain that the first quilt block I made was a 4-patch. I think this may be precisely where most new quilters—not just me—start their quilting journey. Strips of fabric sewn together, then crosscut and sewn again. Nothing magical about any of that. It's just following steps.

However, once that second seam is sewn, a block is born—a real bona fide quilt block. You don't quite know what the block looks like yet because the fabrics were placed right sides together to be sewn. But you slip your thumb in between the layers at the block's edge and open to reveal the pretty sides of the four different fabric pieces now joined together as one.

This is the aha moment, the moment you've been anticipating from the day you selected the fabrics and tools for this very first taste of your new quilting hobby.

The prints and colors of the fabrics you selected and cut, the straight seams, and the crisp intersection in the middle tell you that you are now a quilter. Doesn't matter that the seams aren't *really* perfectly straight, or that the center doesn't *quite* come together in an exact intersection of two seam-lines, or that the fabric prints don't *necessarily* go together as well as you thought they would. The block is yours alone, a product of your creation, and it's perfect. And magical.

Suddenly, you find that you are hungry for more. More colors, more patterns, more challenges. Add triangles, and the 4-patch becomes pinwheels, broken dishes, or pairs of geese: blocks with names that tease the imagination and whet the appetite for even more.

Enter the 9-patch block. More fabric pieces, more seams, and more challenge—but not too much. A 9-patch block is easy enough for a beginner, but it's satisfying for the more experienced sewist. And the options. Where the world of 4-patches can seem limiting, in contrast, the 9-patch—three rows of three elements—creates tons of new territory to explore.

The 9-patch block has a fabric center and different opportunities for symmetry than the 4-patch. The middle of the block connects the pieces that surround it. Friendship and Ohio stars, bear paws, tea leaves, and shoo-fly are among the many, many classic blocks, as well as all their variations, derived from the basic 9-patch formation.

Tiny 9-patch blocks can fascinate in miniature quilts. The same tiny 9-patch in a pincushion shows off piecing prowess in small spaces. Large 9-patches display splashes of color for a fast and easy contemporary quilted throw. Giant 9-patches turn a plain quilt backing into something special.

For me, the 9-patch block and all its derivations represent comfort. It's a sure thing. Doll it up or dress it down, that three-by-three combination feels safe, steady, and grounded.

The ScrapTherapy process has always swirled around cutting, storing, and using 2-in., 3½-in., and 5-in. scrap fabric squares—leftover bits from beloved finished quilt projects. The 3½-in. scrap square size came about because the 2-in. square, when sewn into a 4-patch, measures 3½ in. square. Coincidentally—or maybe not—2-in. scraps can be sewn into a 9-patch that measures 5 in. square, the same as the largest of the three ScrapTherapy scrap sizes.

Making 9-patches work with scraps seems to have become an obsession (the good kind!) in my sewing studio since an online 9-patch challenge several summers ago led to the "99 Bottles" quilt—a quilt that I originally made for the "fun" of it. That quilt, featured on the cover of *ScrapTherapy: Scraps Plus One!*, and its popularity, helped me see that I'm not the only quilter fascinated by the 9-patch block.

The development and introduction of three Scrap-Therapy 9-patch grid interfacing products followed suit, and all three of the original ScrapTherapy scrap sizes could be represented along with 9-patches in sizes to match. More information about the Mini, Middle, and Little Scrap Grid interfacing products and their benefits is found in chapter 2 and within some of the projects. After working with these printed interfacing products rather obsessively for the last couple of years, I'm thrilled to be able to share and document information within these pages about the stability they add to smaller scrap pieces and their role in fundamental 9-patch quilt construction.

It is my hope that in the text and projects that follow, you'll reignite those magical moments from your first few quilt blocks, regardless of whether those moments happened last week, last year, or many years ago.

NAVIGATING THE PROJECTS

The projects that make up the second half of the book are identified by how the 9-patch blocks in the project have been constructed or manipulated. Since quilting and hard-and-fast rules really don't go together well, some projects involve more than one "category" of 9-patch block. The 9-patches for the projects in this book generally fall into one of the five categories described here. You'll find the category next to the project head.

THE BASIC 9-PATCH

Three by three—three rows of three squares. Simple.

Straight set, on-point set, alternate with sashing or solid blocks. Variety rules! Basic 9-patches are simple enough for a novice quilter, yet interesting enough to keep an experienced quilter stimulated.

THE TRANSFORMED 9-PATCH

Now you see it . . . now you don't. Nine equal squares sewn into three rows of three squares. Assuming consistent seam allowances and proper pressing techniques have been applied, the resulting 9-patch block is a larger square. All is in its place, and everything is orderly and mathematically precise, until . . . Slash! Chop! Trim! Cut a little bit off here or there. Chop it through the center. Cover it with a different shape. Sew it back together, and it seems like our 9-patch friend has made an exit. Not to worry, it's still there—it's simply transformed.

THE ELEVATED 9-PATCH

Start with the basic 9-patch block, three by three. Replace some or all of the squares in the basic block arrangement with something else—a half-square triangle unit, a 2-patch, 4-patch, on-point square, or some other element. Oh, the places your 9-patch will go! The patterns, the secondary patterns, the possibilities explode. Suddenly the simple 9-patch is elevated to something new, but still familiar. You've upped the game a bit with an elevated 9-patch project.

THE NESTED 9-PATCH

9-patches within 9-patches. Start with the Scrap-Therapy scrap square sizes—2-in., 3½-in., and 5-in. squares. 4-patches made from 2-in. squares measure 3½ in. 9-patches made from 2-in. squares measure 5 in. square. The three sizes play nicely together. With a little planning, little 9-patches fit nicely within larger 9-patches, which, in turn, fit within even larger 9-patch blocks, a lot like the nested Russian matryoshka dolls. Yet another realm of possibilities awakens, leading to all kinds of scrap fabric busting!

THE HIDDEN 9-PATCH

I'm sure you've heard this saying before: If it walks like a duck and quacks like a duck, then it's a duck. Unfortunately, 9-patch blocks don't quack. To my knowledge, they don't make any noise at all. Without the audible clues for reference, it's probably fair to conclude that if it looks like a 9-patch, then it's a 9-patch. But if it doesn't look like a 9-patch, is it still a 9-patch? The projects in this category will answer these philosophical questions and so much more . . . or not. If nothing else, it's another twist on the 9-patch journey.

MATERIALS AND SUPPLIES

Each pattern in this book begins with charts that detail the amount of scraps, yardage, and other materials needed for that project. Quantities needed for one, two, or all three of the ScrapTherapy scrap sizes—2-in., 3½-in., and 5-in. squares—are highlighted so you have an idea at a glance of the quantity of cut scrap inventory you'll need for the project. Cutting and trimming instructions are provided as well. This is particularly helpful if you are cutting for the project instead of digging into precut scrap storage bins to avoid potential fabric waste as you select and trim your scraps for the project.

Fabric needs in yardage are listed to help you plan and create a cohesive project with swaths of focus prints, solid colors, or neutrals to relax the eye from the onslaught of scrappy color.

COLOR, VALUE, AND SIMPLICITY

Some of the projects rely on color instead of value (dark, medium, and light) descriptions for easy reference to the project photos and illustrations. Clearly, the colors you choose for your projects will reflect the scrap fabrics and yardage in your stash and in the décor for which the project is intended. For some projects, I've provided alternative colorways to help you envision more possibilities. By all means, use the color references as a suggested road map, with lots of alternate routes.

To keep the illustrations clear, some may have been simplified in terms of the scrap coloration to maintain the focus on the steps in the process rather than on the more scrappy appearance of your resulting quilt.

Unless otherwise noted, seams should be sewn using a scant ¼-in. seam throughout all the patterns. For more information on making and recognizing a scant ¼-in. seam, see the additional information on pp. 37–38. Seam pressing direction is shown on the illustrations with small arrows near or crossing over seam intersection lines.

CHAPTER 1
What Is a 9-Patch?

The 9-patch block is a traditional block, a favorite among quilters. The traditional 9-patch usually starts with two high-contrast fabrics cut into squares. Nine squares are arranged into three rows of three squares. Sew, press the seams, and voilà—a basic, traditional 9-patch quilt block is born.

End of story, right? Not even close!

The basic 9-patch is the perfect block for twisting, turning, and creating something that looks completely different. Replace one or more of the 9-patch elements with pieced elements like half-square triangles or 4-patches. Make the 9-patch, then cut it up, and sew it together again. Combine multiple 9-patches for a bigger impact. Take any of these detours, and you have so much more than a basic, traditional 9-patch block!

The projects in this book all use some form of a 9-patch. I identified them based on the end result of the block in the quilted project—the 9-patch transformed, the elevated 9-patch, the nested 9-patch, the hidden 9-patch. You'll find details about these types of 9-patches on pp. 4–5.

Before delving into that exploration, however, let's begin with some common language and definitions that will be referenced throughout this book. Use this information as a road map as you quilt your way through the projects.

THE TRADITIONAL 9-PATCH
PARTS AND PIECES

To me, 9-patch means the same thing as 9-patch block—three rows of three units sewn together with seams pressed alternately (more on that in a bit). For the conversation taking place in this book, each position on the three-by-three grid is identified by name: center, corner, and side. A traditional 9-patch is square, and it has nine equally sized square elements: a center, four sides, and four corners. **1**

1

Center

Obvious, right? The center—the element in the middle—is the only element that touches each of the remaining elements of the block, even if only at its corner points. The center shares a seam with each of the sides, and it shares one intersecting point where it touches each corner. Each of those points is a seam intersection.

Let's say you come across an unfinished 9-patch block in your stash (a block that hasn't been sewn next to anything else yet). The center is the only element of the 9-patch that doesn't require any quilty math (add or subtract ¼ in. for seam allowances) to determine its measured, finished size. Assuming seams were sewn accurately, all you need is a ruler. The sewn center of the 9-patch is sewn into the block on all four of its sides.

Corner

I define the 9-patch element that shares only the seam-intersecting point with the center as the corner of the block. Each basic 9-patch block has four corners.

Sides

Perhaps this element isn't as obvious as the others. Each 9-patch side shares a seam with the center, and each side is sewn comfortably between two corners.

SIZE MATTERS

The easiest way to determine the unfinished size of a traditional 9-patch is to measure the center square, multiply it by three, then subtract ½ in. for seam allowances. Conversely, if you know the finished size of the

Cut Size of Squares	Finished Size of Squares	Unfinished 9-Patch	Finished 9-Patch
1"	½"	2"	1½"
1¼"	¾"	2¾"	2¼"
1½"	1"	3½"	3"
1¾"	1¼"	4¼"	3¾"
2"	1½"	5"	4½"
2¼"	1¾"	5¾"	5¼"
2½"	2"	6½"	6"
2¾"	2¼"	7¼"	6¾"
3"	2½"	8"	7½"
3¼"	2¾"	8¾"	8¼"
3½"	3"	9½"	9"
3¾"	3¼"	10¼"	9¾"
4"	3½"	11"	10½"
4¼"	3¾"	11¾"	11¼"
4½"	4"	12½"	12"
4¾"	4¼"	13¼"	12¾"
5"	4½"	14"	13½"

9-patch block, divide it by three and then add ½ in. to determine the size to make each block element.

For example, if you have a finished 12-in. 9-patch block, divide 12 by 3, and the result is 4. Add ½ in. for seam allowances, and each of the unfinished elements needs to be 4½ in.

Follow the simple chart on the facing page to work backward and forward to determine common traditional 9-patch sizes and the size of the squares to create them.

For a one-page downloadable version of this chart, visit http://hummingbird-highway.com/9chart/

Of course, there are lots of size options in between these dimensions, but the math starts to get pretty strange, and the measurements involve using ⅛-in. (or smaller) markings on the ruler to cut the 9-patch elements.

Why does the math get weird? Let's say you want to make an 8-in. finished 9-patch block. When you divide 8 in. (the finished size of the block) by 3, the result is $2\frac{2}{3}$ in. The imperial measurement system (inches, feet, and yards) doesn't handle thirds very well, so a possible solution would be to select a finished size from the chart that is less than 8 in. and add borders or sashing elements to the block to upsize it—just one example of about a million ways to get creative when building your 9-patch universe of quilts!

HOW MANY SCRAP SQUARES CAN YOU GET FROM A SCRAP?

ONE 2-IN. SQUARE YIELDS:
- Four 1-in. squares
- One 1½-in. square

ONE 3½-IN. SQUARE YIELDS:
- Nine 1-in. squares
- Four 1½-in. squares
- One 2-in. square plus three 1½-in. squares
- One 2½-in. square plus five 1-in. squares
- One 3-in. square

ONE 5-IN. SQUARE YIELDS:
- Twenty-five 1-in. squares
- Nine 1½-in. squares
- Four 2-in. squares
- Four 2½-in. squares
- One 3½-in. square plus five 1½-in. squares

Sewing small scrap squares—by small, I mean anything smaller than 2 in.—is a challenge in and of itself. Making seam allowances consistent is key to keep the end result out of wonky-ville. Color, value, and scale should be considered, particularly when smaller fabric pieces are involved.

Imagine a floral print with big white flowers on a blue background. Overall, the fabric reads medium value or tone. Now imagine that you've cut that square into smaller pieces, and the white flower now covers the entire small scrap, changing the value of the scrap from medium to light.

Be careful to select fabrics, especially in smaller sizes like 1 in. or 1½ in. square, that read solid and have only the smallest of prints.

RECTANGULAR 9-PATCH BLOCK ELEMENTS

9-patch block elements don't have to be square. An elongated 9-patch is still a 9-patch, but it has a larger square center, four smaller square corners, and rectangular sides. **2** Measurement calculations change significantly for this type of 9-patch. To calculate its finished size, determine the finished width of the center, then add two times the finished width of the corners (assuming the corners are the same size). Add ½ in. to the sum to determine the unfinished block size. There is no real standard for an elongated 9-patch; for example, sometimes the corners are half the finished size of the center, but not always. You can't depend on a chart or process for the size calculations for the block parts.

Another exception is 9-patch blocks that are some other shape, like a rectangle. The corners, sides, and centers may be different dimensions, lengths, and widths. So the predictability factor of the block size based on the size of the parts doesn't follow a standard pattern.

Other variations include 9-patch blocks with curved edges or angles other than 90 degrees. With so many options to explore just within the basic parameters of a square 9-patch block, for this book, we'll stick to 9-patch blocks with square or rectangular centers, corners, and sides.

TRADITIONAL 9-PATCH VARIATIONS
DARK/LIGHT CENTERS AND CORNERS

Let's define some common variations.

Dark centers and corners. I use this term for a traditional 9-patch made with five dark-value fabrics and four light-value fabrics. The dark-value center and corners alternate with light-value sides. **3A**

Light centers and corners. A traditional 9-patch made with five light-value fabrics and four dark-value fabrics. The light-value center and corners alternate with dark-value sides. **3B**

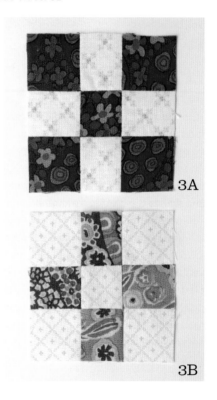

Make a bunch of 9-patch blocks, half of them with dark-value centers and corners and half of them with light-value centers and corners. Then arrange them in rows while alternating blocks with dark-value centers and corners and blocks with light-value centers and corners. Sew the blocks into rows, then sew the rows together, and you have a checkerboard quilt. **4**

Now, take a bunch of 9-patches with dark-value centers and corners and pair them with a bunch of light-value fabric squares that are the same size as the

4

9-patch. Place the 9-patches and fabric squares in an alternating arrangement; sew the blocks into rows, then sew the rows together, and you have an Irish chain quilt.

Similarly, pair 9-patch blocks that have light-value centers and corners with dark-value fabric squares that are the same size as the blocks. Arrange them alternately, and sew. Now, you have an Irish chain quilt in a flipped-value arrangement, much like the center of the "Daisy Fresh Runner" on p. 63.

Add some appliqué or embroidery in the fabric squares in between the 9-patch, and suddenly a basic 9-patch quilt has been transformed into an elegant heirloom quilt—or a fun picnic quilt such as "Beetle Mania" on p. 133.

CROSSING THE LINE

Xs and Os. Squint at a 9-patch with dark-value centers and corners—can you see an X? Look away, blink a couple times, and maybe you'll see a light-value O. The placement of fabrics with strong colors in the block positions can create the illusion of lines, crossed lines, and circles. Expand the possibilities by placing 9-patches side by side with contrasting fabrics in corners, centers, and sides, and shapes, letters, or numbers magically appear. By the way, the O is harder to spot than the X, especially before the 9-patch is sewn into its place in a quilt. It almost looks more like plus sign with a hole in it.

Speaking of **plus signs,** take a 9-patch with centers and corners that are in high contrast to the sides, and replace the center with one that matches the value of the sides, and you have a plus sign (+). Set the plus block on point, and we're back to an X. **5**

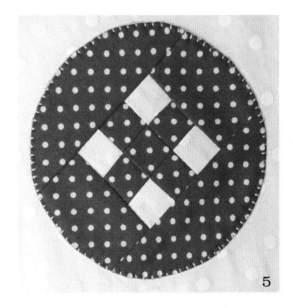

5

Draw the line. Do you prefer lines over Xs? Place a high-contrast fabric in the center and in two opposite corners for a diagonal line impact. When you want your diagonal lines to turn a corner, place a high-contrast square in the center and in two adjacent corners. You'll see both of these used very effectively in "Argyle Dreams" on p. 176.

A single high-contrast square in the center of a 9-patch can resemble a **dot.** Squares in opposite sides of two opposite corners can have a similar impact. Scraps of similar color or value placed in vertical rows mimic a stripe, as was done with the 9-patches in the pocket and main panel of the "Cross-Body Market Sack" on p. 110.

Blend. 9-patch blocks can also represent a mass of a single color, eating up smaller scrap squares in a hurry as larger blocks are assembled from smaller fabric squares. Blocks made from scraps of a similar color appear to be a larger, more interesting version of that color. Blended 9-patches—9-patch blocks made from a playful arrangement of scraps of every color, value, and scale without preference to placement within the block—are the building blocks of a postage stamp quilt. Little bits of varied, blended fabric scraps sewn into long rows that are then sewn together to become a border. Instead, sew those scraps into blended 9-patches for a gradual construction process, breaking the long rows of sewn pieces into smaller, doable, measurable 9-patch chunks. The pieced border from "Argyle Dreams" followed this method. **6**

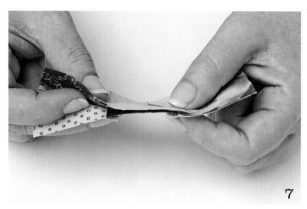

7

6

INNIES, OUTIES, AND FURLS, OH MY!

So far, we've discovered that the 9-patch block can have many faces. Behind the block, almost as many variations can be hiding in the pressing configuration.

For the traditional 9-patch with either dark-value center and corners or light-value center and corners, seams are typically pressed toward the darker fabric. To join the rows, the seams nest and oppose at each intersection. **7**

Within the rows, it's easy to determine which way to press the two seams. For a 9-patch with a dark-value center and corners, the seams will be pressed outward in the first row, inward in the second row, then outward in the third row. **8**

It's not as straightforward for the row seams. Both dark and light values are present in each of the rows. In this case, defer to the value on the outer edge of the block. Continuing with the dark-value center and corners example, the row seams would be pressed outward, or toward the dark-value fabric on the edge of the block. **9**

For a 9-patch block with light-value center and corners, everything is reversed. Seams in the first and third row are pressed inward toward the dark-value sides, and for the center row, the seams are pressed outward. The row seams are pressed inward.

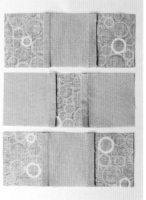

8

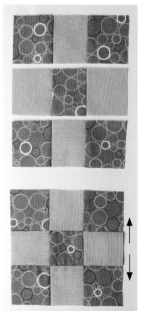

9

Why does it matter? First, there are rules of thumb in pressing hierarchy. The first rule of thumb involves pressing the seam toward the darker fabric to avoid shadowing—when darker fabrics show, or shadow, through lighter colors. The second rule of thumb is to press toward fewer seams to avoid bulk and bunchy seams. But all bets are off and the rule of thumb can be ignored if overall construction issues override what makes the most sense in any one seam. In other words, the pattern author may know a construction issue that shows up later in the process. So if the pressing direction doesn't match the hierarchy stated above, there may be another reason for the pressing direction that goes against the first two "rules" that will materialize later.

Second, it's not uncommon for 9-patch blocks to be sewn right next to each other, dark center and corners next to light center and corners, to create an alternating dark/light or overall checkerboard pattern. This pressing configuration allows for seams joining the blocks to nest. I like this pressing configuration, but you are left with a little bit of bulk at the seam intersections. The way to deal with this is by furling seam intersections.

Furling, also referred to as popping, twisting, and twirling, among other things, is perhaps best known in the 4-patch block universe, but it can be an effective seam-flattening technique in 9-patches or any block where seams are pressed alternately from row to row.

To furl a 9-patch block, or any block for that matter, you have to let go of the "press toward the dark" concept.

Before exploring the furling possibilities in 9-patch blocks, let's consider the furl technique on a 4-patch.

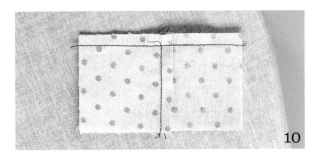

Press from the back so the seams rotate and the center intersection is furled. Note that only the center of the block seam section is open; the rest of the seams are pressed to one side, each rotating around the center. Press from the front. **11**

Seams can furl clockwise or counterclockwise. Also notice that a clockwise seam rotation from the back is counterclockwise from the front. The secret isn't that the seams furl one way or another; it's that they all furl in the same direction for the quilt construction.

In the project patterns, look for a blue circle at a seam intersection to indicate where seams should be furled.

FURLING A 4-PATCH
Sew 2-patch units and press the seams consistently to one side, usually toward the darker fabric. Sew pairs of 2-patches with opposing fabric facing and seams nested. Be sure to feed the 4-patches into the sewing machine exactly the same each time—that is, light fabric first or dark fabric first.

Using a seam ripper, remove the last two or three stitches from the 2-patch seam on each side of the 4-patch unit. Stop removing stitches at the intersection with the longer 4-patch seam. **10**

FURLING A 9-PATCH
Coming back to the 9-patch block, in a 9-patch with dark center and corners, for example, sew the row elements, then press the seams outward in the first row (toward the dark corners), inward in the second row (toward the dark center), and outward in the third row (toward the dark corners). For fun and because it's easier to remember, I've nicknamed the two-seam combinations "innies" and "outies." For a successful "furl," it is important that the seams alternate outie-innie-outie in the row sequence.

Nest and oppose the seams to sew the row seams, exactly like we did for the dark center and corners block. But this time, instead of pressing the center seam in one direction, you will furl each seam intersection. Two intersections will furl clockwise and two counterclockwise, making pressing toward the dark fabric at the outer edge of the block moot.

To furl the seam intersections, use a seam ripper to pick out the last two or three stitches of the block element seam between the longer row seam and the fabric edge. Repeat with the stitches on each side of each of the four 9-patch seam intersections, or eight times. **12**

Place the 9-patch block on the ironing board right side down. Furl one seam intersection at a time. Observe the opposing block element seams at the first seam intersection—they will indicate whether the seams will rotate in a clockwise or counterclockwise direction. Press the remaining two seams in that intersection to follow the rotation established by the two existing seams. **13** As you press the four seams with an iron, a miniature 4-patch will pop open up in the center. Repeat the process for the remaining three seam intersections from the back of the block. Then press the block from the front.

The result will be a block that has two sets of opposite seams on the outer edge of the block pressed outward (outies) and two sets of opposite seams on the outer edge of the block pressed inward (innies). **14** Blocks can then be sewn next to each other, and there will always be a nested seam opportunity by only rotating the neighboring block a quarter turn.

12

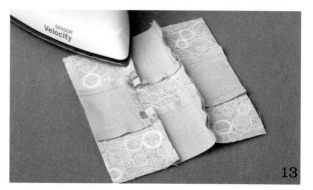
13

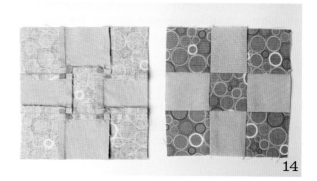
14

A WORD OR TWO ABOUT PRESSING SEAMS OPEN

With a few exceptions, I press seams to one side, and I plan pattern instructions to take best advantage of seam-pressing direction. When piecing, I like the snap of seams pressed to one side when opposing seams are aligned perfectly. More important, over the long haul, the batting has greater potential to migrate through pressed-open seams because a sewing machine stitch length isn't as tight as fabric thread count. Batting is manufactured to stay encased within the fabric thread count, not a typical quilting seam stitch. Additionally, as a machine quilter and a big fan of stitching-in-the-ditch, seams pressed open are more likely to be severed in the process of quilting than seams pressed to one side.

STRIP-PIECING A 9-PATCH

Because I'm focused on using scraps that have been cut into 2-in., 3½-in., and 5-in. squares, I haven't to this point acknowledged a very common 9-patch construction technique—strip-piecing. Strip-piecing is a technique used to sew multiple fabric strips together to create a "strip set" that is then cut apart to yield portions of a quilt block.

Here's an example of strip-piecing a 9-patch. Start with six 2-in. strips at least 7 in. long, three of dark value and three of light value. Sew a dark-value strip to each side of a light-value strip, and press the seams outward toward the dark-value strips. A Separately, sew a light-value strip to each side of a dark-value strip, and press the seams inward toward the dark-value center strip. You'll have two strips sets, each 5 in. wide, one dark/light/dark, one light/dark/light. Cross-cut each strip set to make six 2-in.-wide segments—three dark/light/dark and three light/dark/light. Sew two dark/light/dark and one light/dark/light strip set together, then press the seams outward from the center or furl the seam intersections (more on furling on pp. 12–14). B You'll end up with a 9-patch block with a dark center and corners that measures 5 in. and will finish to 4½ in. square. C1

Repeat the process with two light/dark/light and one dark/light/dark segments, reversing the pressing direction as you sew the segments together, and you'll have a 9-patch block with light-value center and corners with the same measurement. C2

This technique works best when you need an equal quantity of dark- and light-centered 9-patches. To make multiple dark-centered and -cornered 9-patches, plan ahead to have

double the quantity of dark/light/dark strip sets than light/dark/light strip sets, based on your quilt design needs, of course.

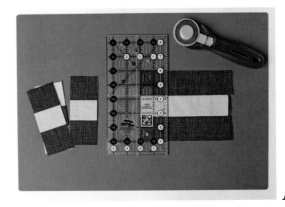

A

B

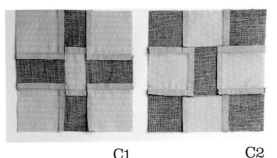

C1   C2

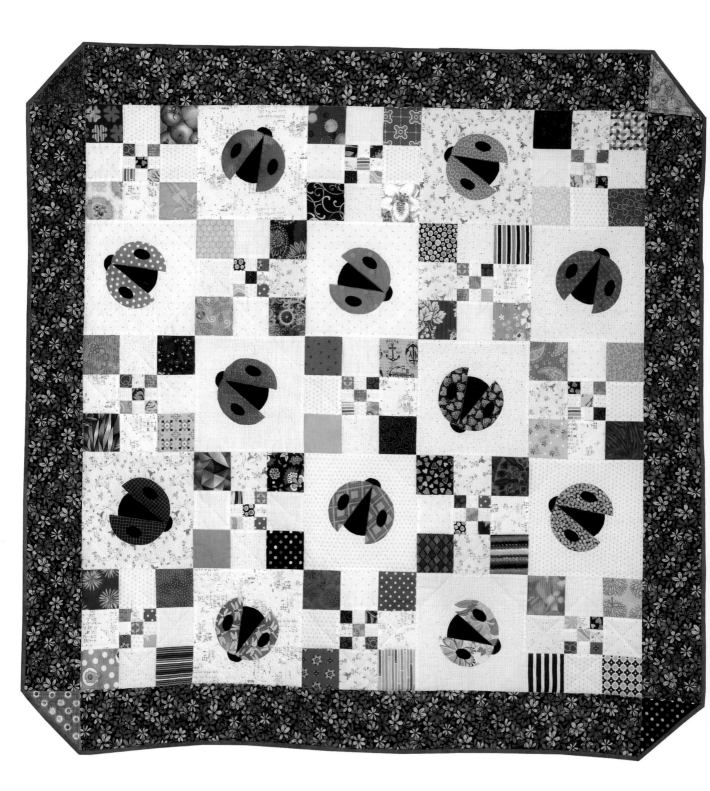

CHAPTER 2

Using the 9-Patch Interfacing

I never set out to create interfacing products to go with the ScrapTherapy method—they just "happened."

It all started with the pattern for the "Bloomin' Steps" quilt from *Scrap-Therapy: Cut the Scraps!* The pattern was initially created in response to many requests to use more of the 2-in. scrap size, the smallest of the three scrap square sizes from the ScrapTherapy scrap-storage system. The 2-in. scrap size really does accumulate more than the other two "official" ScrapTherapy square sizes—3½ in. and 5 in. It seemed the most obvious way to use them up fast was to piece lots of them into a border. In "Bloomin' Steps," five rows of 2-in. squares encircle the entire twin-sized quilt.

The only trouble with this idea was that so many scraps with so many seams were difficult to stabilize with a consistent scant ¼-in. seam. To solve this problem, a printed fusible grid interfacing called the ScrapTherapy Little Scrap Grid was produced. Even though I've used it to simplify the quilt center piecing for other quilts like "Once Upon a Scrap" from *ScrapTherapy: Cut the Scraps!* or "Georgia's Garden" from *ScrapTherapy: Scraps Plus One!*, I like to call the Little Scrap Grid the border interfacing.

At the time the Little Scrap Grid was created for the borders on "Bloomin' Steps," grid interfacing was not a new idea, but the Little Scrap Grid had a specific job and was designed in long, skinny (relatively speaking) grid sections for scrappy borders.

THE BIRTH OF THE 9-PATCH GRID

Fast-forward a couple of years, and *ScrapTherapy: Scraps Plus One!* was published with the "99 Bottles" quilt on its cover. Everyone who sees that quilt loves it.

But one of the first things people say is, "Surely, you didn't sew all those 1-in. squares one at a time." (I did.) Someone at one of the events where the quilt was on display suggested in passing that I should create something similar to the border interfacing to make the 9-patches. And that's how the idea for my line of interfacing products—ScrapTherapy Mini Scrap Grid, ScrapTherapy Middle Scrap Grid, and ScrapTherapy Little Scrap Grid—was hatched.

The interfacing is a lightweight nonwoven material that is printed on one side and fusible on the other. The heat-activated fusible dots create a rough surface on the nonprinted side of the interfacing.

The interfacing exists to do one thing: Make 9-patch blocks more efficient to sew.

The Mini Scrap Grid makes 9-patch blocks that finish to 1½ in. square. With the markings on the grid, the tiny scraps are easier to handle, and the process of placing, fusing, and sewing the scrap squares is quite different from sewing 1-in. squares into 9-patch blocks. As an added bonus, the Mini Scrap Grid is fun to use.

The Middle Scrap Grid interfacing, a 9-patch grid for making 3½-in. blocks (unfinished size) from 1½-in. scrap squares, and the Little Scrap Grid interfacing, the 9-patch grid for making 5-in. blocks (unfinished size) from 2-in. scrap squares, complete the set of three ScrapTherapy 9-patch interfacing products.

Coincidentally—or maybe not—the resulting 9-patch blocks made with the Mini, Middle, and Little Scrap Grid interfacings match the three ScrapTherapy scrap square sizes: 2-in., 3½-in., and 5-in. squares, creating all kinds of combinations of 9-patch blocks with ScrapTherapy scrap square sizes.

Many of the quilted projects in this book can take advantage of the three 9-patch interfacing products, but none of the projects requires it.

MINI SCRAP GRID INTERFACING

The Mini Scrap Grid comes by the panel. Each panel is roughly 1 yd. long and about 22 in. wide and has enough interfacing to make fifty-four 2-in. square 9-patch blocks from 1-in. fabric squares that finish to 1½ in. when sewn into a quilt project.

To make the panel less cumbersome to handle, it is broken into six smaller sections. Each section has enough interfacing to make nine 9-patch blocks. And each section has four different types of lines, each with a specific purpose—dashed lines for cutting, dotted lines for folding, solid lines for sewing, and the crosshairs or "plus" signs for snipping. **1**

1

USING THE INTERFACING
Align and Fuse

To prepare the interfacing, trim on the dashed line around the perimeter of a 9-block section to reduce the risk of the fusible material adhering to the bottom of your iron. Don't cut on the dashed lines within the 9-patch grid section yet. Those dashed lines will be used to separate the 9-patch blocks after they are sewn. **2**

2

Place the interfacing section on your ironing board, with the fusible or rough side facing up. If the lines are difficult to see, place a 10-in. white batting scrap square under the interfacing.

Arrange 1-in. scrap squares into nine 9-patch blocks on the grid using the dotted lines, the dashed lines, and the crosshairs for fabric placement. Place scraps on the grid one 9-patch at a time; don't worry about the 9-patch blocks that are arranged next to each other. Once sewn, the 9-patch blocks will be cut apart, so blocks placed next to each other won't necessarily be sewn next to each other. **3**

Be careful not to follow the solid lines for scrap placement. It's hard to ignore them! They will be used for sewing later.

Once the panel section is filled in with scraps, use a hot iron and a lift-and-press motion to fuse the scrap squares to the interfacing. Proceed carefully so you don't disturb the scraps. Add a puff or two of steam to fuse the scraps in place. **4**

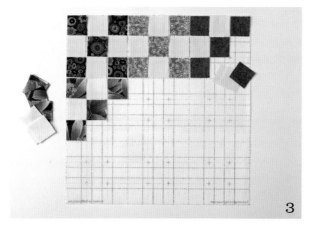

3

4

5

Notice that there is a tiny bit of space in between the fused squares. Don't worry—there is nothing wrong with the scraps or how they are placed on the interfacing. This space will make the folding step—coming up next—easier.

Some may wish to use an appliqué pressing sheet to keep from getting the fusible material on the iron sole plate, but I don't recommend it, as the small scraps may jiggle when the sheet is placed over them. Plus, as long as the interfacing is trimmed around the outside edge of the interfacing segment, and the scraps have been cut and placed accurately, the little gaps between the squares are not enough to create a problem with the iron. Just in case, I keep a tube of iron cleaner handy to clean the bottom of the iron after long sessions of fusing scraps to the grid products.

If you discover that a scrap is out of place, place the iron over the errant fabric scrap and heat for 5 to 10 seconds. Lift one corner of the scrap to peel it off the interfacing, then reposition it. If the interfacing starts to tear, stop and heat again until the fusible material is soft enough to release the fabric square without tearing the interfacing.

Fold, Stab, Sew, and Check

Fold the interfacing along the first vertical dotted line on the right side of the panel section. To keep the bulk away from the sewing machine feed dogs, fold the interfacing toward you throughout the sewing process. The dotted line should be directly on the fold, not to either side of it.

Stab a pin from front to back on the solid line to make sure the pin pierces the line on the front and back. **5**

Adjust the fold as needed to align the solid lines front to back, then secure the layers with pins. **6**

I like to use four or five pins along the length of the fold, stabbing, checking, and securing with each added pin. I also like to place the pins on the inside, so the point of the pin is just outside of the solid sewing line. That way, the pins can stay in place while sewing, avoiding distortion in the seam while sewing and removing pins simultaneously. **7**

Then sew on the line. **8**

Check the sewn seam from the back to make sure the seam follows the line on the front and on the back. **9** If the seam is off the line significantly, the 9-patch may be inaccurate. I've removed plenty of seams that looked okay from the front, but went off the line on the back. The more you practice sewing 9-patch blocks using the grid, the more accurate stitching on the lines will become.

Remove the pins, then repeat the fold, stab, sew, check process with the next set of dotted and solid vertical lines.

Notice that the third set of vertical lines on the Mini Scrap Grid isn't a set of lines at all. It is a single dashed line with no solid lines on either side of it. The dashed lines are cutting lines, used after all the seams are sewn, so this line has no seam. **10**

Follow the same sewing sequence for the next two sets of vertical dotted and solid lines—skip the dashed line, then sew the last two sets of lines—until all six vertical seams are sewn. Do not press. **11**

6

8

7

9

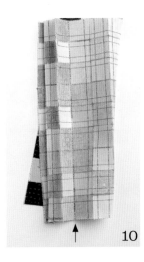

10

11

13

Snip, Nest, and Oppose

With scissors, cut the interfacing at each crosshair on each seam. *Be sure to snip through the stitching line.* Each fold will have six crosshairs and, therefore, six snips. Be very careful to snip on the crosshairs *between* the solid lines. If you snip on the solid lines, you'll be making a tiny hole in the 9-patch block that can't be repaired. **12**

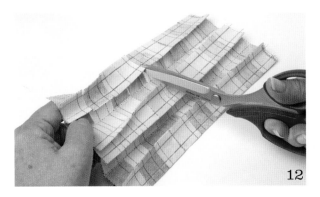

12

Whenever I teach this technique, people always look at me as if I've sprouted a second head when I tell them to cut through the thread. If you don't cut through the thread at the seam, the step that follows won't work. You need to break the thread to allow the seam allowances to rotate freely.

Rotate the panel section to prepare to sew the horizontal seams.

With the right side of the panel section facing you, fold on the first dotted line at the top. Notice that the seams are free to move to one side or the other. **13** Rotate the seam allowances for the first two sets of seams so they nest, oppose, and alternate. Notice that the two seam allowances in front are finger-pressed away from the center, and the two seams on the back side are pressed toward the center.

As I mentioned, I like to refer to 9-patch seams pressed away from each other as "outies" and 9-patch seams pressed toward each other as "innies." As you nest and oppose seams, try to avoid "innie" seams that overlap with a slight outward pull.

At the same time, notice that the fold follows the dotted line exactly, and that pins are placed crosswise to capture both front and back seams at the same time. Notice also that the point of the pin faces the fold, and the tip of the pin is clear of the solid sewing line. **14**

14

Nest, oppose, and secure with pins each of the three sets of 9-patch seams along the first solid sewing line. **15**

Some patterns in this book may call for a specific pressing direction for each set of blocks. Refer to the block diagrams within the patterns for detailed pressing instructions.

Notice that the seams for this panel section are all "innies" in front. And the middle seams are pressed inward on top. Unless otherwise noted in the pattern, it doesn't matter if the seams along the first fold are pressed outward or inward.

Sew on the line. Do not press. **16**

Repeat the fold, nest, oppose, and sew sequence for the next dotted line; skip the dashed lines, then fold, nest, and oppose the following two sets of two seams. You'll notice that the alternating "innie" and "outie" seam directions will naturally fall into place because each row's seam allowance will be the opposite of its predecessor. Each time, fold the unit toward you as the seams are sewn to keep the bulk on top, away from the sewing machine feed dogs. **17**

Cut Apart, Furl, and Press

With all the seams sewn, but not pressed, you'll be able to see the nine 9-patch blocks within the section from the front. **18**

From the back, the panel section looks like a maze of tidy crisscrossing seam allowances. **19**

Turn the panel section right side down, then cut on the dashed lines. You can cut with your rotary cutter and ruler, but I prefer to cut with shears. You should have

nine miniature 9-patch blocks that curl because they haven't been pressed yet. **20**

At this point, the seams could be pressed traditionally, without furling. Just press the seams per the pattern directions, so you have two sets of "innies" and two sets of "outies," or four sets of "innies" or four sets of "outies" (shown). **21**

To reduce bulk at the seam intersections, I like to furl the 9-patch seams. Admittedly, furling seams on 2-in. 9-patch blocks is meticulous and not for the faint of heart. The resulting block that is perfectly flat with evenly distributed seams on the wrong side of the block is worth the effort, though.

Because of the interfacing, the furling process is slightly different than the one shown on pp. 13–14 when no interfacing is present. Start in a similar fashion, removing the last two or three stitches between the longer row seam and the snipped crosshair at the interfacing fold.

Remove the stitches on the short end of both sides of all four-seam intersections; then head to the ironing board. **22**

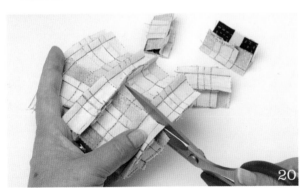

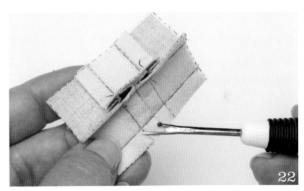

Remember the concern about snipping those seams? For the record, I've inadvertently removed entire mini-seams because I didn't snip completely through the thread at the crosshairs.

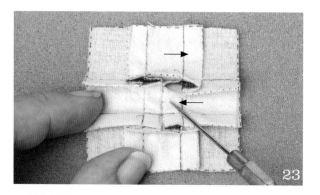

Flatten the cup by pushing its outer edges into a triangle. Then flatten the triangle with the iron. It's a lot like origami! Be careful! Don't burn your fingertips with the iron. **25**

The stage is now set to furl the next seam to the left. That seam will rotate counterclockwise from the wrong side of the block.

Repeat the process with each seam intersection until all four of the seam intersections have been furled. **26**

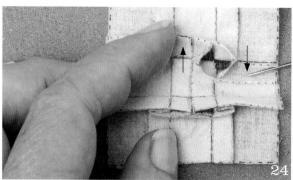

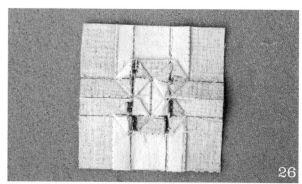

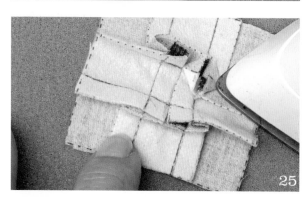

Place the 9-patch block on the ironing board right side down. Working with one seam intersection at a time, notice the pressing direction of the two existing seams at the intersection in the upper right of the block in the photo. **23**

Based on the pressing direction for the two existing vertical seams, the seams at this intersection will furl in a clockwise direction. Use your fingertips to complete the rotation with the remaining two horizontal seams. At the center, because the interfacing is connecting the fabric edges, a miniature cup is formed. **24**

Now press from the front and trim the block to 2 in. square, centering the $\frac{1}{2}$-in.-square 9-patch center. **27** Repeat for the remaining eight blocks made from the panel section. **28**

> The furling process seems insanely detailed for such tiny blocks. At the first attempt, I have no doubt that you might spew a couple of choice words in my direction (with great fondness, of course!). Admittedly, the first few interfaced tiny-block furls don't always go as planned. But stick with it for at least a couple of 9-patch sections. It gets easier and faster as you catch on to the steps. The furling effect is especially nice to reduce bulk on "Fiesta!" on p. 69 or the "Button Collection Pillow" on p. 54. And who wants lumpy seam spots on a quilt like "Argyle Dreams" (p. 176)?
>
> Some fussy techniques are worth the effort. In my humble opinion, this is one of them.
>
> As a small consolation, it goes without saying that furling the seams with interfacing is much easier on the larger Middle and Little Scrap Grid sizes.

MIDDLE AND LITTLE SCRAP GRID INTERFACING

The Middle and Little Scrap Grids are printed on the same lightweight nonwoven fabric as the Mini Scrap Grid. The grid is printed on one side, with heat-sensitive fusible dots on the other side, creating the same rough surface as on the Mini Scrap Grid.

Both the Middle Scrap Grid and Little Scrap Grid are available by the panel, and each panel is approximately 1 yd. long and about 22 in. wide. One panel of the Middle Scrap Grid yields twenty-four $3\frac{1}{2}$-in.-square 9-patch blocks that finish to 3 in. square. A Little Scrap Grid panel yields twelve 5-in.-square 9-patch blocks that finish to $4\frac{1}{2}$ in. square.

In many ways, using the Middle and Little Scrap Grids is a lot like using the Mini Scrap Grid, just on a larger scale. But there are some distinct differences.

The Middle and Little Scrap Grids are so similar to each other that the descriptions that follow along with the accompanying photos feature the Middle Scrap Grid (my favorite!). All instructions for the Middle Scrap Grid apply to the Little Scrap Grid, too. Unless noted below for the Middle and Little Scrap Grids, follow the instructions for using the Mini Scrap Grid.

USING THE INTERFACING

Just like the Mini Scrap Grid, both the Middle and Little Scrap Grid interfacings break down into smaller, easier-to-use sections. However, each of the sections cut from the Middle and Little Scrap Grid yields six blocks each instead of nine Mini Scrap Grid blocks. Like the Mini Scrap Grid, each section has four different types of lines—dashed, dotted, solid, and crosshairs. Whereas the Mini Scrap Grid does not have solid lines on either side of the dashed cutting lines, the Middle and Little Scrap Grids do, making them particularly useful when joining 9-patch blocks to make flying geese units like those in the "Fiesta!" on p. 69.

As for Mini, prepare Middle Scrap Grid interfacing by trimming any extra interfacing on the dashed line along the perimeter of the six-block section of interfacing. Don't cut on the dashed lines between the 9-patch blocks yet.

Align and Fuse

Place the section of interfacing on your ironing board, with the fusible or rough side facing up. Place a white batting rectangle slightly larger than the interfacing—about 10 in. by 15 in. for a section of Middle Scrap Grid or about 14 in. by 20 in. for a section of Little Scrap Grid—under the interfacing if you're having difficulty seeing the printed interfacing lines. Since each section is a rectangle, orient the section so the long ends are the top and bottom and the short ends are the sides.

Just as for the Mini Scrap Grid, arrange $1\frac{1}{2}$-in. scrap squares (2-in. scrap squares for Little) on the grid using the dotted lines and the crosshairs for fabric placement. Be careful not to follow the more bold solid sewing lines for scrap placement.

Place scraps on the grid one 9-patch at a time, and unless otherwise noted by the pattern instructions, don't worry about the 9-patch blocks that are arranged next to each other.

Once the grid section is filled in with scraps, use a hot iron to fuse the scrap squares to the interfacing with a lift-and-press motion. Proceed carefully without disturbing the unfused scraps. Use no more than a puff or two of steam to fuse the scraps to the interfacing. **29**

As with the Mini Scrap Grid, you can remove and replace scraps by heating up the interfacing with the iron, peeling off the fabric, and then repositioning it.

The Middle and Little Scrap Grids have built-in space between the scrap squares so scraps tend not to overlap, which makes the next steps easier.

All three of the 9-patch grids can accommodate pieced elements, too! For example, the grid can be used to stabilize half-square and quarter-square triangle units for "Laptop Sleeve" on p. 191 and "Citrus Coverlet" on p. 140. When placing pieced units on the interfacing, try to place the units so they are perfectly centered and square between the dotted and dashed lines.

Fold, Stab, Sew, and Check

With the long edges of the interfacing section at the top and bottom, fold the interfacing along the first vertical dotted line on the right of the unit.

Follow the steps outlined on pp. 19–20 for the Mini Scrap Grid to fold and sew along the first two sets of vertical dotted and solid lines. Don't forget to fold directly on the dotted line, stab a pin from front to back at several points along the solid lines, and check that the pin stabs through the solid line underneath. Secure with pins across the seam; then sew on the line and check the line of sewing on both sides of the interfacing. **30**

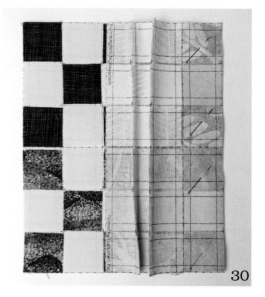

Once you've sewn the second vertical seam, notice that the next seam looks a lot like the first two. Both Middle and Little Scrap Grids include the solid sewing lines along dotted folding lines as well as dashed cutting lines, both vertically and horizontally. Use these sewing lines only when the pattern calls for 9-patch blocks that are joined. For now, to stay on track to make 9-patch blocks, we'll skip every third set of lines.

Sometimes, to keep myself from getting confused, I'll repeat a short phrase to keep me on track: Sew two, skip one . . . sew two, skip one . . .

31

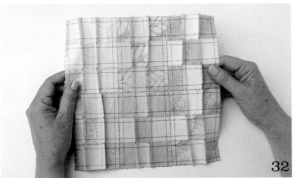

32

33

Continue to follow the Mini Scrap Grid instructions on pp. 21–22 to sew the four longer horizontal seams with the Middle or Little Scrap Grid panels (skip the set of lines and seam in the center unless otherwise instructed by the pattern). Remember, do not press until the blocks are cut apart. **31, 32**

> Repeat after me: "Snip two, skip one . . . Snip two, skip one . . . " Remember, it's important to snip through the stitching line, breaking the thread.

Note that some 9-patch blocks can be rotated without affecting the pattern, like the 3-in. 9-patch blocks in the center of the larger 9-patch blocks for "Beetle Mania" on p. 133. Therefore, pressing direction and furling are not critical. But some blocks cannot be rotated into place without impacting the pattern, like those created for "Citrus Coverlet" on p. 140, "Laptop Sleeve" on p. 191, or "Cross-Body Market Sack" on p. 110. Be careful to follow the pressing diagrams shown within the patterns.

Sew on the line. Do not press.

Cut Apart, Furl, and Press

As with the smaller blocks made with the Mini Scrap Grid, once all the seams are sewn, cut the larger 9-patch blocks made from the Middle or Little Scrap Grid on the dashed lines with scissors. As with the Mini Scrap Grid, the seams could be pressed traditionally without furling.

To reduce bulk at the seam intersections, I like to furl the 9-patch seams. Follow the same steps for furling the Mini Scrap Grid blocks to furl the larger blocks made with the Middle and Little Scrap Grids. You'll find it's much easier when you're working with larger blocks. **33**

Snip, Nest, and Oppose

Follow the steps outlined on pp. 21–22 for the Mini Scrap Grid to snip the interfacing at the crosshairs, cutting past the stitching line for each seamline. You'll make four snips for each line of sewing.

CHAPTER 3
The Seven Steps Revisited

STEP ONE: GETTING STARTED

It's so hard to keep from jumping right into the projects! Oh what fun to rifle around in messy scrap bags and bins to dig out the perfect scraps in just the right sizes and colors to start sewing up one of the quilts or bags or accessories found in the section that begins on p. 42. You know exactly how many scraps you need in certain colors or values—the pattern tells you that. But something always seems to get in the way.

You've got the perfect focus print, but you can't find the right scrap colors to go with it. The scraps are ready to go, but nothing from your stash excites you like the main-player fabric. Before too long, the hunt is called off and the project is left for another day, or worse, the project gets a grand start but falls apart, and the excitement wanes every time you have to go digging for more scraps to match the blocks you've started.

Without a process, finding just the right scraps for your next scrappy quilt can be a lot like looking for a speck of gold in a mountain stream. The dream has a grand scale, but the chances of striking it big and carrying the process to completion are small. Let's go back to the beginning with a review of the seven steps outlined in my first book (*ScrapTherapy: Cut the Scraps!*) to cut, store, and use scrap fabrics. The steps walk you through the process of preparing your fabric, defining a theme for your project, and making it happen. Not every scrappy quilt project needs to follow these steps. But having a process keeps you focused and headed down a sensible path.

JUST START

It has been said that knowing you have a problem is the first step in solving it. The ScrapTherapy pattern series started as a result of my issues with unused scrap fabrics in my own stash, stored away in my basement. You shouldn't have issues associated with a hobby that you love to do. Period.

When I started quilting, I kept several shoebox-size clear plastic bins full of fabric scraps—pieces of fabric, strips, half strips, quarter strips, rectangles, triangles, you name it. The bins were stored, out of the way, unseen on the bottom shelf in a dark corner of the basement. They contained leftovers from hundreds of quilts and samples created in less than 10 years of quilting. The bins were rarely touched. Instead of using what I had, I ran to the quilt shop to purchase a fat quarter or a yard or two of fabric when a piece of scrap fabric would have been fine.

Stored away in all those bins in the basement were treasured memories of quilts I made and had given away, commemorating a variety of life's passages, like graduations, weddings, and births.

It made me cringe to think that, someday, someone might be digging through my stash without me. They would wonder, "What did she have in mind for all this?" And it also drove me over the edge thinking that someone else might be using my favorite pieces of cloth—my memories, my investment! I am very selfish when it comes to my fabric stash.

So when I headed to a quilt retreat weekend with some friends, I brought those bins out of my basement. I cut for much of the first day of the retreat. I cut until I had lots of scraps stored right back in those shoebox-size bins, now neatly cut and ready to sew, plenty to choose from in each size.

Once I had enough to choose from, I pulled out some background fabric from my stash, as well as a few specialty rulers, and started to work. By the end of the evening, I had assembled four blocks into a small baby-size quilt, using background, accent fabric, a border, and, of course, my scraps. Every thread of fabric came from my stash, and it looked great. And I felt terrific. I was on to something.

STEP TWO: CUT!

Now that you've decided to begin, where do you start? Accept that old habits die hard, and small steps and manageable goals will keep you on track. Next, keep it simple. I propose cutting your scraps into just three square sizes that store easily and play well together. And finally, cut more scraps than you need for the next project, so you can pick and choose scraps that go with your theme as you build your scrappy quilt.

DEFINE "SCRAP"

Everyone will have his or her own definition of what constitutes a scrap piece of fabric. For me, it's a scrap if the piece of fabric is less than ¼ yd. by the width of the fabric: 9 in. by 42 in. Usually, my fabric scraps are much smaller than that: leftovers from a fabric strip, an extra rectangle or square, odd shapes remaining from appliqué or borders, and long, skinny strips of leftover backing. These pieces are tossed into a basket as I work on the latest quilt project. In between projects,

I pull the leftovers from the basket and replenish my scrap bins with fresh-cut scraps. It's an ongoing cycle.

In my mind, if the leftover fabric is more than ¼ yd. and is completely intact, it goes back into the stash of running yardage. My stash also has dedicated space for fat quarters (18 in. by 21 in.) and large but odd-shaped fabrics—usually leftovers from backings. Running yardage is stored on several shelves, folded edge out for easy access.

THE RIGHT STUFF

Here's a list of tools you'll want to have on hand for your cutting session.

STRAIGHTEDGE RULER

Any straightedge, laser-printed acrylic ruler used for quilting will work. Consider a ruler that has strong, distinct vertical lines typically used to cut strips with dimensions shown clearly in whole and half inches. It's not about any one brand of ruler, it's about how comfortable you are with its accuracy and speed to get the job done. My favorite ruler sizes to use are 6 in. by 12 in., 4 in. by 14 in., and 6 in. by 6 in.—or in those size neighborhoods.

CLEAR STORAGE BINS

Shoebox-size bins allow the cut-up scraps to be stored neatly in stacks. Clear plastic makes it easy to find colors later. Although plastic bins aren't optimal for long-term fabric storage, our goal is to use the scraps, not *store* them for the long haul.

ROTATING CUTTING MAT

A 12-in. rotating cutting mat has an even cutting surface that turns or rotates. Because the surface turns easily, cutting is fast and accurate, plus its size makes it portable for cutting sessions on the go! A new rotating mat not in your budget? No problem. I find a 12-in. by 18-in. mat is a convenient size for any space and is portable.

ROTARY CUTTER AND FRESH BLADE, 45 MM

A fresh blade at the beginning of a big cutting session makes the job so much more pleasant and allows you to cut through more layers of scraps with confidence and accuracy. To avoid fabric shifting, don't cut more than six layers of fabric at a time.

VINYL FABRIC STRIP GUIDE

I like to use Qtools™ Cutting Edge and Sewing Edge. These orange and purple vinyl strips help make cutting fast and accurate. Put a strip on the bottom of the ruler, precisely on the cutting measurement line—orange for smooth-bottom rulers and purple for rulers with a rough or frosted finish. The orange vinyl clings to smooth surfaces, the purple vinyl sticks with a light adhesive to the ruler without leaving residue, and the thickness creates a guide that stops the ruler at the edge of the fabric and makes the cutting process nearly thought free.

SCRAPTHERAPY SIZES

Gather your cutting tools and, from the basket of fabrics to cut, pull out a small clump of scrap fabric. Grab just one handful without being selective about size, color, or value. We'll discuss sorting later. Go to your ironing board and press each scrap neatly, and make a stack of ready-to-cut fabrics near your cutting area. Don't grab more scraps than can be cut in a 10-minute or 15-minute cutting session.

The ScrapTherapy sizes are 2-in., 3½-in., and 5-in. squares. Every ScrapTherapy quilted project starts with

scraps cut into one, two, or all three of these sizes. Why these sizes? The logic starts with squares—not strips, not triangles.

The 5-in. scrap size was the first one I decided on; it's a versatile size with lots of potential. Next came the 2-in. size, because a 2-in. square was about as small a piece of fabric as I wanted to fuss with, in terms of stacking and storing. If I needed a smaller scrap piece, I could always trim it down, as is the case for many of the smaller 9-patch projects like "Argyle Dreams" on p. 176 or "Fiesta!" on p. 69.

It felt as though a size in between the two was missing. Employing a little quilter's math, a 2-in. scrap will finish to $1\frac{1}{2}$ in. (subtract $\frac{1}{2}$ in. for seam allowances). A 4-patch made from 2-in. scrap squares will finish to 3 in. ($1\frac{1}{2}$ in. + $1\frac{1}{2}$ in. = 3 in.), which is $3\frac{1}{2}$ in. unfinished. That's how $3\frac{1}{2}$ in. became the third ScrapTherapy size.

Store the cut scraps in a couple of clear shoebox–size bins. Two stacks of 5-in. scrap squares fit perfectly into one bin. Three stacks of $3\frac{1}{2}$-in. plus five stacks of 2-in. scraps fit very well into a second bin.

The three ScrapTherapy sizes play well together; it's as simple as that. Quick quilts appear like magic from your scrap bins when you sew 4-patches from the 2-in. scrap squares and then sew them alternately with $3\frac{1}{2}$-in. scrap squares. Likewise, 9-patches made from 2-in. scrap squares can be sewn alternately with 5-in. squares.

SCRAP SIZES AMENDED

Some of my followers have recently asked me if I've amended my favored scrap size list to include 1-in. and $1\frac{1}{2}$-in. squares in my storage bins to accommodate the sizes needed to make the smaller 9-patch blocks used in several of the quilt projects in this book. In fact, I have not—well, not really. I continue to cut and collect the prescribed 2-in., $3\frac{1}{2}$-in., and 5-in. scrap squares as outlined in my first two ScrapTherapy books. I still feel that scraps smaller than 2 in. square are a chore to stack and store. When I need smaller scraps for the smaller 9-patch blocks, I typically select scraps from the inventory of three larger scrap sizes and cut them to size. In addition, I do keep a separate small container-style bin for 1-in. and $1\frac{1}{2}$-in. scrap squares that were cut for projects but not used. Even though I

keep the cut leftover squares, I don't make an effort to add to that collection by cutting more.

One adjustment I have made to my scrap storage collection is adding a separate storage bin just for 2-in. and $2\frac{1}{2}$-in. strips in any length. I still like to start with squares, not strips, for my scrappy projects, but the strips represent a storage unit for 2-in. and $2\frac{1}{2}$-in. squares. I realized that if I cut all the leftover strips I have into 2-in. squares to store in my bins, I'd soon be out of space for the larger $3\frac{1}{2}$-in. and 5-in. scraps! Those smaller scraps tend to multiply like bunnies, don't you agree?

CUTTING TIPS

Cutting scraps can be a little different than cutting from yardage. For starters, the pieces are often smaller. Many scraps don't have a straight, trued-up edge. And the grain may not be as easily identified if the selvages are gone. As you cut, you'll find your own tricks to reduce effort and increase efficiency. Here are a few tips I find helpful when I cut my scraps:

- Try to avoid cutting fabric squares with bias edges. Hold an odd-shaped fabric in front of a light source or a window to identify the horizontal and vertical lines in the fabric weave.
- Cut multiple layers at once but try not to cut more than six layers at a time.
- Select fabrics randomly and try not to sort by color or print at this stage.
- Sort fabrics into three stacks as they are cut, one stack for each size.
- Cut the largest size possible from each scrap. Larger scrap squares can always be cut down if needed.
- For a scrap that will become a 5-in. square, make a fresh cut a little more than 5 in. away from one raw edge. **1**
- Turn the fabric 180 degrees (or use a rotating cutting mat, and you won't have to disturb your newly cut fabric), and then make a parallel cut exactly 5 in. away from the first cut, using the lines on the ruler, not the lines on the cutting mat. You can see how using the orange (or purple) vinyl strips can make this step easier. **2**
- Then turn the fabric (or rotating mat) a quarter turn, and make the third cut perpendicular to the first two

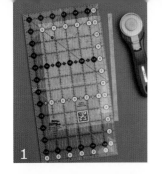
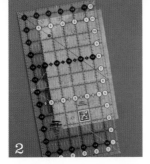

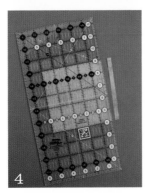

cuts and a little more than 5 in. away from the raw edge while lining up the first two cuts with horizontal ruler lines that are 5 in. away from each other. **3**

- Turn the fabric (or mat) one last 180-degree turn and make the final cut to make the 5-in. square. **4**

- Cutting seems to work hand in hand with sorting, which not so coincidentally leads us to the third step.

PALMING THE RULER

Many quilting classes teach us to place the ruler on the mat with thumb and three fingers on the ruler and the pinkie just off the edge of the ruler to keep it from slipping. Add a little pressure during an extended cutting session, and your fingers are going to be tired, creating the potential for the ruler to shift while cutting. Instead, consider forming a new habit.

   Place your hand on the ruler as shown in photo 3 (cutting 5-in. squares), then drop your palm onto the surface of the ruler. Immediately, you'll notice the pressure on your hands and fingers is much more comfortable, and the energy to hold the ruler in place comes from your shoulder rather than the muscles in your fingers and hands. You'll find that you tire less quickly and therefore can extend your cutting sessions.

STEP THREE: SORT

Sort your cut fabric scraps by value or type of collection so they are ready to use and easy to find. I like to compare how I sort my scraps to how I sort laundry—darks, lights, and everything else.

   For each mini cutting session, I arrange three short stacks at my cutting station, with one small stack for each size. Once the cutting session is done, the stacks get placed in the scrap bins by size. But that's not all. As I cut, I also sort, not necessarily by color, but by value. Why? I try to stay mindful of the next step. When I'm cutting, I'm evaluating how I might use what I'm cutting. If it seems I have a growing pile of small scraps, and I notice that as I cut, I make a mental note to make the next project heavy in the 2-in. scrap department. It's the same with value.

VALUE

What is value? Lots of quilters have difficulty determining value. For purposes of filling the scrap bins, dark generally means the scrap piece is darker than 90 percent of the rest of your scraps—dark, dark blues; deep, rich purples; blacks with just a bit of print in them. Conversely, light scraps are lighter in value than 90 percent of everything else—white-on-white prints, white with bits of print, pale yellows, pinks, and blues.

Then there's everything else. Simply put, if a scrap is not dark and not light, it falls into the "everything else" category, or medium value. Brights nearly always fall into the everything-else category.

When sewing scrap fabrics next to each other in a scrap quilt, it's important that the value is different. Sometimes it's not enough that the color is different; the value also needs to contrast for the pattern to stand out.

As I place cut scraps into the bins, I have a separate bin for extreme dark scraps and extreme light fabrics; these are separate from everything-else, or medium-value, scraps, which make up the bulk of my scrap collection. The values are determined as I cut.

Since several of the quilt projects in this book include scraps that have been trimmed from the larger sizes to 1½ in. or 1 in. square, it's worth mentioning that value and scale should be considered as scraps are selected for these sizes. Choosing scraps in high contrast to one another or to the background fabric will help the smaller pieces shine.

The scale of the scrap print squares selected for a scrappy quilt project should contribute to a successful scrappy project. Scraps with large-scale prints—like a print of a large pink flower on a black background—when cut into smaller pieces may produce scraps that are dramatically different. Some pink, some black, and maybe some green leaves could all be cut from that same large-scale scrap fabric square. Be careful that you haven't lost the quilt's theme when cutting larger-scale prints into smaller pieces.

STEP FOUR: SELECT A THEME

I've said it before; I'll say it again: I don't like scrap quilts! I don't like weird combinations of fabrics that feel forced together. Just because it's a scrappy project doesn't mean it can't be cohesive. My solution? Determine a theme for the quilt, then select the scraps according to that theme. The theme will be the common thread that pulls all the elements of the project together. Now, that's a scrap quilt I can fall in love with!

CHOOSING A THEME

When you start thinking about your next scrappy project, selecting the theme for that project usually falls into one of four broad categories.

FOLLOW YOUR HEART

See a ScrapTherapy pattern you love? Make it happen—it's as simple as that. Follow the color scheme and value suggestions and select the scraps, background fabrics, and focus prints suggested. Your quilt will be unique to you because it will contain your favorite scraps and fabric pieces, but it will look similar to the photograph in the book.

USE WHAT YOU HAVE

Stand back and take a look at your scraps. What kind of fabrics do you have in excess? For example, have you been making lots of baby quilts lately, generating a ton of baby prints in your scrap bins? Consider making a kid-oriented pattern and have that baby quilt ready before the baby shower announcement! It's easy to turn scrap overkill into over-the-top quilt treasures and move those out-of-control scraps out of your scrap bins.

USE WHAT YOU WANT

I just love blue and purple. When I buy fabric, I almost always go heavy on blue and purple prints. That means many of my non-scrappy quilts are blue, which in turn

means blue scraps are always at my fingertips. What to do? Make blue scrappy quilts, of course!

What's your favorite color? If you have a lot of one color or type of fabric print, don't worry about selecting the focus print, typically used for the border, right away. Make a few blocks within your favorite theme, then take the blocks to the stash or the quilt shop to "audition" some focus or main-player fabric selections.

LET THE FABRIC DECIDE

When using what you have and using what you want, the focus print or theme might be decided after several blocks are constructed based on what the blocks look like. Another approach starts with selecting the focus print or inspiration fabric—the fabric that is usually reserved for the border—and then selecting the scrap fabrics around the colors predominant in that print.

If you are out and about and happen to stop into a quilt shop, do you ever see a focus print that speaks to you? The next thing you know, it's going home with you. When that happens, build a scrappy quilt around it. Why fight it? Some of the best projects can be inspired by the colors in the main-player and accent fabrics—even if you don't use the fabric in the quilt.

THEME BINS

You may find, as you are cutting your stash, that there's a recurring theme happening. Let's say every time you reach in to start a new batch to cut, you pull out some holiday-themed prints. If this is the case, you might need separate bins for fabric themes in all three sizes. That way, if you decide to work on a scrappy holiday project, for example, you don't have to sort through everything just to find the holiday fabrics.

MAKE A TEST BLOCK

Once a theme is decided and scraps are selected, make a sample block. Place your test block on a design wall and stand back and take a good look at it from more than a few feet away. Does the block work? Do the mediums hold up against the lights and darks or the background fabrics? If they do, carry on and make more blocks. If they don't, the completion of one block is the best time to reconsider scrap selections.

It's so easy to get caught up in the excitement of seeing your first quilt block coming together. Try not to wait until all of the quilt blocks are done before you step back and evaluate. Often, the original test block can still be included in the quilt, even though fabric selection for the remaining blocks is tweaked a little bit.

STEP FIVE: USE TRADITIONAL TECHNIQUES AND TRY ALTERNATIVES

All the patterns in this book can be made with basic quilting supplies. Some patterns may suggest alternatives to more traditional methods, incorporating updated processes and tools to make the construction simpler, faster, or more efficient. With so many options available, choose the method, tool, or gadget that works best for you. This is a hobby, after all, and it's supposed to be fun!

GOTTA LOVE GADGETS

I love gadgets and sewing notions. If a tool makes a time-honored technique more accurate or simpler, it's a winner! Scrap quilts lend themselves especially well to testing and using the latest sewing notions. Because sewing small fabric scraps can sometimes become tedious, the infusion of sewing notions changes up familiar methods, refreshes standard techniques, and improves results.

TRIMMING TOOLS

Trimming tools are rulers with a specific job. Most quilters have a 6-in. or 7-in. square ruler with a bias line. These lined square rulers are the most-used trimming tools in my sewing room. Some trimming tools have a more specific, single-purpose use like trimming half-square and quarter-square triangle units.

As you contemplate a trimming tool purchase, consider the added value you'll have from using that tool in multiple projects and for trimming block units in a variety of sizes.

FUSIBLES

Printed fusible interfacing and fusible web can add ease and stability to a variety of scrap sewing projects. Fusible interfacing is available with a variety of printed grids, patterns, and appliqué shapes and comes unprinted as well.

Fusible web is a favorite for machine appliquérs. However, it also makes a quick and easy stabilizer. Fusible web usually comes with protective paper on one or both sides of the actual adhesive. When applying, be sure to follow the manufacturer's instructions for the specific brand you're using.

THE "BEST" TECHNIQUE OF ALL

Quilting is *your* hobby. The best gadget in the world for me might be the worst gadget for you. Just because all your friends have it doesn't mean you have to have it, too. Quilting creates an opportunity to choose from multiple methods and tools to complete almost any task. I like to try new techniques, notions, and gadgets, but sometimes the tried-and-true methods are the best.

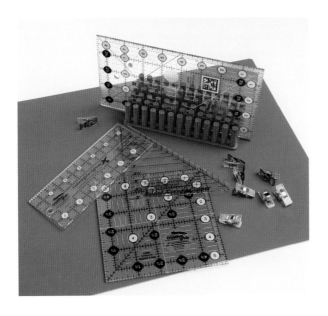

STEP SIX: PIECE AND SEW

As you sew your scraps together, keep this short list of tips in mind to help you make assembling your ScrapTherapy projects fun and problem free.

SCANT VERSUS TRUE ¼-IN. SEAMS

Most quilts are sewn together using a scant ¼-in. seam allowance, which is just one or two thread-widths shy of a true ¼-in. seam allowance. Many sewing machines have a ¼-in. foot for piecing quilts. As you sew, be sure to place the fabrics right sides together with raw edges aligned. Piecing accuracy starts by aligning your fabrics properly. The machine needle should enter the aligned fabric pieces just a little bit less than ¼ in. away from the aligned raw edges for a scant ¼-in. seam allowance.

CHAIN PIECING

Chain piecing is sewing two pieces of fabric together, taking two or three stitches off the edge, then sewing the next set of fabric pieces together. Cut the stitches in between, and press the seams as needed.

Because ScrapTherapy projects work with smaller fabric pieces, not strips, chain piecing is a logical sewing strategy. Sew a test block first, so any piecing issues or light/dark value questions are worked out. Once you're satisfied with the test block, sew multiple blocks using the chain-piecing technique.

TRUING UP FINISHED BLOCKS

Simply put, I don't like to trim finished blocks. Instead, I troubleshoot the problem and make adjustments to the construction steps. The problem almost always comes down to one of three issues: cutting, seam allowance, or pressing.

Take a close look at the block, first from the front. Are the block parts the correct size? Turn the block over. Are there any obvious out-of-shape pieces? Gently unpress some of the seams with your fingers. Measure the size of the cut pieces. Were the fabric pieces cut the correct size?

Check your seams. One seam that is too small or too big isn't really a big deal. But several seams that are off can be a real problem. Think about it. If a quilt block has seams consistently sewn too small, resulting in a block that is off by ¼ in., then it takes only four blocks sewn together in a row for the quilt to be off by a whole inch!

Finally, check the pressing. Place your fingernail right up against the seam. Does the tip of your nail disappear under an extra little flap in the seam? Are the seams stretched so piecing threads are showing?

Try making the block again, testing each unit size at each step. If you follow these steps and sleuth out what's creating the inaccuracy, it won't be necessary to true up the final block. I promise!

TRIMMING SUCCESS

When trimming block elements like half-square triangles, be sure to trim all four sides. Place the unit on your cutting mat, line up seams with the chosen trimming tool or ruler, and cut one or two sides, usually along the side and across the top. Then rotate the partially trimmed unit 180 degrees, line up the chosen trimming tool or ruler with the appropriate seams, and trim the remaining two sides. Work carefully when trimming across the top of the ruler.

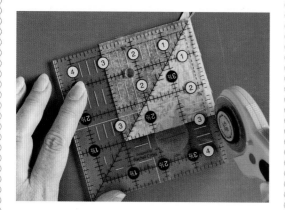

A TEST SEAM

A scant ¼-in. seam accommodates the thickness of the fabric as the seam is pressed to one side. To be completely confident of your seam accuracy, try a test seam using scraps from your bin.

Align and sew two 2-in. scrap squares. Press the seam to one side. For the best results, make the extra effort to press the seam with an iron instead of finger pressing. Place the pressed scrap 2-patch on your ruler. It should be exactly 2 in. by 3½ in.

If the test 2-patch is larger than 3½ in., your seam allowance is too small. Move the needle farther away from the edge of the fabric to make a larger seam allowance. If the test 2-patch is less than 3½ in. wide, then your seam allowance is too big. Move the needle closer to the edge of the fabric to make a narrower seam allowance.

Continue making test 2-patches until you have accurate results—or until you run out of 2-in. scrap squares!

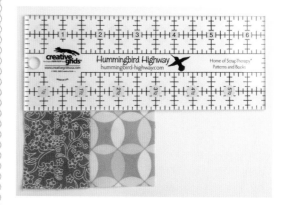

STEP SEVEN: FINISH THE QUILT

Some quilters enjoy the piecing, but not the quilting. Some prefer hand quilting or tying to hold the layers together. Choose your preference, and get the job done! Consider these finishing elements as you complete your project.

BACKING

Whether you quilt your project yourself or hire someone else to do it, all quilts need backing. As you work with it, the backing should be roughly 4 in. to 6 in. larger than the quilt top in each direction.

Most of the quilts in this book require that you piece the backing with at least two sections, assuming a standard 42-in. usable fabric width. You can avoid the math and the seams by using extra-wide backing fabrics, which are between 108 in. and 110 in. wide.

Backing yardage calculations are provided for each quilt. If the backing needs to be seamed, cut the yardage length in half (4 yd. becomes two 2-yd. pieces), and trim the selvage off one side of each backing fabric

piece. Sew a $\frac{1}{4}$-in. seam along the cut lengthwise edge and press the seam open. For better wear, avoid having a seam directly in the center of the quilt back.

LAYERING AND BASTING

The following steps assume that the quilt will be machine-quilted on a standard home machine. The layering and basting process can be different, depending on the quilting method, such as hand quilting or long- or short-arm quilting on a frame.

Layering and pin basting may seem tedious, but it's a critical step in the quilting process. With your work of art so close to being finished, it's easy to short-change these important steps; try to avoid that temptation.

SANDWICHING

Once the backing is seamed and pressed, firmly secure the flat backing, right side down, to a large worksurface. Use residue-free adhesive tape, such as painter's tape, to secure the backing to the worksurface.

Center the batting on the backing and smooth it with your hands from the center out until it's completely flat. Avoid the temptation to trim the batting at this stage.

Place the quilt top, right side up, on top of the batting. Starting in the center and working outward, smooth out any wrinkles, puckers, and folds. Rough-cut the batting layer 1 in. to 2 in. beyond the quilt top's edges.

PIN BASTING

Beginning at one corner of the quilt center, place curved safety pins through all three layers of the quilt.

Place pins 2 in. to 3 in. apart. Once the quilt center is pinned, pin the borders. When the entire top is pin-basted, remove the tape from all four sides of the quilt

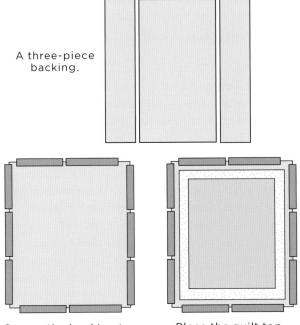

A three-piece backing.

Secure the backing to the worksurface.

Place the quilt top, right side up, on top of the batting.

backing. If there is enough extra backing material, fold the backing edge over the raw edges of the quilt to protect them from fraying during quilting. Pin the fold to the edge of the quilt through all layers with another series of curved safety pins. Don't be surprised if you use several hundred pins to baste a twin-size quilt.

QUILT AS DESIRED

For some quilters, *quilt as desired* are the three most dreaded words in pattern instructions. I say, "Bring it on!" If you have a walking foot or an integrated dual-feed foot, you can easily machine-quilt your own project on a standard sewing machine. With a little practice and a darning foot, you can add some free-motion quilting. Or walk away from the sewing machine and do some hand quilting.

QUILTING ON A STANDARD SEWING MACHINE

Machine quilting can be fast and fun but sometimes intimidating. Machine-quilting classes at your local quilt shop can help you hone your skills. Excellent instructional DVDs and online videos are also available. However, the best way to improve your machine-quilting skills is experience. Roll up your sleeves and dive in! Look for more tips on machine quilting on p. 209.

HAND QUILTING

Hand quilting is traditional, beautiful, relaxing, and perfectly suited for scrappy quilts. Hand quilting can be done with or without hoops and frames. Seek out a local hand-quilting expert and take some classes to perfect this time-tested skill.

TIED QUILTS

Tied quilts offer another classic effect perfectly suited to scrappy projects. To tie a quilt, use yarn or heavy thread (like perle cotton) to make the ties. The finished knots can be on the right or wrong side of the quilt, depending on your preference.

Thread a needle with the yarn or thread and insert it straight into the quilt from the side on which you want the finished knots. Leave about a 2-in.-long tail. Take a

small stitch and bring the thread back up through all the layers. Tie off in a square knot.

Ties should be no more than 3 in. to 4 in. apart across the quilt surface. After the tying is complete, clip all thread tails evenly to about $3/4$ in. long.

BINDING

When all the quilting is done, it's time to encase the raw edges of the quilt with binding.

To prepare the binding, cut the recommended number of $2\frac{1}{4}$-in.-wide binding strips. Most of the projects in this book assume cross-grain binding cuts. Bias binding may be substituted for a different look and for a more stretchy binding, particularly nice when curved edges are involved, as in "Cross-Body Market Sack" on p. 110. However, the yardage and number of cuts needed may vary slightly between cross-grain and bias binding. Join the strips end to end using a diagonal seam. Fold the binding in half, wrong sides together.

Prepare the quilt for binding by trimming the batting and backing even with the quilt top's edges. Beginning along one straight side (never at the corner), sew the binding to the quilt with the raw edges aligned. Miter the binding at each of the corners. Fold the binding over the quilt edge and sew the folded edge to the back of the quilt by hand. For additional instructions on binding your quilt, see pp. 210–213.

LABEL

The label is the quilt's voice. Reach into your scrap bin for one more square of light-value fabric. Grab a permanent fabric-marking pen and a piece of fine-grain sandpaper. Place the fabric on the sandpaper for stability, and jot down the important stuff!

The label doesn't have to be complicated; all you need is a square, rectangle, or other shape and enough space to write. Jazz it up with embroidery, computer graphics, cross-stitch, or running stitches.

To sew the label to the back of the quilt, fold and press under a $1/4$-in. seam allowance around the edges, then pin the label in place with appliqué pins on a lower corner of the backing. Secure the label by hand using an appliqué stitch through the backing.

The handwritten label on the quilt reads:

Pomegranate Rose
Table Topper
Scraps to the 9's
designed & stitched by
JonJone
January 2016
gentle wash & cool dry

LABEL DETAILS

Use the label to detail information about the quilt. Here are a few suggestions:

- the name of the quiltmaker
- the date the quilt was finished and how long it took to complete
- the pattern name, source, and designer
- the city, state, and country in which it was made
- special care instructions, to accommodate batting fiber content or embellishments
- the occasion it commemorates

PICTURE THIS!

Only one more task needs to be completed before the quilt is officially and truly done. Before your quilt goes to the lucky recipient, take a picture of it and its label.

Why bother with a picture? One finished quilt leads to another, and you can easily forget the details associated with your quilts. A printed or digital photo is all you need to keep a record of your projects. Be sure to include a photo of the label, too.

FINISHED SCRAP QUILTS

The beauty of scrap quilts is that no two are exactly alike. Two quilters digging into their own scrap bins to make the same exact pattern could end up making quilts that look wildly different from each other. And that's when the fun really begins!

The Projects

Moody Blue

FEATURING THE ELEVATED 9-PATCH

FINISHED QUILT SIZE: **59 in. by 75 in. (lap quilt); 90 in. by 90 in. (bed-size quilt)**
PATTERN DIFFICULTY: **Easy**

I'm an avid fan of new fabric purchasing. Sometimes, as is the case for this quilt project, the scraps become the background to the combination of prints and solids chosen by the yard, wrapped up in a pretty bag to come home with me from the quilt shop.

For this quilt, the spotted-splashy cool-tone fabric used for the block sashing came first. It was then joined by lots of cool-tone scraps that coordinated with the spots. The soft yellow yardage used for the blocks and sashing strips added a little warmth to all the cool scraps and dots. And the purple border jumped in at the very end to encircle the quilt with deep, rich color.

No matter what prints and colors you choose for your scrappy creation, you'll find that this 9-patch project, based on the classic churn dash block, goes together smoothly and quickly. The 9-patch elements aren't perfectly matched in size, but they use up ScrapTherapy scraps with very little trimming and waste.

The lap quilt shown in the photograph on the facing page is one of two quilt sizes included in this pattern.

SCRAPS NEEDED FOR LAP QUILT

Square Size	Description	Quantity Needed	Notes and Cutting Instructions
2"	To coordinate with sashing print	40	
5"	To coordinate with sashing print	54	

FABRICS AND OTHER MATERIALS FOR LAP QUILT

Materials	Quantity Needed	Notes and Cutting Instructions
Background print	2 yd.	• Cut seven 5″ width-of-fabric strips; then cut fifty-six 5″ squares for the blocks. Following diagram **1**, with a pencil, draw a diagonal line from corner to corner on the back of 24 squares. • Cut eleven 2″ width-of-fabric strips for the pieced sashing units. • Cut two 2″ width-of-fabric strips for the cornerstone piecing.
Accent print	3⁄4 yd.	• Cut eleven 2″ width-of-fabric strips for the pieced sashing units.
Border print	1½ yd.	• Cut eight 5½″ width-of-fabric strips for the borders.
Binding	½ yd.	• Cut seven 2¼″ width-of-fabric strips for the binding.
Backing	5 yd.	
Batting	64″ x 80″	

SCRAPS NEEDED FOR BED-SIZE QUILT

Square Size	Description	Quantity Needed	Notes and Cutting Instructions
2″	To coordinate with sashing print	72	
5″	To coordinate with sashing print	112	

Materials	Quantity Needed	Notes and Cutting Instructions
Background print	3²⁄₃ yd.	• Cut fifteen 5″ width-of-fabric strips; then cut one hundred thirteen 5″ squares for the blocks. With a pencil, draw a diagonal line from corner to corner on the back of 50 squares. See diagram **1**. • Cut twenty 2″ width-of-fabric strips for the pieced sashing units. • Cut four 2″ width-of-fabric strips for the cornerstone piecing.
Accent print	1¼ yd.	• Cut twenty 2″ width-of-fabric strips for the pieced sashing units.
Border print	1½ yd.	• Cut nine 5½″ width-of-fabric strips for the borders.
Binding	²⁄₃ yd.	• Cut ten 2¼″ width-of fabric strips for the binding.
Backing	8½ yd.	
Batting	95″ x 95″	

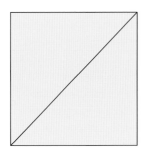

1

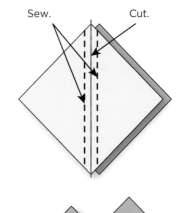

Sew.   Cut.

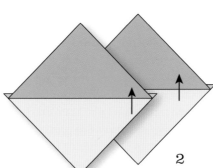

2

MAKE THE BLOCKS

FOR THE LAP QUILT

Select a 5-in. scrap square and a 5-in. background square (with drawn diagonal line) **1**, and place them right sides together with the background fabric on top. Sew a ¼-in. seam on both sides of the drawn line. Cut on the line, then press the seams toward the scrap fabric. **2** Trim each of the half-square triangle (HST) units to 4½ in. square. Repeat to make 48 HST units that measure 4½ in. square.

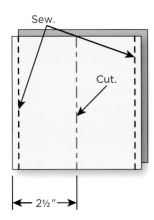

Sew.

Cut.

2½"

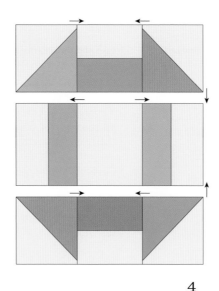

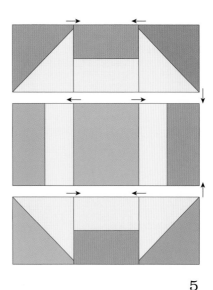

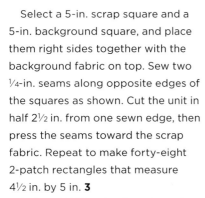

3

4

5

Select a 5-in. scrap square and a 5-in. background square, and place them right sides together with the background fabric on top. Sew two ¼-in. seams along opposite edges of the squares as shown. Cut the unit in half 2½ in. from one sewn edge, then press the seams toward the scrap fabric. Repeat to make forty-eight 2-patch rectangles that measure 4½ in. by 5 in. **3**

Select 4 HST units, four 2-patch rectangles, and one 5-in. background square, and arrange them into a 9-patch block with the background square in the center and with background fabrics along

all outer edges of the block. Sew the units into rows, press the seams as shown, and then sew the rows together and press. Repeat to make six 13-in. square background blocks for the lap quilt. Set aside. **4**

Select 4 HST units, four 2-patch rectangles, and one 5-in. scrap square, and arrange them into a 9-patch block with the scrap square in the center and with scrap fabrics along all outer edges of the block. Sew the units into rows, press the seams as shown, and then sew the rows together and press. Repeat to make six 13-in. square scrap blocks for the lap quilt. Set aside. **5**

FOR THE BED-SIZE QUILT

Select a 5-in. scrap square and a 5-in. background square (with drawn diagonal line), and place them right sides together with the background fabric on top. Sew a ¼-in. seam on both sides of the drawn line. Cut on the line, then press the seams toward the scrap fabric. Trim each of

the half-square triangle (HST) units to 4½ in. square. Repeat to make 100 HST units that measure 4½ in. square. **2**

Select a 5-in. scrap square and a 5-in. background square, and place them right sides together with the background fabric on top. Sew two ¼-in. seams along opposite edges of the squares as shown. Cut the unit in half 2½ in. from one sewn edge, then press the seams toward the scrap fabric. Repeat to make one hundred 2-patch rectangles that measure 4½ in. by 5 in. **3**

Select 4 HST units, four 2-patch rectangles, and one 5-in. background square, and arrange them into a 9-patch block with the background square in the center and with background fabrics along all outer edges of the block. Sew the units into rows, press the seams as shown, and then sew the rows together and press. Repeat to make thirteen 13-in. square background blocks for the bed-size quilt. Set aside. **4**

Select 4 HST units, four 2-patch rectangles, and one 5-in. scrap square, and arrange them into a 9-patch block with the scrap square in the center and with scrap fabrics along all outer edges of the block. Sew the units into rows, press the seams as shown, and then sew the rows together and press. Repeat to make twelve 13-in. square scrap blocks for the bed-size quilt. Set aside. **5**

MAKE THE SASHING
FOR THE LAP QUILT
Sew each 2-in. background fabric strip to a 2-in. accent fabric strip on one long edge as shown. Press the seams on 5 of the strip sets toward the accent fabric, then cross-cut the strips into fifteen 3½-in. by 13-in. horizontal sashing units. Press the seams on the remaining 6 strip sets toward the background fabric; then cross-cut the strips into sixteen 3½-in. by 13-in. vertical sashing units. Keep the horizontal and vertical sashing strips together, but separate from each other, and set aside. **6**

FOR THE BED-SIZE QUILT
Sew each 2-in. background fabric strip to a 2-in. accent fabric strip on one long edge as shown. Press the seams on 10 of the strip sets toward the accent fabric, then cross-cut the strips into thirty 3½-in. by 13-in. horizontal sashing units. Press the seams on the remaining 10 strip sets toward the background fabric; then cross-cut the strips into thirty 3½-in. by 13-in. vertical sashing units. Keep the horizontal and vertical sashing strips together, but separate from each other, and set aside. **6**

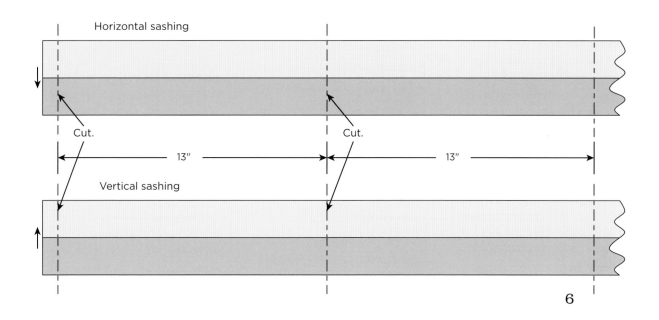

Horizontal sashing

Cut.   Cut.

|←——— 13" ———→|←——— 13" ———→|

Vertical sashing

6

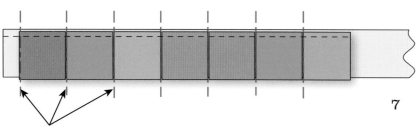

Cut between sewn units.

7

MAKE THE CORNERSTONES

FOR THE LAP QUILT

Randomly select and align a 2-in. scrap square on a 2-in. background strip, right sides together. Sew the scrap square to the background strip on the long edge with a ¼-in. seam. Without breaking the thread, align and sew a second scrap square to the background strip, leaving minimal space between the sewn scrap squares. Continue adding scrap squares to the background strips until the forty 2-in. scrap squares are sewn to the two 2-in. background strips. Cut the 2-patch units apart, even with the scrap squares, and press the seams toward the scrap fabric to make forty 2-in. by 3½-in. 2-patch units. Press the seams toward the scrap square. **7**

Pair two 2-patch units randomly and sew them together to make twenty 4-patch units. Furl the 4-patch scraps as shown on p. 13.

Important! Sew 10 pairs of the 2-patch units so each feeds into the sewing machine with the background fabric first, **8A** and sew 10 pairs of the 2-patch units so each feeds into the sewing machine with the scrap fabric first. **8B** Press and furl the seams as shown. Separate the blocks into 2 stacks based on the direction of the furl.

Based on how the 4-patch units are sewn, the 4-patch seams will furl in opposite directions, clockwise or counterclockwise (as seen from the front of the 4-patch). This technique, where half of the cornerstones furl in one direction and half furl in the other direction, will come in handy when the quilt is assembled. By following the cornerstone and sashing pressing direction carefully, all the connecting sashing and cornerstone element seams will nest and oppose as they are sewn to each other.

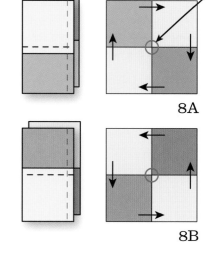

Furl.

8A

8B

FOR THE BED-SIZE QUILT

Randomly select and align a 2-in. scrap square on a 2-in. background strip, right sides together. Sew the scrap square to the background strip on the long edge with a ¼-in. seam. Without breaking the thread, align and sew a second scrap square to the background strip, leaving minimal space between the sewn scrap squares. Continue adding scrap squares to the background strips until the seventy-two 2-in. scrap squares are sewn to the four 2-in. background strips. Cut the 2-patch units apart, even with the scrap squares, and press the seams toward the scrap fabric to make seventy-two 2-in. by 3½-in. 2-patch units. Press the seams toward the scrap square. **7**

Pair two 2-patch units randomly and sew them together to make thirty-six 4-patch units.

Important! Sew 18 pairs of the 2-patch units so each feeds into the sewing machine with the background fabric first, **8A** and sew 18 pairs of the 2-patch units so each feeds into the sewing machine with the scrap fabric first. **8B** Press and furl the seams as shown. Separate the blocks into 2 stacks based on the direction of the furl.

ASSEMBLE THE QUILT

Arrange the cornerstones, horizontal and vertical sashing units, and blocks into rows (for the lap quilt, 4 rows of 3 blocks; for the bed-size quilt, 5 rows of 5 blocks). Alternate the placement of the clockwise (identified with a red "C" on the illustration) and counterclockwise (identified with a red "X" on the illustration) cornerstones in the quilt arrangement. At the same time, alternate the placement of background blocks and scrap blocks.

Sew the cornerstones and horizontal sashing units into sashing rows. Nest the cornerstone and sashing seams at each intersection. Press the seams toward the sashing unit. Sew the vertical sashing units and blocks into block rows, and press the seams toward the sashing units. Sew the rows together, nesting all the sashing, cornerstone, and block seam intersections. Press the seams between the blocks toward the sashing rows. **9**, **10**

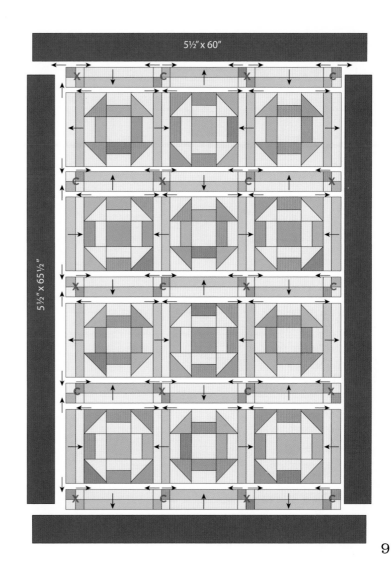

9

MAKE THE BORDERS
FOR THE LAP QUILT

Sew two 5½-in. width-of-fabric border strips together end to end with a diagonal seam as shown on p. 205, and press the connecting seams open to make a strip 5½ in. by approximately 80 in. long.

Repeat to make a total of four 80-in. border strips. Trim 2 strips to 5½-in. by 65½-in. side borders. Trim the remaining 2 border strips to 5½-in. by 60-in. top and bottom borders. Sew the borders to the quilt, sides first, then top and bottom. Press the seam toward the border after each addition. **9**

FOR THE BED-SIZE QUILT

Sew all nine 5½-in. width-of-fabric border strips together end to end with diagonal seams. Press the connecting seams open. Cut two 5½-in. by 81-in. side borders and two 5½-in. by 91-in. top and bottom borders. Sew the borders to the quilt,

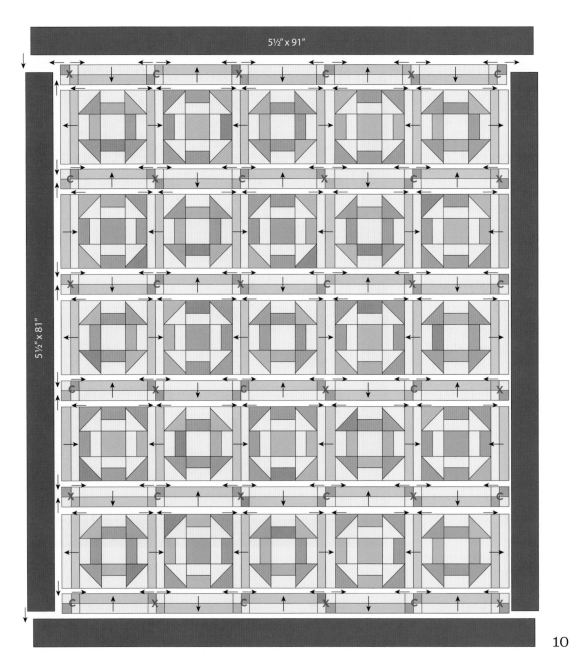

5½" x 91"

5½" x 81"

10

sides first, then top and bottom. Press the seam toward the border after each addition. **10**

QUILT AND BIND
Layer the backing, batting, and quilt top; baste. Quilt as desired.

Refer to the charts on pp. 46–47 for the number of strips to cut for the lap and bed-size quilts. Sew the binding strips together end to end using a diagonal seam. Press the connecting seams open; then press the binding in half lengthwise, wrong sides together.

Trim the batting and backing even with the quilt top. With the raw edges aligned, sew the binding to the front of the quilt using a ¼-in. seam. Miter the binding at the corners.

Turn the folded edge of the binding to the back of the quilt and hand-stitch it in place.

Button Collection Pillow

FEATURING THE NESTED 9-PATCH

FINISHED SIZE: 24 in. by 24 in.
PATTERN DIFFICULTY: Easy

When I was growing up, my father smoked cigars, and the best part of those cigars was definitely not the stinky smell when he smoked them, but the box they came in. With a little paint and creativity, that sturdy cardboard box with its flip-top lid could hold all kinds of treasures! I remember one brightly painted cigar box, in particular, that I filled with crayons and stored in the basement, where my sister and I created colorful masterpieces on seasonal bulletin boards.

My mother used one of those boxes to store her massive button collection. She kept a huge variety of buttons in all colors and sizes in an old cigar box, just in case she needed a button to fix a garment. You could reach in and pull out handfuls of buttons at a time—they made gentle, tinkling *chink-chink* sounds as they spilled back into the box through your fingers. There must have been several hundred buttons, in many different sizes and shapes, in that magical box!

The scrappy buttons tossed across this 24-in. pillow remind me of that old button collection. Each colorful button on the pillow is made from a single 5-in. scrap square plus a couple of squares of the pillow background fabric. A 9-patch block at the center of each playful button simulates the buttonholes.

SCRAPS NEEDED

Square Size	Description	Quantity Needed	Notes and Cutting Instructions
5″	Novelty print scrap squares	18	Follow diagram **1** to cut each square: • One 1″ x 5″ strip, subcut into five 1″ squares. • Two 1½″ x 4″ strips. • Two 1½″ x 2″ rectangles.

Materials	Quantity Needed	Notes and Cutting Instructions
White fabric	1½ yd.	• Cut two 24½" width-of-fabric strips. From one strip, cut one 24½" square pillow front. From the second strip, cut two 18" x 24½" pillow back panels. • From the leftover fabric, cut seventy-two 1" squares.
12" wide paper-backed fusible web	¼ yd.	• Cut four 2" x 12" strips.
20" wide plain fusible interfacing	½ yd.	
24" square pillow form		

RECOMMENDED MATERIALS

Materials	Quantity Needed	Notes and Cutting Instructions
ScrapTherapy Mini Scrap Grid Interfacing	1 panel	• 2 sections of 1 panel will be used.
Quiltsmart ZigZapps!™ circles	2 panels	

MAKE THE BUTTONS AND PILLOW FRONT

Select the prepared scraps cut from one 5-in. square. Arrange five 1-in. scrap squares and four 1-in. background squares into a 9-patch block with background corners and scrap center and sides. Sew as for a basic 9-patch with furled seams as shown on pp. 13–14. Each 9-patch block measures 2 in. square. **2**

Sew a 1½-in. by 2-in. scrap rectangle to opposite sides of the 9-patch block. Press the seams toward the scrap rectangles.

Sew a 1½-in. by 4-in. strip to each side of the 9-patch unit. Press the seams toward the scrap strips. The button unit measures 4 in. square. Repeat to make 18 button units from the cut pieces from each unique 5-in. scrap square. **3**

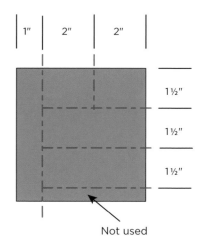

Not used

1

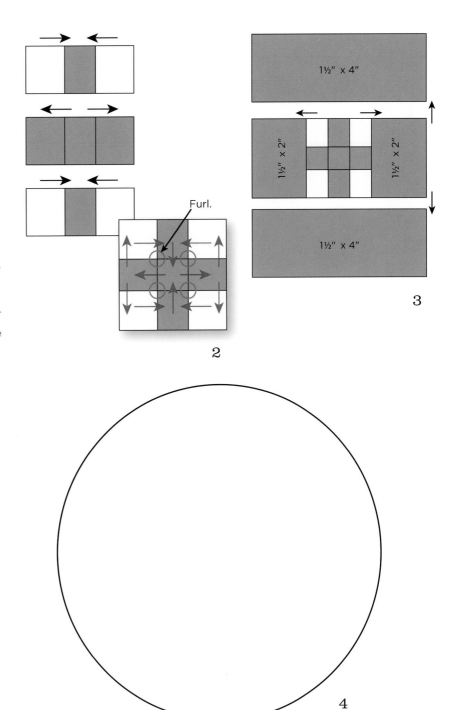

Furl.

2

1½" x 4"

1½" x 2"   1½" x 2"

1½" x 4"

3

4

Two sections of the ScrapTherapy Mini Scrap Grid Interfacing help to stabilize the 1-in. squares forming the button centers. Follow the instructions on pp. 18–24. Once the 1-in. squares are fused on the interfacing, you are only 24 longer seams away from having the itty-bitty blocks sewn. Cut the blocks apart, furl the seams, and trim to 2 in. square. The miniature 9-patches are ready to sew to the 1½-in.-wide strips to complete the button blocks.

Using a permanent fabric marker, trace eighteen 3½-in.-diameter circles on the smooth side of the plain fusible interfacing, leaving about ½ in. between the shapes. Rough-cut the shapes at least ¼ in. away from the drawn lines. Fold each interfacing circle in half, and make a cut about 1 in. long. You'll use the cut for turning later. **4**

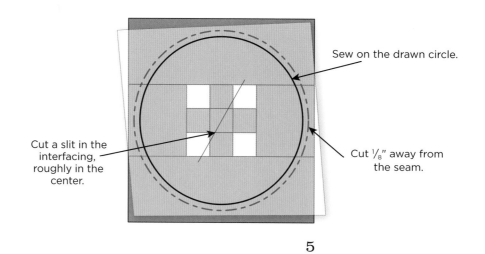

Sew on the drawn circle.

Cut ⅛" away from the seam.

Cut a slit in the interfacing, roughly in the center.

5

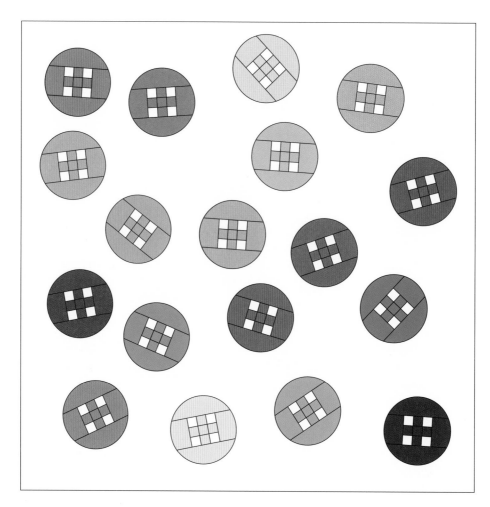

6

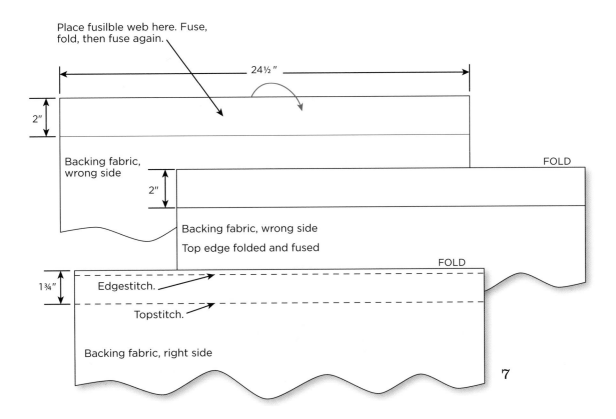

Place fusilble web here. Fuse, fold, then fuse again.

24½″

2″

Backing fabric, wrong side

FOLD

2″

Backing fabric, wrong side

Top edge folded and fused

FOLD

1¾″

Edgestitch.

Topstitch.

Backing fabric, right side

7

Place each interfacing circle on a button block with the fusible side of the interfacing facing the right side of the block. Center the 9-patch block within the drawn circle. Pin the interfacing to the block; then sew on the drawn line carefully. A shorter stitch length may help to maintain the curved line. Trim the block and the interfacing ⅛ in. away from the sewn line. **5**

Turn the shape right side out through the opening in the interfacing. Repeat with all 18 button blocks to make 18 round interfaced buttons.

Arrange the interfaced buttons playfully on the 24½-in. pillow background fabric, placing them at least 1 in. away from the fabric edges.

Fuse the buttons with a hot iron and a puff of steam. **6**

Secure the button edge with a machine blanket or zigzag stitch. Set aside.

> In lieu of plain fusible interfacing, substitute Quiltsmart printed circle interfacing, which can be purchased by the panel. The number of circles on each panel may vary; you'll need enough panels to make 18 circles that are 3½-in. finished size.

MAKE THE PILLOW BACK

Place the fusible side of two 2-in. by 12-in. fusible web strips end to end and aligned with one 24½-in. edge of a backing rectangle. Fuse the web in place, then remove the paper. Fold the fabric 2 in. from the edge and fuse in place. Edgestitch, then topstitch 1¾ in. away from the fold. Repeat with the second pillow backing rectangle. **7**

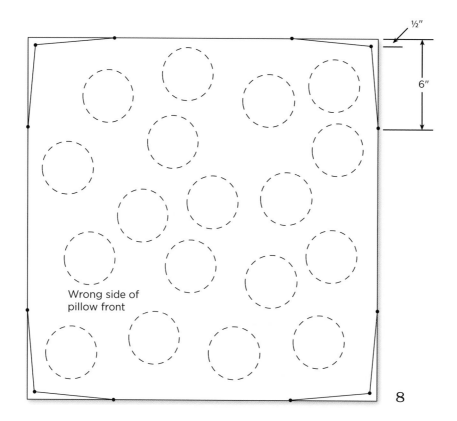

½"

6"

Wrong side of
pillow front

8

ASSEMBLE THE PILLOW

Place the pillow front right side down on your worksurface. Make a mark ½ in. from the corner, as shown. Then make a second mark on each adjacent side 6 in. from the corner. Draw a line connecting the marks. Repeat for all four corners. **8**

Place the pillow front right side up on a large worksurface. Make sure it is completely flat.

Place one backing piece, right side down, on the pillow front, with raw edges aligned.

Place the second backing piece, right side down, on the pillow front assembly, aligning the raw edges on the opposite side of the pillow top. Pin liberally around the entire pillow assembly to secure the edges. **9**

Flip the entire assembly so the wrong (marked corner) side of the pillow front is facing up. Sew a ¼-in. seam allowance around the entire outside edge and along the corner markings following the dashed line. Remove the pins as you sew. Trim on the lines. **10**

Turn the pillow assembly right side out through the opening in the back. Insert a 24-in. square pillow form.

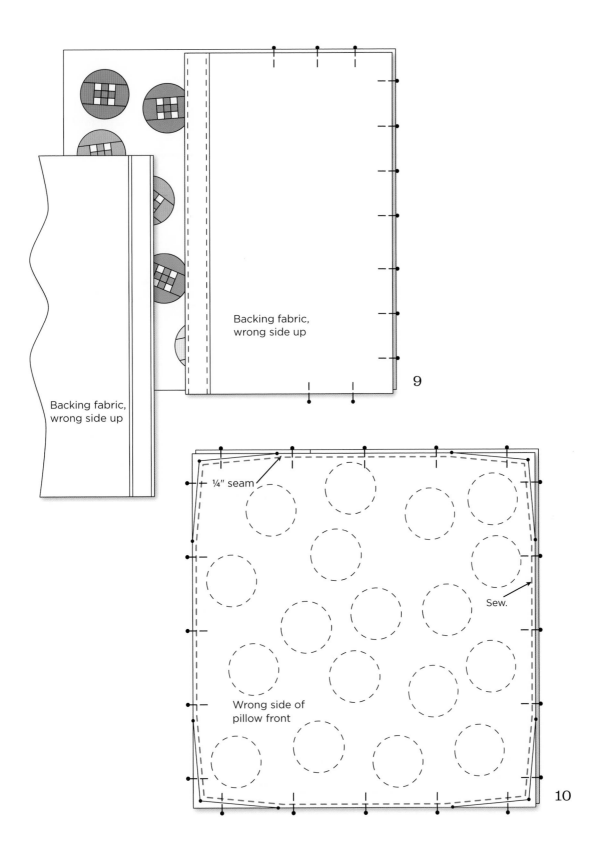

Backing fabric,
wrong side up

Backing fabric,
wrong side up

9

¼" seam

Sew.

Wrong side of
pillow front

10

Daisy Fresh Runner

FEATURING THE BASIC 9-PATCH AND THE NESTED 9-PATCH

FINISHED SIZE: **17 in. by 53 in.**

PATTERN DIFFICULTY: **Easy +**

I've heard some say, "A little yellow goes a long way in a quilt," meaning yellow is one of those colors that can steal the attention away from the main-player fabrics in a typical quilted project. Yellow has a tendency to be boastful and brave when placed next to colors that may not hold up to its "personality." Therefore, using it sparingly in your quilts can be well advised, with *can* being the operative word.

Yellow has a broad range, from rusty-golden, nearly brown to lemony bright yellow. For this bright and sunny runner, I decided to take on yellow's challenge and make it the main player. Smaller 9-patches fit within larger 9-patches composed of bright yellow scraps offset with bright white squares cut from yardage to form the cheery Irish chain center of the runner. A border of blended 9-patches encircles the runner for a postage stamp finish and adds shades of light green and gray in the mix of bright yellow scraps. This runner makes me think of an early summer garden filled with bright yellow buds and crisp white daisies with spring greenery encircling the garden.

SCRAPS NEEDED

Square Size	Description	Quantity Needed	Notes and Cutting Instructions
$3\frac{1}{2}''$	Bright yellow scrap squares	22	
$1\frac{1}{2}''$ or larger	Bright yellow scrap squares	96	• Cut ninety-six $1\frac{1}{2}''$ squares from a combination of 2″, $3\frac{1}{2}''$, and 5″ squares.
$1\frac{1}{2}''$ or larger	Bright yellow, light green, and light gray scrap squares	360	• Cut a total of three hundred sixty $1\frac{1}{2}''$ squares from a combination of 2″, $3\frac{1}{2}''$, and 5″ squares.

Materials	Quantity Needed	Notes and Cutting Instructions
White fabric	½ yd.	• Cut nine 1½" width-of-fabric strips. From 5 strips, cut one hundred fifteen 1½" squares for the block. Reserve 4 strips for the borders.
Backing fabric	⅞ yd.	
Light green binding fabric	⅓ yd.	• Cut four 2¼" width-of-fabric strips for the binding.
Batting	20" x 56"	

RECOMMENDED MATERIALS

Materials	Quantity Needed	Notes and Cutting Instructions
ScrapTherapy Middle Scrap Grid Interfacing	3 panels	• 2 full panels plus 2 sections of 1 panel will be used.

Use the sidebar on p. 9 to calculate how many larger ScrapTherapy scraps will yield enough of the smaller scraps needed for this project.

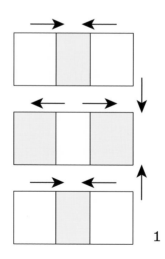

1

MAKE THE BLOCKS
NESTED 9-PATCHES
Randomly select four 1½-in. bright yellow scrap squares and five 1½-in. white squares. Arrange and sew the squares into a basic 9-patch with a yellow scrap center and corners and white sides. Sew the squares into a basic 9-patch. Press the seams within the rows toward the darker fabric. Press the row seams toward the center of the block. Repeat to make twenty-three 3½-in. square yellow-and-white 9-patches. **1**

Randomly select four 3½-in. bright yellow scrap squares and five 3½-in. square 9-patches. Arrange the squares into a basic 9-patch with a 9-patch center and corners and

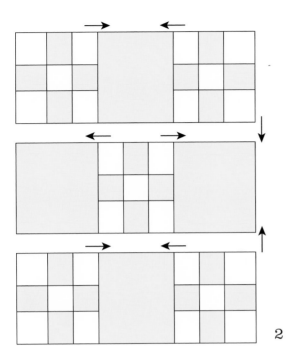

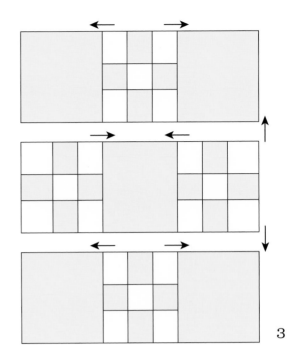

2

3

bright yellow scrap sides. Sew the squares into a basic 9-patch. Repeat to make three 9½-in. square nested 9-patches. **2**

Randomly select five 3½-in. bright yellow scrap squares and four 3½-in. 9-patches. Arrange the squares into a basic 9-patch with 9-patch sides and a bright yellow scrap center and corners. Sew the squares into a basic 9-patch. Repeat to make two 9½-in. square nested 9-patches. **3**

Sew the nested 9-patches together, alternating the blocks, starting and ending with a 9½-in. square patch that has five smaller 9-patches, one in the center and in each corner. Press the seams as shown. **4**

MAKE THE BORDERS

Randomly select nine 1½-in. bright yellow, light green, and light gray scrap squares. Arrange the squares into a basic blended 9-patch with randomly placed scraps, then sew the squares into a basic blended 9-patch. Press and furl the seams as shown on pp. 13–14. Repeat to make forty 3½-in. square blended 9-patches. **5**

Select 15 blended blocks and arrange them randomly in a row. Sew the blended 9-patch blocks together, rotating the blocks so the connecting seams nest and oppose to make a postage stamp side border that measures 3½ in. by 45½ in. Furl the seams connecting the blended 9-patch blocks. Repeat to make a second postage stamp side border. **6**

Similarly, select and sew 3 blended blocks and arrange them randomly in a row. Sew the blocks together, rotating them so the connecting seams nest and oppose to make a postage stamp top border that measures 3½ in. by 9½ in. Furl the seams connecting the blended 9-patch blocks. Repeat to make a second postage stamp bottom border. Set aside all 4 borders along with the 4 remaining blended 9-patch blocks.

Sew three 1½-in. white width-of-fabric strips end to end using a diagonal seam as shown on p. 205 to make a strip that is approximately 120 in. long. Cut two 1½-in. by 45½-in. side inner borders.

From the remainder of the pieced strip and from the remaining width-of-fabric strip, cut two 1½-in. by 9½-in. strips and eight 1½-in. by 3½-in. strips.

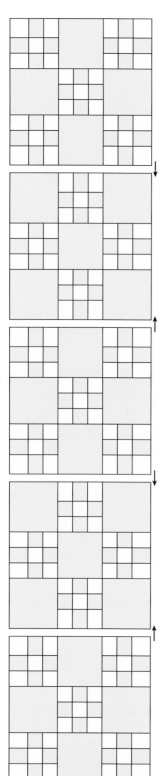

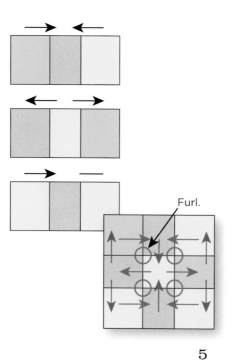

Furl.

5

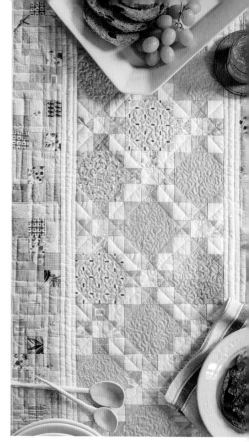

4

Pieced borders can be tricky. I often get nervous that the pieced border will not be long enough to fit on the quilt, so I make my seam allowances extra scant. The result: Too-scant seams create a border that is too long! To fix this situation, lay the border next to the quilt center on a flat surface to assess the variance. If your border is a bit too long for the quilt center, maybe about ½ in. or so, don't grab for the seam ripper! Instead, select a few seams along the row of 9-patches that can benefit from a larger seam allowance, and sew a seam just to the inside of the existing seam. You would be surprised how much difference that small correction on only a few 9-patch seams will make in the border length. Keep laying the border back on the flat surface next to the center until you're satisfied that the center is in harmony with the borders.

If your border is a bit too short, take another look at the seams connecting the blended 9-patch blocks. If there are any that appear to be more than a scant ¼ in., remove and re-seam to tighten up the border so it fits perfectly.

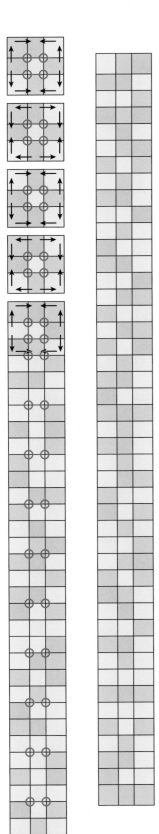

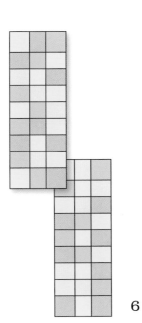

6

Arrange the table runner center, the white strips, the postage stamp border, the remaining four 1½-in. yellow scraps, and the blended 9-patch blocks as shown. Sew the elements into rows, then sew the rows together, using a ¼-in. seam allowance. Press the strips as shown. **7**

QUILT AND BIND

Cut the backing in half along the lengthwise grain to make two 21-in. by 31-in. rectangles. Sew the 2 halves together along a shorter side to make a 21-in. by approximately 62-in. rectangle for the backing. Press the backing seam open.

Layer the backing, batting, and table runner top; baste. Quilt as desired.

Sew the binding strips together end to end using a diagonal seam. Press the connecting seams open; then press the binding in half lengthwise, wrong sides together.

Trim the batting and backing even with the table runner top. With the raw edges aligned, sew the folded binding to the front of the quilt using a ¼-in. seam. Miter the binding at the corners.

Turn the folded edge of the binding to the back of the quilt and hand-stitch it in place.

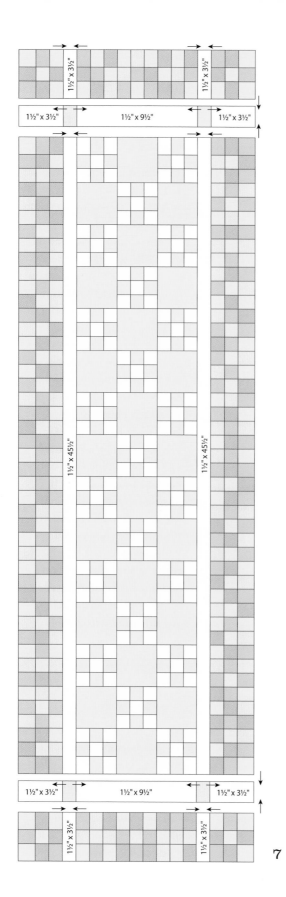

1½" x 3½"

1½" x 3½"

1½" x 3½" 1½" x 9½" 1½" x 3½"

1½" x 45½" 1½" x 45½"

1½" x 3½" 1½" x 9½" 1½" x 3½"

1½" x 3½"

1½" x 3½"

7

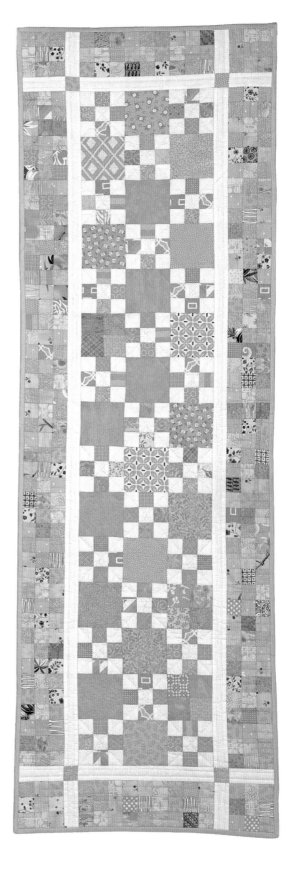

Fiesta!

FEATURING THE HIDDEN 9-PATCH

FINISHED QUILT SIZE: **58 in. by 73 in.**
PATTERN DIFFICULTY: **Intermediate**

My motivation for this quilt, aside from using tons of scraps, started with the purchase of a luscious fat quarter bundle of solid, intensely colored fabrics. The bright print border came next. The border fabric reminds me of a Mexican market with lots of visual stimulation. The rest fell together easily. Initially, I thought about making each block with one fat quarter color and scraps—adding scraps in light tones from its paired deep, dark fat quarter.

After assembling the block elements, the quilt called to me to mix things up a bit in the blocks to continue the chaotic cheerfulness of the border. The fat quarter leftovers along with some crisp white yardage were used in the sashing elements featuring—you guessed it!—9-patch cornerstones.

The key to making this quilt is staying organized. I'll walk you through a series of smart techniques to make the flying geese for each block from a pair of 9-patches sewn side-by-side with stitch-and-flip corners (see pp. 72–73). Nothing goes to waste. One element leads to another—block elements, then blocks, then the quilt.

The block itself is an elongated 9-patch with lots of elevated pieced elements.

To keep from being overwhelmed with small scraps and lots of fat quarter parts, cut incrementally. A set of block elements will be constructed from 1 fat quarter plus sixty-eight $1\frac{1}{2}$-in. squares. To make the quilt shown, I selected scraps in a lighter tone that matched the fat quarter color. For example, for a block based on a dark blue fat quarter, select scraps in a significantly lighter version of the dark blue. To avoid a "muddy" block without defined elements, be careful to select scraps high in contrast to the fat quarter you are working with.

Square Size	Description	Quantity Needed	Notes and Cutting Instructions
1½"	Light-value scrap squares	816	Cut from a combination of 2", 3½", and 5" scrap squares.

FABRICS AND OTHER MATERIALS

Materials	Quantity Needed	Notes and Cutting Instructions
Bright solid-color fat quarters	12	• From each fat quarter, cut eight 3½" squares, two 1½" x 4½" strips, two 1½" x 6½" strips, and four 1½" squares for the block corners. Draw a diagonal line from corner to corner on the back of each 3½" square. • From the fat quarter remainders, cut a total of thirty-one 1½" by 12½" strips for the pieced sashing elements, and one hundred 1½" squares for the 9-patch cornerstones. Mix up the colors.
White-on-white print fabric	1⅔ yd.	• Cut three 12½" width-of-fabric strips; subcut into sixty-two 1½" x 12½" strips for the sashing. • Cut two 3½" width-of-fabric strips; subcut into forty-eight 1½" x 3½" strips for the blocks. • Cut two 2½" width-of-fabric strips; subcut into forty-eight 1½" x 2½" strips for the blocks. • Cut three 1½" width-of-fabric strips; subcut into eighty 1½" squares for the cornerstones.
Focus print fabric	1¼ yd.	• Cut seven 5½" width-of-fabric strips for the borders.
Binding fabric	½ yd.	• Cut seven 2¼" width-of-fabric strips for binding.
Backing fabric	4¾ yd.	

RECOMMENDED MATERIALS

Materials	Quantity Needed	Notes and Cutting Instructions
ScrapTherapy Middle Scrap Grid Interfacing	4 panels	

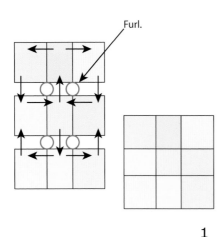

Furl.

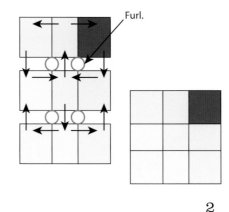

Furl.

1

2

The instructions will walk you through using 1 fat quarter to make all the elements needed for 1 block. Once you've made the block elements, you can decide whether you'd like to keep all the parts from the same fat quarter together and create the block or wait until you have all the block parts complete, so you can mix them up in your final blocks.

MAKE THE BLOCK ELEMENTS

9-PATCHES

Select sixty-eight 1½-in. light-value scraps that coordinate with one of the fat quarter colors. Use thirty-six 1½-in. scrap squares to make four 3½-in. blended 9-patch blocks with furled seams as shown on pp. 13–14. **1**

Use the remaining thirty-two 1½-in. squares plus four 1½-in. fat quarter colored squares to make four 3½-in. 9-patches with one colored corner and furled seams. **2**

FLYING GEESE UNITS

Sew together 1 blended 9-patch block with 1 colored corner 9-patch block as shown.

Rotate the blended 9-patch so the adjoining seams nest and oppose. Furl the connecting seams. Repeat to make 4 scrap rectangles that measure 3½ in. by 6½ in. **3**

Choose four 3½-in. squares cut from a different fat quarter than the one used for the colored corner 9-patch. Place a 3½-in. fat quarter square right sides together on one side of the scrap rectangle as shown. Sew on the diagonal line. **4**

Before pressing or cutting the additional layers at the edge of the rectangle, turn the rectangle over and draw a 45-degree line on the wrong side of the pieced scraps so that the line intersects at the 9-patch corner seam intersection; sew on the line. **5A** Cut ¼ in. away from each seam as shown to create 1 in-progress flying geese unit and 1 smaller half-square triangle (HST) unit, **5B** then press the seams toward the colored triangle on each unit. **5C**

Repeat with a second matching 3½-in. fat quarter square aligned with the other end of the scrappy rectangle. Sew on the line, turn the rectangle over, mark the wrong

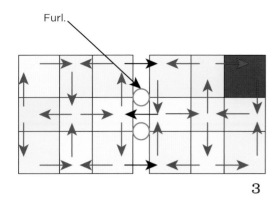

Furl.

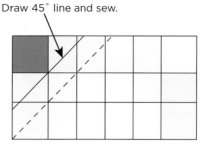

Draw 45° line and sew.

5A

Wrong side of flying geese unit
(in progress)

3

Then cut ¼" away from each seam.

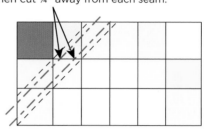

5B

Right side of flying geese unit
(in progress) and HST unit

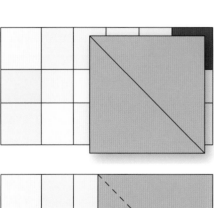

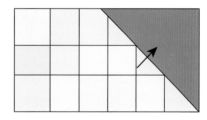

5C

4

side of the pieced scrap rectangle through the corner scrap seam intersection, sew on the line, cut ¼ in. away from the lines as before, and press. The flying geese unit measures 3½ in. by 6½ in., and each corner HST unit measures 2½ in. square. **6**

Repeat to make a total of 4 flying geese units and 8 HST units, 4 with scrappy corners and 4 with a colored corner. Set aside.

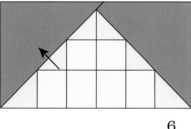

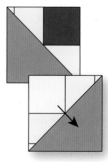

6

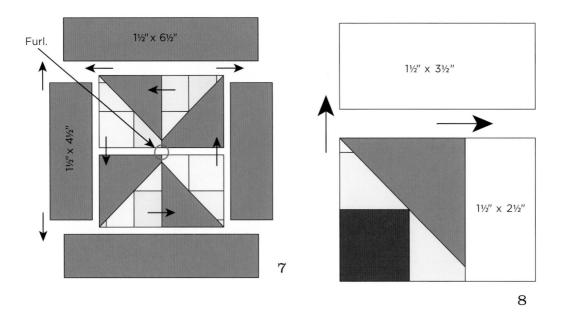

7

8

BLOCK CENTER
Arrange the four 2½-in. HST units with scrappy corners into a 4-patch pinwheel as shown. Sew the HST units into 2 rows, press the seams toward the colored triangle, then sew the rows together and furl the seam intersection to reduce bulk as shown on pp. 13–14. The pinwheel measures 4½ in. square. Sew a 1½-in. by 4½-in. colored strip to each pinwheel side, and press the seams toward the strips. Sew a 1½-in. by 6½-in. strip to the top and bottom of the pinwheel, and press the seams toward the strips. The block center measures 6½ in. square. Set aside. **7**

BLOCK CORNERS
Sew a 1½-in. by 2½-in. white strip to the side of a 2½-in. square HST unit with the colored corner as shown. Press the seam toward the strip. Sew a 1½-in. by 3½-in. white strip to the adjacent side of the HST unit as

shown. Press the seam toward the strip. Repeat to make 4 matching block corners that measure 3½ in. square. **8**

ASSEMBLE THE BLOCKS
With the remaining fat quarter colors, scrap squares, and white strips, make a total of 48 flying geese units, 12 block centers, and 48 corner units. Keep block elements with matching fat quarter colors together.

Arrange 4 matching flying geese units, 1 block center, and 4 matching block corners into the block as shown. Sew the block units into 3 rows, then sew the rows together. Press the seams as indicated. Repeat to make 12 blocks that measure 12½ in. square. **9**

For each block in the sample quilt, I chose to match the fat quarter color used for the center unit with the fat quarter color used in the block corners. Consider mixing up the colors even more.

MAKE THE SASHING AND CORNERSTONES
VERTICAL SASHING STRIPS
Randomly select a 1½-in. by 12½-in. colored strip; then sew a 1½-in. by 12½-in. white strip to both sides of the colored strip. Press the seam toward the colored fabric. Repeat to make 16 vertical sashing strips that measure 3½ in. by 12½ in. Set aside. **10**

HORIZONTAL SASHING STRIPS
Randomly select a 1½-in. by 12½-in. colored strip; then sew a 1½-in. by

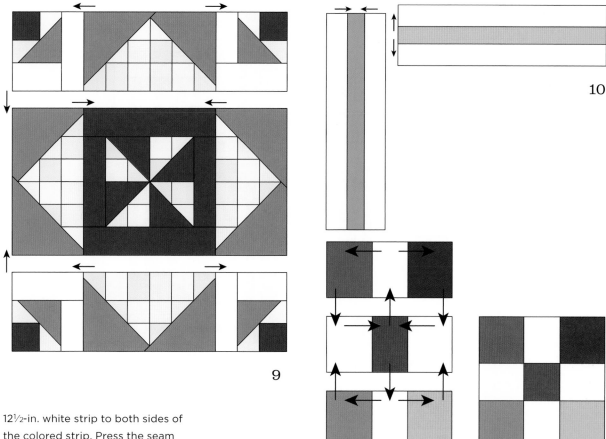

9

10

11

12½-in. white strip to both sides of the colored strip. Press the seam toward the white fabric. Repeat to make 15 horizontal sashing strips that measure 3½ in. by 12½ in. Set aside. **10**

CORNERSTONES

Randomly select five 1½-in. colored squares and four 1½-in. white squares. Arrange them into a 9-patch block with colored corners and center and furled seams as shown. Repeat to make 20 cornerstones that measure 3½ in. square. **11**

COMPLETE THE QUILT TOP

Arrange the blocks, vertical and horizontal sashing, and the cornerstones as shown on p. 76. Rotate the cornerstones so the seams will nest

and oppose at the seam intersections. Sew the cornerstones and horizontal sashing into rows. Sew the vertical sashing and blocks into rows. Press the seams toward the sashing strip in each row. Sew the rows together, and press the row seams toward the sashing.

MAKE THE BORDERS

Sew 2 of the 5½-in. width-of-fabric border strips together end to end with a diagonal seam as shown on p. 205; press the connecting seams open to make a 5½-in. strip that is approximately 80 in. long. Sew 2

more width-of-fabric strips together to make a second 80-in. border strip. From each strip, cut one 5½-in. by 63½-in. side border.

Sew the remaining 3 width-of-fabric strips together end to end with diagonal seams, and press the seams open to make a 5½-in. strip that is approximately 120 in. long. From this strip, cut two 5½-in. by 58½-in. top and bottom borders.

Sew the borders to the quilt, sides first, then top and bottom. Press the seam toward the border after each addition. **12**

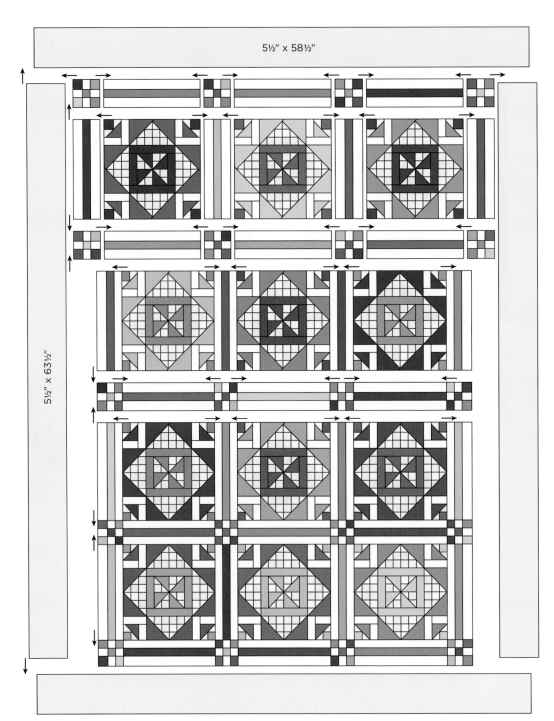

5½" × 58½"

5½" × 63½"

12

QUILT AND BIND

Layer the backing, batting, and quilt top; baste. Quilt as desired.

Sew the binding strips together end to end using a diagonal seam. Press the connecting seams open; then press the binding in half lengthwise, wrong sides together.

Trim the batting and backing even with the quilt top. With the raw edges aligned, sew the folded binding to the front of the quilt using a ¼-in. seam. Miter the binding at the corners.

Turn the folded edge of the binding to the back of the quilt, and hand-stitch it in place.

USING THE 9-PATCH INTERFACING

The ScrapTherapy Middle Scrap Grid Interfacing can be used to make the 3½-in. 9-patch blocks for this project.

Follow the steps on pp. 25–26 to arrange the scraps on each section of the interfacing. Be sure to arrange one 1½-in. colored fat quarter square on the corner of 4 of the eight 9-patches needed

for each block. Follow the instructions on pp. 26–27 to make the basic 9-patch blocks with interfacing. Start by sewing the vertical seams, marked with the red arrow on the diagram. Then snip, fold, and sew *all 5* of the horizontal seams, using the same process to nest, oppose, and furl the seams as described on p. 27.

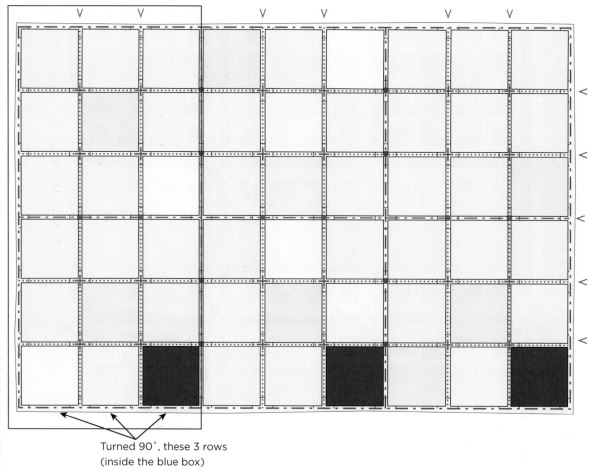

Turned 90°, these 3 rows
(inside the blue box)
make 1 flying geese base.

Pomegranate Rose Table Topper

FEATURING THE TRANSFORMED 9-PATCH

FINISHED SIZE: 43 in. by 43 in.
PATTERN DIFFICULTY: Intermediate

When I was a kid, my family celebrated holidays and important events with a significant meal served in our tiny dining room. The special-occasion china with painted pink roses manufactured at world-famous Syracuse China (right in my hometown!) always accompanied the meal. Those delicate pink roses of my memory set the stage for this topper. The bright floral inspiration fabric galvanized the scrap selection in bright pinks, greens, and yellows, overthrowing the dainty pink-and-gray china color palette.

To make the scraps and block elements pop, I selected a really bold but playful dark fabric for the star points and a crisp white-on-white print for the sashing and background elements. A favorite technique borrowed from the popular "Stained Glass" quilt from *ScrapTherapy: Scraps Plus One!* makes the skinny strips a breeze to sew. Top it off with squished prairie points around the perimeter of the quilt for a playful, dimensional border.

SCRAPS NEEDED

Square Size	Description	Quantity Needed	Notes and Cutting Instructions
2"	Pink scrap squares	162	
2"	Green scrap squares	45	
2"	Yellow scrap squares	36	
2"	Green/pink print scrap squares	9	
5"	Pink scrap squares	9	• Trim each scrap square to 4" square.
5"	Green scrap squares	32	• Select 32 squares for the prairie points. Following diagram **1**, fold each diagonally, right sides together, then fold diagonally a second time. Press.

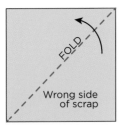

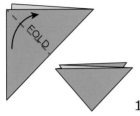

1

2

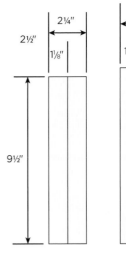

3

FABRICS AND OTHER MATERIALS

Materials	Quantity Needed	Notes and Cutting Instructions
Black print	⅔ yd.	• Cut two 4″ width-of-fabric strips; subcut into eighteen 4″ squares. Following diagram **2**, draw a diagonal line from corner to corner on the wrong side of each square. • Cut five 2¼″ strips for the binding.
White-on-white print	1 yd.	• Cut one 9½″ width-of-fabric strip; subcut into eighteen 2¼″ x 9½″ strips. Following diagram **3**, on the **right side** of each strip, draw a line down the center, 1⅛″ away from the long edge of each strip. • Cut one 4″ width-of-fabric strip; subcut into nine 4″ squares. • Cut six 2″ width-of-fabric strips; subcut into three 2″ x 10″ strips, one 2″ x 30″ strip, and seventy-two 2″ squares. Following diagram **3**, on the **right side** of each 2″ x 10″ strip and the 2″ x 30″ strip, draw a line down the center, 1″ away from the long edge of each strip. • Cut four 1½″ width-of-fabric strips. Set aside for the inner borders.
Focus print	1 yd.	• Cut four 2¾″ width-of-fabric strip. Set aside for the middle borders. • Cut five 4″ width-of-fabric strips. Set aside for the outer borders.
Backing	2¾ yd.	
Batting	48″ x 48″	
Large square ruler		10½″ or larger.
Miniature buttons	32	

Materials	Quantity Needed	Notes and Cutting Instructions
ScrapTherapy Little Scrap Grid Interfacing	3 panels	

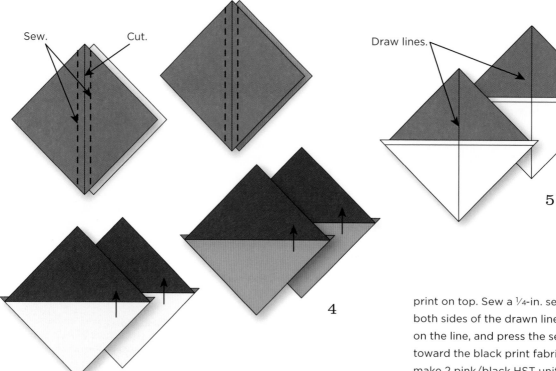

MAKE THE BLOCKS

QUARTER-SQUARE TRIANGLE UNITS

Place a 4-in. black print square and a 4-in. white square right sides together with the black print on top. Sew a ¼-in. seam on both sides of the drawn line. Cut on the line, and press the seam toward the black print fabric to make 2 white/black half-square triangle (HST) units. Leave untrimmed.

Similarly, select a trimmed 4-in. pink scrap square. Place a 4-in. black print square and the pink square right sides together with the black print on top. Sew a ¼-in. seam on both sides of the drawn line. Cut on the line, and press the seam toward the black print fabric to make 2 pink/black HST units. Leave untrimmed. **4**

Draw a line perpendicular to the existing seam on the wrong side of each of the white/black HST units. **5**

Place a white/black HST unit right sides together with a pink/black HST unit, with the black fabric facing the white and pink fabric. Make sure the seams are nested. Pin to secure and sew a ¼-in. seam on both sides of the drawn line. Cut on the drawn line and furl the seams (see pp. 13–14) to reduce bulk. Repeat with the second set of white/black and pink/black HST units. Make 4 matching quarter-square triangle (QST) units. **6**

9-patch blocks made from 2-in. scraps will be trimmed after they are sewn, making some scraps very small in the final block. To keep the scraps from getting lost in the quilt, be sure to select bold, solid-reading fabrics for the yellow and green scraps, in particular.

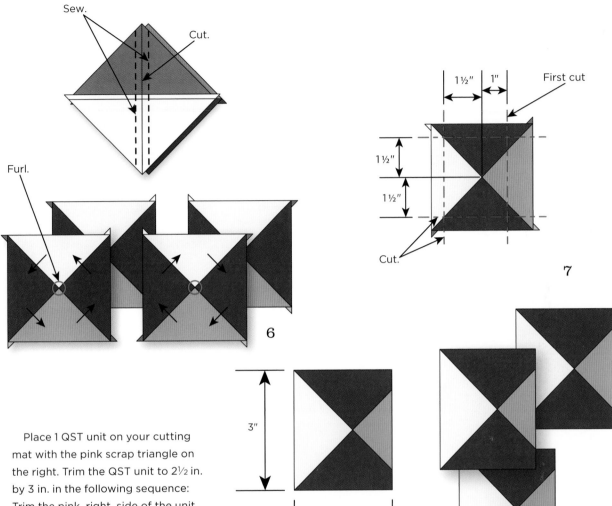

Sew.

Cut.

Furl.

1½" 1" First cut

1½"

1½"

Cut.

7

6

3"

2½"

8

Place 1 QST unit on your cutting mat with the pink scrap triangle on the right. Trim the QST unit to 2½ in. by 3 in. in the following sequence: Trim the pink, right, side of the unit 1 in. away from the center as shown. Rotate the unit to cut the remaining three sides of the QST unit, one at a time, 1½ in. away from the center seam intersection. Each trimmed QST is 2½ in. by 3 in. **7**

Trim all 4 matching QST units the same. **8**

Repeat to make 9 sets of 4 matching trimmed QST units. Keep each set together. Set aside.

Trim the QST units one at a time with a ruler that has a 45-degree line. Use the 45-degree marking on the ruler to make sure the trimmed edges maintain a 45-degree angle with the seams.

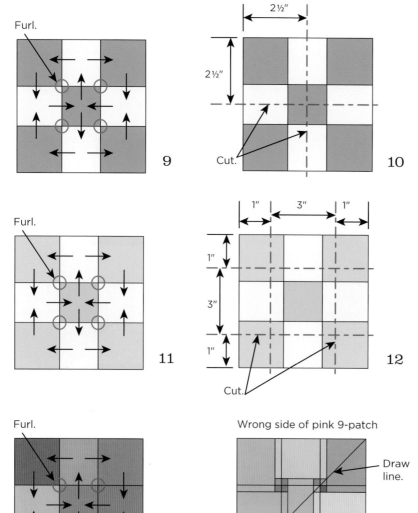

Furl.

2½"

2½"

Cut.

9

10

Furl.

1" 3" 1"

1"

3"

1"

Cut.

11

12

Furl.

Wrong side of pink 9-patch

Draw
line.

13

14

and 1 green/pink print 2-in. scrap square for the star block center. Arrange the squares into a basic 9-patch with a print center, yellow corners, and white sides. Sew the squares into a furled 9-patch following the instructions on pp. 13–14. Repeat to make nine 5-in. square yellow 9-patches. **11**

Place a yellow 9-patch on your cutting mat and cut 1 in. off each side of the block, leaving a 3-in. square yellow center. The 1-in. by 5-in. pieces are not used. **12**

> For best results, cut and trim 9-patch blocks one at a time!

Randomly select 9 different pink 2-in. scrap squares for the star block setting triangles. Arrange the squares into a blended basic 9-patch (all positions in the 9-patch are basically the same color and value square). Sew the squares into a furled 9-patch following the instructions on pp. 13–14. Repeat to make eighteen 5-in. square 9-patches. **13** Draw a diagonal line from corner to corner on the wrong side of each pink 9-patch. Note that the line will intersect two of the four seam intersections. Set aside. **14**

MAKE THE 9-PATCHES
Randomly select five 2-in. green scrap squares and four 2-in. white squares for the star block corner 9-patches. Arrange the squares into a basic 9-patch with a green scrap center and corners and white sides. Sew the squares into a furled 9-patch following the instructions on

pp. 13–14. Repeat to make nine 5-in. square green 9-patches. **9**

Place a green 9-patch on your cutting mat, and cut the block into equal quarters as shown to make four 2½-in. square green 9-patch corners. **10**

Similarly, select 4 yellow 2-in. scrap squares, 4 white 2-in. squares,

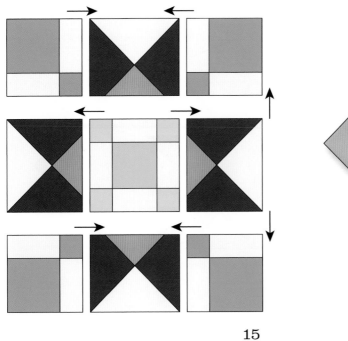

15

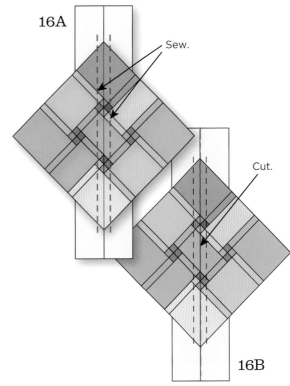

16A

Sew.

Cut.

16B

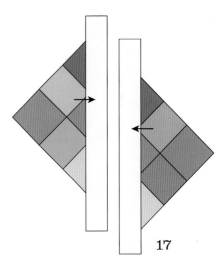

17

The Little Scrap Grid Interfacing can be used to make the green, yellow, and pink 9-patch blocks. Follow the steps on pp. 22–25 for the furled 9-patch with interfacing to make nine 9-patch blocks with 2-in. green scrap corners, 2-in. green scrap centers, and 2-in. white sides; nine 9-patch blocks with 2-in. yellow scrap corners, 2-in. print scrap centers, and 2-in. white sides; and eighteen 9-patch blocks each with 9 different 2-in. pink scrap squares.

MAKE THE BLOCK CENTER

Arrange 4 green 9-patch quarters, 4 trimmed QST units, and 1 yellow center into a 9-patch as shown. Sew the units into rows, then sew the rows together. Press as indicated. Furl the seams, if desired, to reduce bulk. The block measures 7 in. square. Repeat to make nine 7-in.-square star blocks. Set aside. **15**

COMPLETE THE BLOCK

Place a 5-in. pink 9-patch on a white 2$\frac{1}{4}$-in. by 9$\frac{1}{2}$-in. strip, right sides together, with the 9-patch on top. Roughly center the 9-patch on the strip and align the line drawn on the wrong side of the pink 9-patch square with the one on the right side of the 2$\frac{1}{4}$-in. by 9$\frac{1}{2}$-in. strip.

Sew a $\frac{1}{4}$-in. seam on both sides of the drawn line. **16A**

Cut on the line. **16B** Press the seam toward the white strip on each of the 2 resulting triangular corner units. Don't worry about trimming the white strips to match the 9-patch edges. **17**

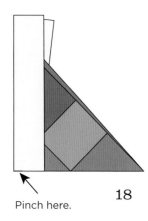

Pinch here. 18

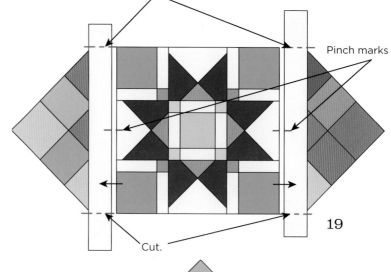

Cut after sewing.

Pinch marks

Cut.

19

Repeat to make a total of 36 corner units from 18 sets of pink 9-patch blocks and white strips.

Select a 7-in. star block and a corner unit. Find the center of one side of the block by folding the block in half, right sides together, and pinching the center at the very edge of the block, leaving a depression in the fabric at the pinch.

Likewise, find the center of the long side of the corner unit by folding the unit in half, wrong sides together, and pinching the center of the strip; match the sides of the triangle rather than the ends of the rectangular strip to find the center. **18**

Using the pinch marks, center a corner unit onto one side of the 7-in. star block, right sides together. Sew with a ¼-in. seam.

Similarly, sew a second corner unit to the opposite side of the block. Mix up the pink 9-patch blocks as they are sewn to the star blocks. Trim the excess corner unit fabric even with the unsewn sides of the star block, and then press the seams toward the corner. **19**

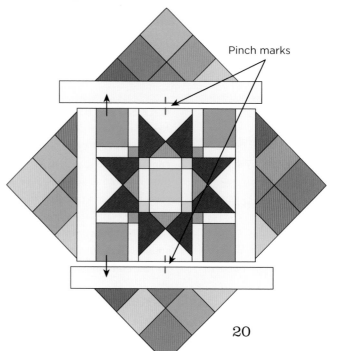

Pinch marks

20

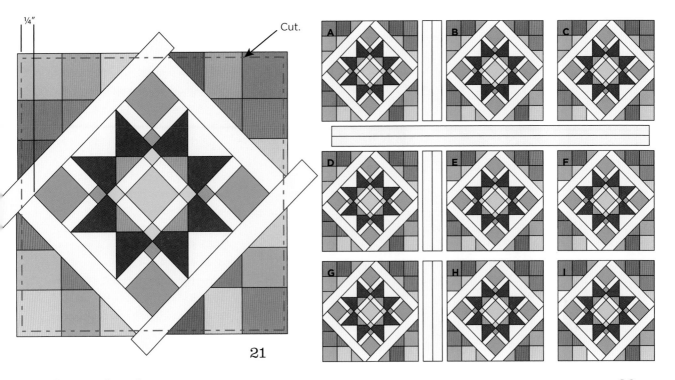

21

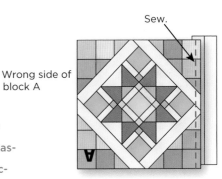

22

Center and sew 2 more corner units to the remaining two sides of the star block unit. Press the seams toward the corner units. **20**

With a large square ruler, center and trim all four sides of the block to 10 in. square. Be sure the center block points are at least ¼ in. away from the trimmed block edge and that the side points, where the sashing strips intersect, align with the 5-in. markings on the ruler. Trim one or two sides at a time, then rotate the block at 90-degree intervals to trim the remaining sides, measuring after each rotation. **21**

Repeat to make nine 10-in. blocks.

Arrange the blocks in 3 rows of 3 blocks. Label each block with a pin and a piece of scrap fabric to identify its location within the quilt center. In between, add three 2-in. by 10-in. and one 2-in. by 30-in. white strips as shown. **22**

Avoid cutting and sewing very narrow lattice strips that can easily distort during quilt construction. Instead, sew block units to the lattice strips aligned with the center of the strip, then cut them apart. To stay organized, follow the sequencing carefully, and return partially sewn elements to your worksurface with the block placed right side up in its position between sewing steps.

Wrong side of block A

23

When sewing the blocks to the white strips, keep the white strip right side up as you align the blocks and sew. Align the inner edge of block A with the line drawn on the 2-in. by 10-in. white strip, right sides together. Sew with a ¼-in. seam from the edge of block A. **23**

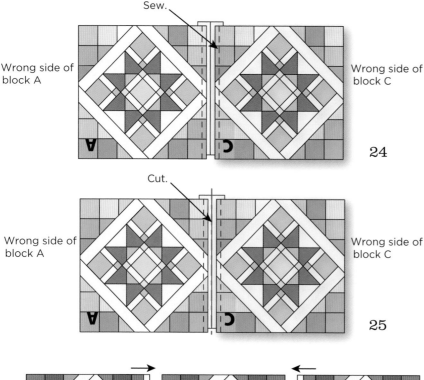

Sew.

Wrong side of
block A

Wrong side of
block C

24

Cut.

Wrong side of
block A

Wrong side of
block C

25

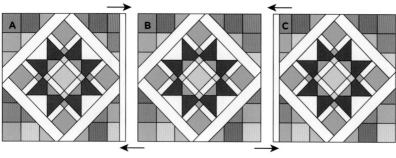

A B C

26

Similarly, align the inner edge of block C with the drawn line on the opposite side of the same 2-in. by 10-in. white strip, right sides together. Sew with a ¼-in. seam from the edge of block C. **24**

With the wrong side of the block units facing up, cut the white strip on the drawn line, exactly where the edges of A and C meet. Press the seams toward the strips. **25**

Return block units A and C to the quilt center arrangement on the worksurface. Sew block B to block unit A; then sew block unit C to block B to complete the row. Press the seams toward the strips. **26**

Repeat the sequencing to make rows D-E-F and G-H-I.

Sew the rows in the same way you sewed the block units. Align the bottom edge of row A-B-C with the drawn line on the 2-in. by 30-in. white strip, right sides together. Sew with a ¼-in. seam from the edge of row A-B-C.

Align the top edge of row G-H-I with the drawn line on the opposite side of the same 2-in. by 30-in. white strip, right sides together. Sew with a ¼-in. seam from the edge of row G-H-I.

Cut the white strip on the drawn line, exactly where the edge of row A-B-C and row G-H-I meet. Press the seams toward the white strips. Return the rows to the block arrangement on the worksurface.

Sew row D-E-F to the white strip edge of row A-B-C, then sew the white strip edge of row G-H-I to row D-E-F to complete the quilt center. Press the seams toward the white strips. The quilt center is 30 in. square. **27**

MAKE THE BORDERS

From the four 1½-in. inner border strips, cut two 1½-in. by 30-in. side inner borders and two 1½-in. by 32-in. top and bottom inner borders.

Sew the 1½-in. by 30-in. white side inner borders to the quilt; then sew the 1½-in. by 32-in. white top and bottom inner borders to the quilt. Press the seams toward the border after each addition.

From the four 2¾-in. focus print middle border strips, cut two 2¾-in. by 32-in. side middle borders and two 2¾-in. by 36½-in. top and bottom middle borders.

Sew the 2¾-in. by 32-in. focus print side middle borders to the quilt; then sew the 2¾-in. by 36½-in. focus print top and bottom middle borders to the quilt. Press the seams toward the border after each addition.

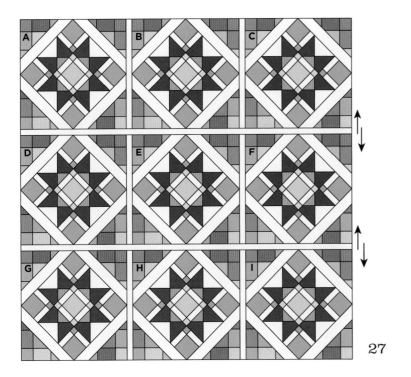

27

28

PRAIRIE POINTS

Lay the quilt top right side up on a large worksurface. With raw edges aligned, arrange and pin 8 prairie points to each side of the quilt top as shown. Prairie points should be evenly spaced, and the single-fold edge of the prairie point rotates around the quilt perimeter consistently. Prairie points will overlap slightly in the seam allowance along the quilt edge. Baste the prairie points in place within 1/4 in. of the edge of the quilt top. **28**

From 2 of the 4-in. focus print outer border strips, cut two 4-in. by 36½-in. side outer borders. Connect the remaining three 4-in. strips end to end using a diagonal seam as shown on p. 205 to make one strip approximately 120 in. long. From this strip, cut two 4-in. by 43½-in. top and bottom outer borders.

Sew the focus print outer borders to the quilt, sides first, then top and bottom, sandwiching the prairie points between the middle and outer borders. Press the seams toward the border after each addition. The quilt top measures 43½ in. square.

QUILT AND BIND

Layer the backing, batting, and quilt top; baste. Quilt as desired.

> To avoid quilting over the prairie points, pin them to the outer border while quilting the middle border, and pin them to the middle border while quilting the outer border.

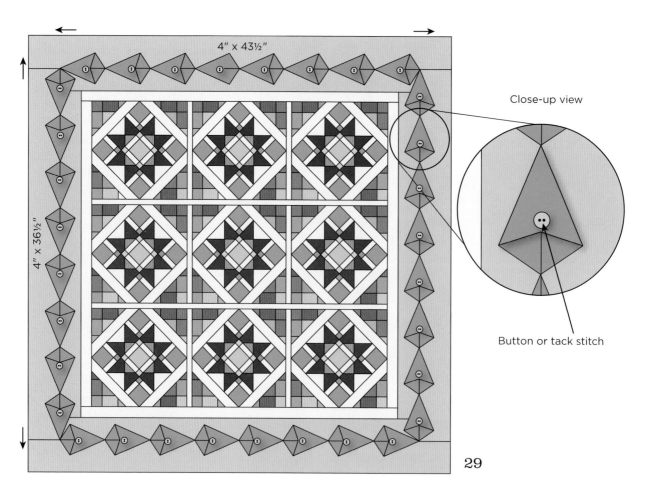

4" x 43½"

4" x 36½"

Close-up view

Button or tack stitch

29

Once the quilting is complete, open and compress each prairie point and secure it with a miniature button sewn through all the quilt layers. **29**

Instead of buttons, consider a variety of options to secure the compressed prairie points:

- a sewing machine bar-tack stitch (a zigzag stitch sewn in one place)
- a French knot made with contrasting embroidery thread
- a button or large bead sewn through all the layers

Sew the binding strips together end to end using a diagonal seam. Press the connecting seams open; then press the binding in half lengthwise, wrong sides together.

Trim the batting and backing even with the quilt top. With the raw edges aligned, sew the folded binding to the front of the quilt using a ¼-in. seam. Miter the binding at the corners.

Turn the folded edge of the binding to the back of the quilt and hand-stitch it in place.

This project would also be an excellent baby quilt. To secure the prairie point elements, omit the buttons or any object that could cause a potential choking hazard, and secure the prairie points with stitching.

Mix 'n' Match Mug Mats

FEATURING THE BASIC, TRANSFORMED, AND ELEVATED 9-PATCH

FINISHED SIZE (ONE MUG MAT): 6 in. by 9 in.
PATTERN DIFFICULTY: Easy+

Part of the fun of starting a new scrappy project is figuring out which special scrap fabrics will become my next spectacular creation. For these adorable mug mats, not only do you get to choose the scrap fabrics that go together for each one, but you can also choose from four different appliqué shapes and three different side panel options. To add to the fun, each appliqué shape, if cut carefully, will yield two variations, the shape you cut out and its reverse, making it even harder to make just one.

SCRAPS NEEDED FOR ONE MUG MAT

Square Size	Quantity Needed	Notes and Cutting Instructions
2" scrap squares in similar colors	9	
5" scrap square that contrasts with 2" scrap square fabric	1	
3½" scrap squares for backing	6	
1½" or 2" light- and dark-value scrap squares (see notes and cutting instructions)		• For the **Simple Double Side Panel Option:** Select or cut nine 1½" scrap squares from two different colors. • For the **Super Stripe Side Panel Option:** Select or cut four 1½" and five 2" dark-value scrap squares. Select or cut five 1½" and five 2" light-value scrap squares. On the back of each 2" light-value square, draw a diagonal line from corner to corner (see diagram **1**). • For the **Break and Take Side Panel Option:** Select nine 2" dark-value scrap squares. Select nine 2" light-value scrap squares. On the back of each 2" light-value square, draw a diagonal line from corner to corner (see diagram **1**).

Materials	Quantity Needed	Notes and Cutting Instructions
Light-value print fabric	Fat eighth (9" x 21")	• Cut two 1¼" x 21" strips. From each, cut one 1¼" x 5" accent strip and one 1¼" x 6½" accent strip.
Binding fabric	One 2¼" width-of-fabric strip	
5" square paper-backed fusible web	1	
6½" x 9½" double-sided fusible fleece	1	

RECOMMENDED MATERIALS

Materials	Quantity Needed	Notes and Cutting Instructions
ScrapTherapy Little Scrap Grid Interfacing	1 panel	
ScrapTherapy Middle Scrap Grid Interfacing	1 panel	

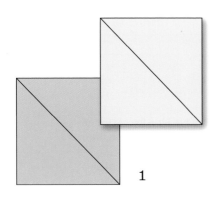

1

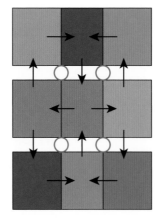

2

One panel of ScrapTherapy Little Scrap Grid Interfacing will make enough 9-patch blocks for the appliqué blocks for 12 mug mats. A panel of the ScrapTherapy Middle Scrap Grid Interfacing will make up to 12 pieced side panels.

Consider substituting a 5-in. scrap square for the 9-patch for the appliqué base.

MAKE THE APPLIQUÉ BLOCKS

Sew nine 2-in. scrap squares into a basic 9-patch block with furled seams. Set aside. **2**

Choose one of the 4 appliqué shapes shown on p. 98. **13, 14, 15, 16** If needed, enlarge the shape. Trace the shape onto the fusible web paper backing. The shapes are reversed.

Fuse the web to the wrong side of the 5-in. scrap chosen for the appliqué shape. Starting on a straight section of the shape in the center of the appliqué, cut carefully around the shape to remove it from the center of the scrap square, leaving its reverse shape intact.

Center and fuse either the shape or the reverse to the right side of the 9-patch block. Reserve the remaining shape for a second mug mat. **3**

Secure the appliqué or reverse appliqué edge with a buttonhole, zigzag, or satin stitch, or skip this step for now and secure the appliqué edges after the mug mat has been sandwiched. That way, the stitching to secure the appliqué will do double duty as quilting.

Sew a 1¼-in. by 5-in. accent strip to each side of the appliqué block. Press the seams toward the strips.

Sew a 1¼-in. by 6½-in. accent strip to the top and bottom of the appliqué block. Press the seams toward the strips. **4**

Set aside the 6½-in. square appliqué block.

3

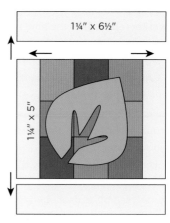

1¼" x 6½"

1¼" x 5"

4

MAKE THE SIDE PANEL

Select one of three different side panel options, outlined below, for your mug mat. Each side panel measures 3½ in. by 6½ in.

SIMPLE DOUBLE SIDE PANEL

Select or cut eighteen 1½-in. scrap squares, split evenly between two contrasting colors or values. Arrange the blocks into two 9-patches as shown, and sew each set of scraps into a 3½-in. basic 9-patch block with furled seams as shown on pp. 13–14. Notice that the row seams are pressed toward the darker fabric for each block, resulting in a slightly different pressing configuration for each block.

Sew the two 9-patch blocks together and furl the connecting seams. **5**

SUPER STRIPE SIDE PANEL

Place a 2-in. dark-value and a 2-in. light-value scrap square right sides together with the light-value scrap on top. Sew a ¼-in. seam along both sides of the drawn line. Cut on the line, and press the seam toward the

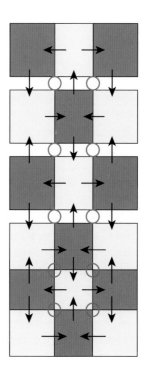

5

darker fabric. Trim the half-square triangle (HST) unit to 1½-in. square. Repeat to make 10 HST units. **6**

Arrange nine HST units, the 4 dark-value 1½-in. scrap squares, and the 5 light-value 1½-in. scrap squares into two 9-patch blocks as shown; you will have 1 HST unit left over. Sew the units into two 3½-in. square basic 9-patch blocks with furled seams as described on pp. 13–14. Press and furl the seams as shown.

Sew the 9-patch blocks together to form a diagonal stripe and furl the connecting seam intersections. **7**

BREAK AND TAKE SIDE PANEL

Place a 2-in. dark-value and a 2-in. light-value scrap square right sides together with the light-value scrap on top. Sew a ¼-in. seam along both sides of the drawn line as shown for the Super Stripe panel. Cut on the line and press the seam toward the darker fabric. Trim the half-square triangle (HST) unit to 1½ in. square. Repeat to make 18 HST units. **8**

Arrange the 18 HST units into two 9-patch blocks as shown. Sew the units into two 3½-in. square basic 9-patch blocks with furled seams as described on pp. 13–14. Press and furl the seams as shown.

Arrange the two 9-patch blocks into a vertical row. Sew the 9-patch blocks together and press and furl the seams. **9**

ASSEMBLE THE MAT

Sew the side panel to the appliqué block. Press the seam toward the appliqué block. The mug mat top measures 6½ in. by 9½ in. **10**

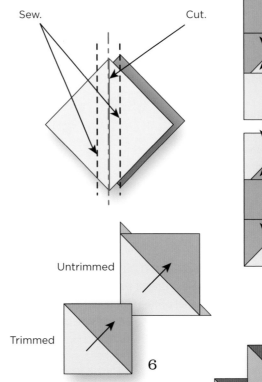

Sew.   Cut.

Untrimmed

Trimmed

6

7

MAKE THE BACKING

Arrange six 3½-in. scrap squares into 2 rows of 3 squares. Sew the scraps into rows, press the seams as shown, then sew the rows together; press and furl the seams. **11**

QUILT AND BIND

Layer the backing, fusible fleece, and mug mat top; fuse. Quilt as desired.

Trim the 2¼-in. binding strip to 34¼ in. long. Press the binding strip in half lengthwise, wrong sides together.

Unfold one end of the binding and lay it flat on your worksurface, right side up. Unfold the opposite end of the binding strip and align it perpendicular to the opposite end of the

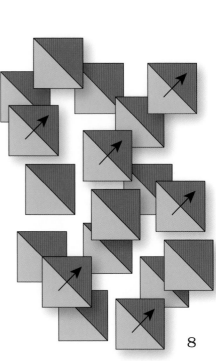

8

strip, forming a loop. Be careful not to twist the strip. Draw a diagonal line from corner to corner where the strip ends intersect. **12**

Pin to secure the layers and sew on the line. Trim ¼ in. away from the seam. Press the connecting seam open; then refold the binding strip, wrong sides together.

Secure the folded binding to the front of the mug mat edge with a ¼-in. seam. Start in the lower middle of one of the long sides of the rectangular mat, and sew one side at a time, just as for the binding on a large quilt. Miter the binding at the corners.

Turn the folded edge of the binding to the back of the mug mat and hand-stitch it in place.

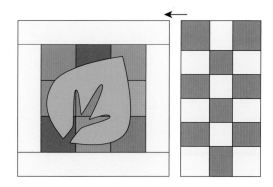

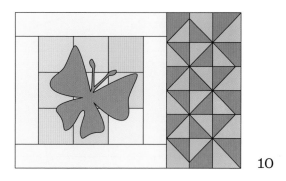

10

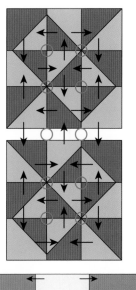

9

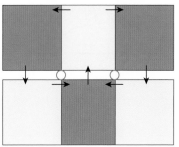

11

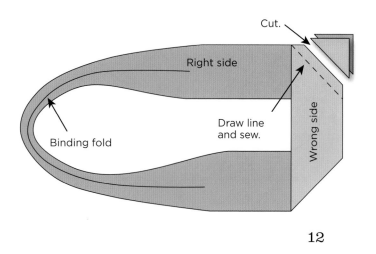

Cut.

Right side

Draw line
and sew.

Binding fold

Wrong side

12

Full size   **13**

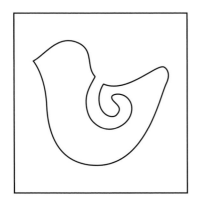

Enlarge 267%   **14**

Enlarge 267%   **15**

Enlarge 267%   **16**

USING THE 9-PATCH INTERFACING

A single panel of the ScrapTherapy Little Scrap Grid will yield enough 9-patch blocks with interfacing for the appliqué base for a dozen mug mats.

Any of the side panels can be made using the Middle Scrap Grid Interfacing, particularly if you are making three side panels at a time— any three, they don't have to be matching panel styles.

Then follow the steps on pp. 25–27 to arrange the elements for three side panels on a section of the interfacing as shown below. Follow the instructions on pp. 26–27 to make the 9-patch blocks with interfacing. Start by sewing the six vertical seams, marked with the red arrow on the diagram. Then snip, fold, and sew *all five* of the horizontal seams, using the same process to nest, oppose, and furl the seams as described on p. 27.

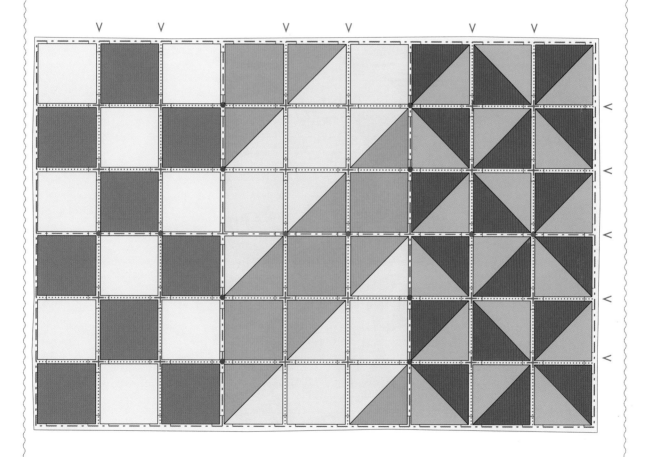

Split the Check

FEATURING THE TRANSFORMED 9-PATCH

FINISHED QUILT SIZE: 59 in. by 77 in.

PATTERN DIFFICULTY: Easy+

9-patch blocks in alternating dark-light-dark/light-dark-light values sewn together without sashing make a checkerboard postage stamp quilt. "Split the Check" is just that, with a little twist. Each block is split by a super-narrow fabric strip in a high-contrast color. I suspect you already know how much I dislike sewing long, skinny strips because they tend to distort during the sewing and pressing process. In case you didn't know that, you'll see a variation on this technique with the "Pomegranate Rose Table Topper" on p. 79.

For this quilt, the added distraction of stretchy bias edges where the 9-patch blocks are split in half diagonally creates the potential for a royal mess on your hands. But never fear—follow the steps carefully, and you'll find that the long, skinny strips inside the blocks are easy to make. I started by targeting two different colors—blue and brown—for my lap-size quilt. I chose about a yard each of light blue and light tan for the light-value block elements. For the alternating dark and medium values, my scrap bins were my playground. Throw in a bold solid-reading fabric for the luminous sashing and border, and the end result is a fast-finish, fun-to-make quilt with a mystifying twist.

SCRAPS NEEDED

Square Size	Description	Quantity Needed	Notes and Cutting Instructions
3½"	Dark-value blue print scrap squares	108	
3½"	Dark-value brown print scrap squares	108	

Materials	Quantity Needed	Notes and Cutting Instructions
Light or light-value blue solid fabric	1⅛ yd.	• Cut ten 3½″ width-of-fabric strips; subcut into one hundred eight 3½″ squares.
Light or light-value brown solid fabric	1⅛ yd.	• Cut ten 3½″ width-of-fabric strips; subcut into one hundred eight 3½″ squares.
Bold green solid fabric	1½ yd.	• Cut two 14″ width-of-fabric strips; subcut into twenty-four 2″ x 14″ sashing strips. • Cut seven 3″ width-of-fabric strips for the borders.
Binding fabric	½ yd.	• Cut seven 2¼″ width-of-fabric strips.
Backing fabric	4¾ yd.	
Batting	64″ x 83″	

RECOMMENDED MATERIALS

Materials	Quantity Needed	Notes and Cutting Instructions
Strip ruler		• 14″ or larger.
Light- and dark-value marking pens or pencils		

Since the scraps are never side by side in the quilt, other than where they might intersect at a corner, choose a variety of scrap prints including solids, botanicals, and geometrics without too much concern about placing varied scrap prints next to each other.

MAKE THE BLOCKS

Randomly select five 3½-in. dark blue scrap squares and four 3½-in. light blue squares. Arrange and sew the squares into a basic 9-patch with a dark scrap center and corners and light sides. Sew the squares into a basic 9-patch following the instructions on p. 10. Make sure seams are pressed toward the scrap fabric at the block edge. Repeat to make twelve 9½-in. square blue scrappy-corner 9-patches. **1**

Make a sample block from start to finish so you become familiar with the techniques involved. The quilt is straightforward to make, but the blocks are dependent on accurate scant ¼-in. seams, cutting, and pressing for the best results—and for a happy quilter!

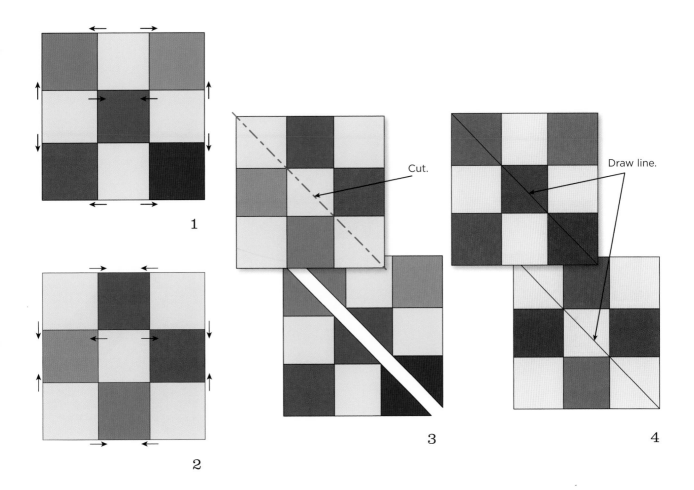

1

2

Cut.

3

Draw line.

4

Randomly select four 3½-in. dark blue scrap squares and five 3½-in. light blue squares. Arrange the squares into a basic 9-patch with a light center and corners and dark scrap sides. Sew the squares into a basic 9-patch following the instructions on p. 10. Repeat to make twelve 9½-in. square blue scrappy-side 9-patches. **2**

Cut each blue block once diagonally to form 2 half-square 9-patches (HS9). You have 48 blue HS9s. **3** Keep HS9s in two separate stacks: HS9s with scrap corners and HS9s with light corners. Set aside.

Follow the same process used to make the blue 9-patches to make twenty-four 9½-in. square brown 9-patches, 12 with a dark scrap center and corners (scrappy corner) and 12 with a light center and corners (scrappy side). Draw a diagonal line from corner to corner on the right side of each brown 9-patch block and separate into two stacks: scrappy-corner blocks and scrappy-side blocks. Don't cut the brown 9-patches as you did the blue 9-patches. **4**

Depending on the value of the scraps you've selected, it may be helpful to use a light-colored marking pen or pencil to draw the lines on the dark 9-patch blocks.

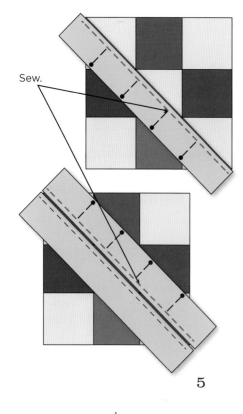

Sew.

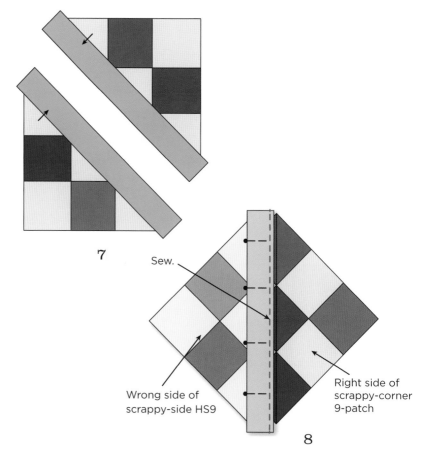

5

7

Sew.

Wrong side of
scrappy-side HS9

Right side of
scrappy-corner
9-patch

8

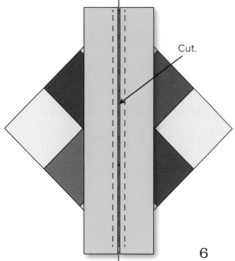

Cut.

6

ADD SASHING TO THE BLOCKS

Select a 9½-in. brown scrappy-side block, and place it right side up on your worksurface. Align the long edge of a 2-in. by 14-in. bold green sashing strip with the drawn line as shown. Roughly center the block under the strip; the strip will be a little longer than the block diagonal. Pin the strip to secure it to the block, and sew a ¼-in. seam along the strip edge. Similarly, align the edge of a second 2-in. by 14-in. green strip on the other side of the drawn line. Sew a ¼-in. seam along the strip edge. **5**

Cut the block in between the two seams **6** and press toward the green strip. **7**

Pin liberally to secure the strip to the block before sewing. Only cut after both seams are sewn. Cut carefully!

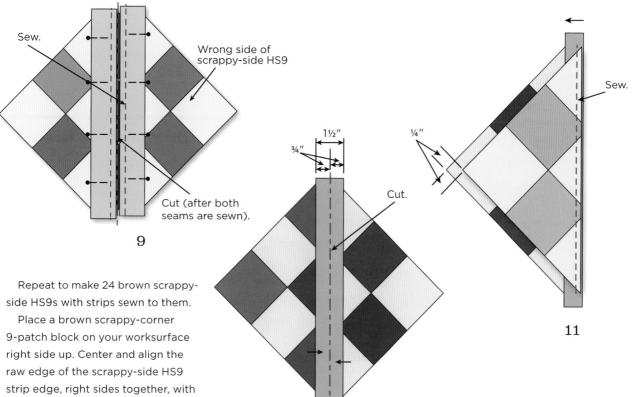

Sew.

Wrong side of scrappy-side HS9

Cut (after both seams are sewn).

9

1½"

¾"

Cut.

10

¼"

Sew.

11

Repeat to make 24 brown scrappy-side HS9s with strips sewn to them.

Place a brown scrappy-corner 9-patch block on your worksurface right side up. Center and align the raw edge of the scrappy-side HS9 strip edge, right sides together, with the drawn line on the uncut scrappy-corner 9-patch. Don't worry about perfectly centering the 9-patch blocks opposite each other; they will be cut apart in the next step. Pin to secure the layers; then sew a ¼-in. seam along the strip edge. **8**

Align and secure a second brown scrappy-side HS9 on the other side of the drawn line on the brown scrappy-corner 9-patch. Sew a ¼-in. seam along the strip edge; then cut in between the two seams and press toward the strip. **9**

Cut down the center of the green strip, ¾ in. away from either HS9 seam to separate the brown scrappy-side HS9 from the brown scrappy-corner HS9. You have 48 brown HS9s with a green sashing strip. **10**

Measure the width of the center strip before you cut. If it isn't 1½ in. wide, divide the strip width equally between the two halves to make the cut. Double-check your seam allowance and pressing technique, and make adjustments if needed before sewing additional blocks.

Congratulations! Now you have a 1-in. sashing strip sewn along the 9-patch block diagonal, without ever handling a pesky 1-in. strip!

Randomly select a blue scrappy-side HS9 and a brown scrappy-side HS9 with a green strip. Center the blue HS9 right sides together with the brown HS9 so the diagonal edge of the blue HS9 is aligned with the strip edge of the brown HS9. The block edges will be about ¼ in. from each other. Pin liberally to secure the layers before you sew. Sew; then press the seam toward the sashing strip as shown. **11**

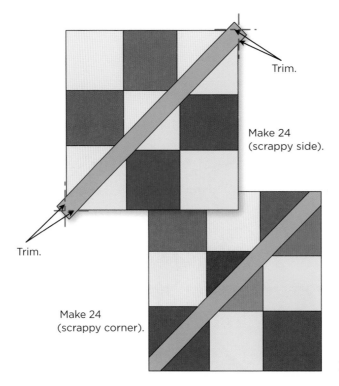

Trim.

Make 24
(scrappy side).

Trim.

Make 24
(scrappy corner).

12

Trim the strip points to make the blue/brown scrappy-side block 9½ in. square. Repeat to make 24 blue/brown scrappy-side blocks and 24 blue/brown scrappy-corner blocks, following the same process as for the blue/brown scrappy-side blocks. Each sashed block has a blue and a brown HS9 separated by a ½-in. sashing strip. **12**

Arrange the blocks into 8 rows of 6 blocks, alternating scrappy-side and scrappy-corner sashed blocks. Rotate every other block so the sashing strips create a chevron pattern. Sew the blocks into rows; then sew the rows together. **13**

ADD THE BORDERS

Sew 2 of the 3-in. border strips together end to end with a diagonal seam as shown on p. 205, and press the connecting seams open to make a 3-in. strip approximately 80 in. long. Sew 2 more strips together to make a second 80-in. border strip. Trim each strip to 3 in. by 72½ in. for the side borders. Sew the remaining 3 strips together end to end with a diagonal seam and press the seams open to make a 3-in. strip approximately 120 in. long. Cut two 3-in. by 59½-in. top/bottom borders from the 120-in. strip.

Sew the borders to the quilt, sides first, then top and bottom. Press the seams toward the border after each addition. The quilt top measures 59½ in. by 77½ in.

QUILT AND BIND

Layer the backing, batting, and quilt top; baste. Quilt as desired.

Sew the binding strips together end to end using a diagonal seam. Press the connecting seams open; then press the binding in half lengthwise, wrong sides together.

Trim the batting and backing even with the quilt top. With the raw edges aligned, sew the folded binding to the front of the quilt using a ¼-in. seam. Miter the binding at the corners.

Turn the folded edge of the binding to the back of the quilt and hand-stitch it in place.

3" x 59½"

3" x 72½"

13

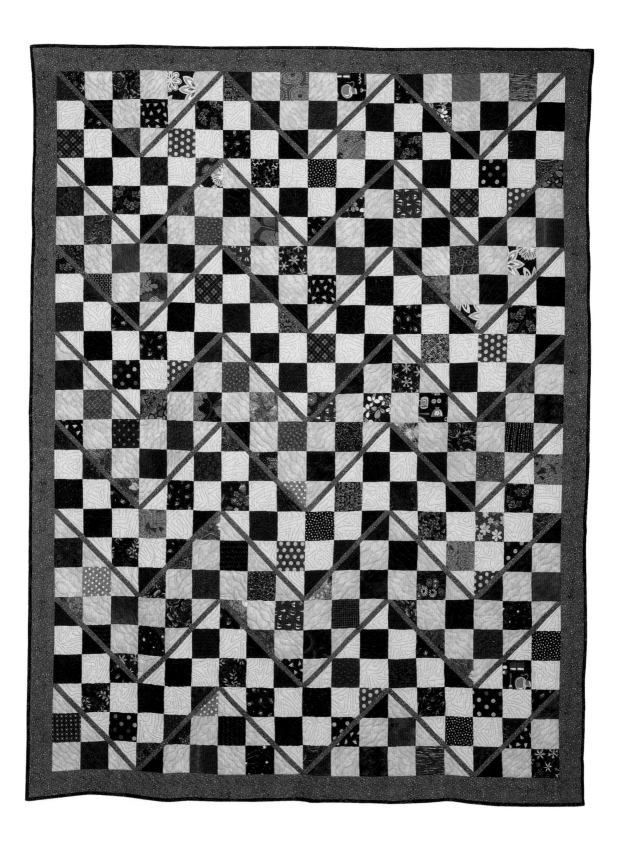

CHANGE UP THE SIZE

"Split the Check" is easy to upsize or downsize. Make the blocks, arrange them in the alternating pattern as for the quilt shown, and then rotate the blocks in place—a whole new quilt emerges. It's hard to imagine that the toddler quilt in the photo at right is made with the same pattern as the lap-size quilt!

For the 41-in. by 59-in. toddler size, you'll need the following:

- Fifty-four 3½-in. pink scraps
- Fifty-four 3½-in. orange scraps
- ⅔ yd. each solid pink and solid orange for the blocks. Cut fifty-four 3½-in. squares from 5 strips in each color.
- 1 yd. contrasting print for the sashing and borders. Cut one 14-in. width-of-fabric strip; then subcut into twelve 2-in. by 14-in. sashing strips. Cut five 2-in. width-of-fabric strips for the borders.
- ½ yd. binding. Cut six 2¼-in. width-of-fabric binding strips.
- 45-in. by 63-in. batting
- 3 yd. backing fabric, seamed horizontally

Start by making twenty-four 9½-in. square 9-patch blocks, then follow the steps on pp. 102–106 to make 12 blocks with scrappy corners and 12 blocks with scrappy side sashes.

Arrange the blocks in 6 rows of 4 blocks each, alternating scrappy-corner blocks with solid-corner blocks. Rotate the blocks to create the pattern shown, or make up your own variation! Finish the toddler quilt following the directions for the lap-size quilt.

Cross-Body Market Sack

FEATURING THE BASIC AND TRANSFORMED 9-PATCH

FINISHED SIZE: 15 in. by 17 in. by 3 in. deep (without the strap)
PATTERN DIFFICULTY: Intermediate

Almost every Saturday morning during the summer, I head to the farmers' market to get fresh local produce. I throw a quilted bag over my shoulder as I hop out of the car to make my way to my favorite fruit and veggie stands. By the time I get to the end of the first row of vendors, my bag is already weighing heavy on my shoulder, filled with farm-fresh goodies.

When I decided to create a market sack, I knew one thing for sure: it needed an extra-long, comfortable cross-body strap. In addition, I wanted it to be flexible enough to wrap around and hug my body, be sturdy and roomy enough for a successful market shopping spree, and have an accessible zippered pocket to stash essentials like keys and cash. The "Cross-Body Market Sack" is the result. This scrappy sack isn't just for veggies. I take it along on all kinds of shopping expeditions, like a big sale at the local quilt shop!

For my sack, I harvested a yard or two of an earthy botanical print from my fabric stash, unearthed some scraps in two distinct coordinating colors—purple and green—and dug up some binding fabric. I added a zipper, a ceramic button, and a few interfacing products like the ScrapTherapy Middle and Little Scrap Grid Interfacing, and the seeds were sown (or should that be *sewn*? *Wink!*) for this practical quilted sack.

Square Size	Description	Quantity Needed	Notes and Cutting Instructions
5"	Green scrap squares	2	• Following diagram **1**, cut two 2" x 5" rectangles from each square.
5"	Purple scrap squares	2	• Following diagram **1**, cut two 2" x 5" rectangles from each square.
3½"	Green scrap squares	22	• Following diagram **2**, cut two 2" x 3½" rectangles and two 1½" squares from each square.
3½"	Purple scrap squares	22	• Following diagram **2**, cut two 2" x 3½" rectangles and two 1½" squares from each square.
2"	Green squares	54	
2"	Purple squares	54	
1½"	Green scrap squares	47	• Cut from a combination of 2", 3½", and 5" squares.
1½"	Purple scrap squares	47	• Cut from a combination of 2", 3½", and 5" squares.

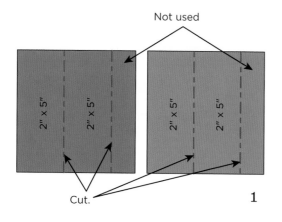

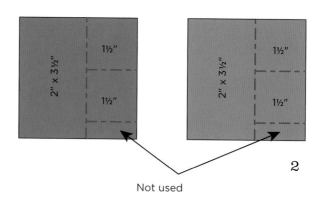

Materials	Quantity Needed	Notes and Cutting Instructions
Focus print	2 yd.	Cut two 17″ width-of-fabric strips; subcut into the following: • Three 15½″ x 17″ rectangles; fuse 1 rectangle with single-sided fusible batting; face 2 rectangles with Face-It Soft (see below). • One 13″ x 17″ rectangle; face with Face-It Soft. • One 3½″ x 17″ lining rectangle; face with Face-It Soft. Cut one 5″ width-of-fabric strip; subcut into six 5″ squares. Cut three 4½″ width-of-fabric strap lining strips. Cut six 1½″ width-of-fabric strips; subcut into one hundred thirty-five 1½″ squares for the strap. From the remaining scraps, cut the following: • Two 2″ x 3½″ zipper tab strips. • One 1½″ x 9″ strip for the button loop. • One 1½″ x 2½″ rectangle for the button loop cover.
Face-It Soft interfacing by Lazy Girl Designs	1½ yd. (22″ wide)	• Cut two 15½″ x 17″ rectangles. • Cut one 13″ x 17″ rectangle. • Cut one 3½″ x 17″ rectangle.
12″-wide paper-based fusible web	½ yd.	• Cut into six 5″ squares.
Binding	½ yd.	
Single-sided fusible batting	Craft size (36″ x 46″)	• Two 15½″ x 17″ rectangles, one 13″ x 17″ rectangle, one 3½″ x 17″ rectangle.
Batting	1	• One 4″ x 90½″ strip; note: this is not fusible.
22″ zipper	1	

Materials	Quantity Needed	Notes and Cutting Instructions
ScrapTherapy Middle Scrap Grid Interfacing	2 panels	
ScrapTherapy Little Scrap Grid Interfacing	1 panel	
Clover Wonder Clips		

USING THE 9-PATCH INTERFACING

The ScrapTherapy Little Scrap Grid Interfacing can be used to make the 9-patch blocks for the front and back exterior panels of the sack, and the ScrapTherapy Middle Scrap Grid Interfacing can be used to make the 9-patch blocks for the strap.

To make the 9-patch leaf blocks for the exterior panels, use both sections from one full panel of the interfacing. Since the blocks form directional stripes with the scrap placement, they can't be rotated into position within the panel to make the seams nest. Therefore, if you take special care when arranging, sewing, and pressing the seams using the grid, the 9-patch blocks will nest and oppose as they are sewn into the panel.

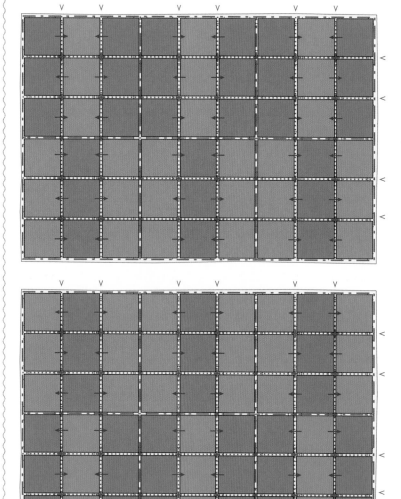

Arrange the scraps as shown on the diagram, then follow the steps to make the furled 9-patch blocks with interfacing as shown on pp. 22–25. Take note of the pressing direction used for the first set of 6 blocks (identified with the blue arrows in the diagram).

The second set of blocks looks similar, but pay close attention to the pressing direction and scrap placement; then follow the steps to make furled 9-patch blocks with interfacing.

To make the 9-patch blocks for the strap, follow the steps for the furled 9-patch with interfacing. Since these blocks *can* be rotated so the block seams nest and oppose where they intersect, you don't need to be as fussy about fabric placement and pressing as you do with the external panel blocks. You'll need one full panel and one full section from a second panel of the Middle Scrap Grid. Make 30 blocks, half with scrap centers and corners and half with scrap sides.

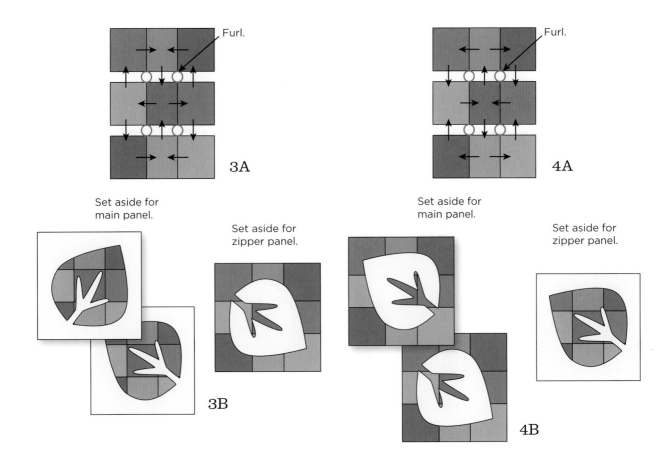

Furl.

3A

Set aside for
main panel.

Set aside for
zipper panel.

3B

Furl.

4A

Set aside for
main panel.

Set aside for
zipper panel.

4B

MAKE THE 9-PATCH LEAF BLOCKS

Trace six of the leaf and 5-in. square shapes from the "Mix 'n' Match Mug Mats" pattern on p. 98 onto the fusible web paper backing. The shape is reversed.

Cut on the square and fuse the web to the wrong side of each of the six 5-in. focus print squares. Starting on a straight section of the shape in the center of the appliqué, cut carefully around the shape to remove it from the center of the scrap square, leaving its reverse shape intact. Set aside.

Select six 2-in. purple scrap squares and three 2-in. green scrap squares. Arrange the 2-in. squares into a 9-patch to form 3 purple/green/purple vertical stripes. Sew the scraps into rows, and press the seams as shown—the seam pressing direction is important. Then sew the rows together and furl the seams as shown on pp. 13–14. Repeat to make 3 purple 9-patches (these 9-patches have more purple than green) that measure 5 in. square. **3A**

Center and fuse a reverse shape to the right side of two 9-patch blocks. Center and fuse a leaf shape to one 9-patch block. Rotate the leaf shapes 90 degrees randomly for each block before fusing.

Secure the appliqué and reverse appliqué edges with a buttonhole, zigzag, or satin stitch. Set the 2 reverse appliqué blocks aside for the main panel and the appliqué block for the zipper panel. **3B**

Similarly, select six 2-in. purple scrap squares and three 2-in. green scrap squares. Arrange the 2-in. squares into a 9-patch to form 3 purple/green/purple vertical stripes. Sew the scraps into rows, and press the seams as shown, reversing the pressing direction from the first three 9-patch blocks. Then sew the rows together and furl the seams. Repeat to make 3 purple 9- patches that measure 5 in. square. **4A**

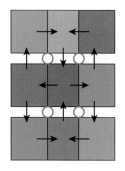

5A

Set aside for
zipper panel.

Set aside for
main panel.

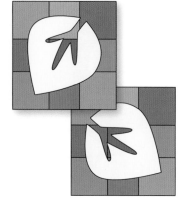

5B

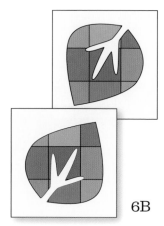

6A

Set aside for
zipper panel.

Set aside for
main panel.

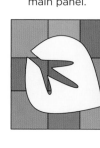

6B

Center and fuse a leaf shape to the right side of two 9-patch blocks. Center and fuse a reverse shape to one 9-patch block. Rotate the leaf shapes 90 degrees randomly for each block.

Secure the appliqué and reverse appliqué edges with a buttonhole, zigzag, or satin stitch. Set the appliqué block aside for the main panel and the 2 reverse appliqué blocks for the zipper panel. **4B**

Repeat the process to make 2 sets of 3 green/purple/green 9-patch blocks, each made with 6 green 2-in. scrap squares and three 2-in purple scrap squares.

Press the first set of 3 blocks as shown and furl the seams. Center and fuse a reverse appliqué shape to

the right side of one 9-patch block. **5A** Center and fuse 2 leaf shapes to the right side of two 9-patch blocks. Rotate the shapes 90 degrees randomly before fusing.

Secure the appliqué and reverse appliqué edges with a buttonhole, zigzag, or satin stitch. Set the reverse appliqué block aside for the main panel and the two appliqué blocks aside for the zipper panel. **5B**

Press the second set of 3 green/purple/green blocks as shown, reversing the pressing direction from the last set of blocks. **6A** Center and fuse a leaf shape to the right side of one 9-patch block. Center and fuse a reverse shape to two 9-patch blocks. Rotate the shapes 90 degrees randomly before fusing.

Secure the appliqué and reverse appliqué edges with a buttonhole, zigzag, or satin stitch. Set the appliqué block aside for the main panel and the 2 reverse appliqué blocks aside for the zipper panel. **6B**

MAKE THE LEAF PANELS

Arrange and sew the 6 appliqué and reverse appliqué blocks set aside for the main panel into 2 rows of 3 blocks, alternating purple and green stripes within the blocks while also alternating blocks with appliqué leaf shapes and reverse appliqué leaf shapes. Sew a green 2-in. by 5-in. scrap to each end of each row. Press the seams as indicated on the

Main panel leaf assembly

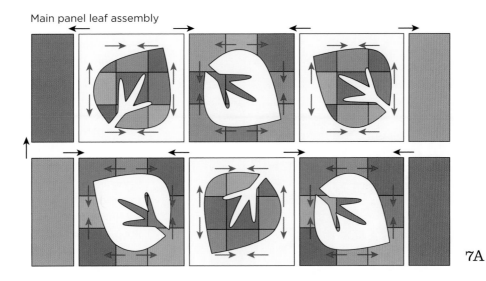

7A

Zipper panel leaf assembly

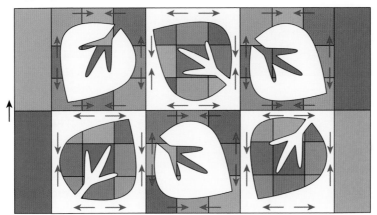

7B

diagram. Sew the rows together and press the row seams in one direction. The main panel leaf assembly measures 9½ in. by 17 in. **7A**

Similarly, arrange and sew the 6 appliqué and reverse appliqué blocks set aside for the zipper panel into 2 rows of 3 blocks, alternating green and purple stripes within the blocks while also alternating blocks with appliqué leaf shapes and reverse appliqué leaf shapes. Sew

a purple 2-in. by 5-in. scrap to each end of each row. Press the seams as indicated on the diagram. Sew the rows together and press the row seam in one direction. The zipper panel leaf assembly measures 9½ in. by 17 in. **7B**

COMPLETE THE MAIN PANEL

Arrange and sew two sets of six 2-in. by 3½-in. green strips and five 2-in. by 3½-in. purple strips cut from 3½-in. scrap squares. Start and end with a green strip, and alternate purple and green strips in between. Press the seams as indicated on diagram **8**. Repeat to make 2 striped strips that measure 3½ in. by 17 in.

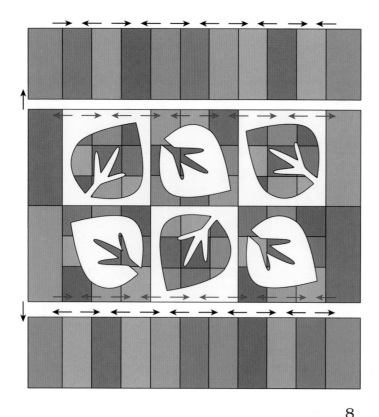

8

Sew a striped strip to the top and bottom of the main panel leaf assembly. Press the seam toward the striped strip. The main panel measures 15½ in. by 17 in. **8**

Fuse a 15½-in. by 17-in. single-sided fusible batting rectangle to the wrong side of the main panel. Place the main panel and a 15½-in. by 17-in. faced lining rectangle right sides together with raw edges aligned. Sew a ¼-in. seam along the top edge of the panel. **9A** Fold the panel in half, wrong sides together so the seam runs along the turn of the fold at the top of the panel. Edgestitch along the fold. **9B** Pin-baste and quilt the main panel as desired. Set aside.

COMPLETE THE ZIPPER PANEL

Arrange and sew 2 sets of six 2-in. by 3½-in. purple strips and five 2-in. by 3½-in. green strips cut from the 3½-in. scrap squares. Start and end with a purple strip and alternate green and purple strips in between. Press the seams as indicated. **10A** Repeat to make 2 striped strips that measure 3½ in. by 17 in.

Fuse a 3½-in. by 17-in. single-sided fusible batting rectangle to the wrong side of 1 striped strip.

Sew the remaining striped strip to the bottom of the zipper panel leaf assembly. Press the seam toward the striped strip. The lower zipper panel measures 12½ in. by 17 in. **10B**

Fuse a 12½-in. by 17-in. single-sided fusible batting rectangle to the wrong side of the lower zipper panel.

Sew.   Main panel   9A

Lining

Place the lining right sides together with the main panel, and sew a ¼" seam along the top edge.

Edgestitch.

Fold

9B

PREPARE THE ZIPPER

Retrieve the zipper, move the zipper pull to the center, and trim each end of the zipper to make it 15½ in. long. Retrieve the 2-in. by 3½-in. focus print lining fabric zipper tab strips. Make a ½-in. fold, wrong sides together, on each short end of the 2-in. by 3½-in. zipper tab strip. Press.

> Warning! When you trim the zipper, you'll cut off all the stuff that keeps the zipper pull from sliding off either end! Keep the zipper pull safely in the center of the zipper until the fabric zipper tabs are sewn.

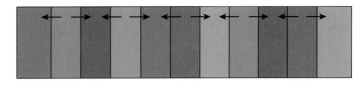

10A

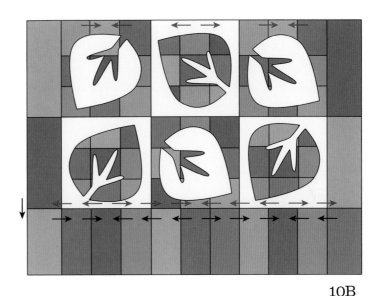

10B

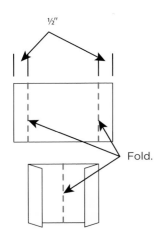

½"

Fold.

2"

1¼"

11

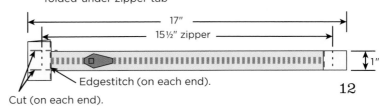

Zipper end aligned with folded-under zipper tab

17"

15½" zipper

1"

Edgestitch (on each end).

Cut (on each end).

12

Fold the zipper tab strip in half, wrong sides together. Press.

Repeat to make a second zipper tab that measures 1¼ in. by 2 in. **11**

Open the zipper tab center fold and align one end of the zipper with the raw edge of the folded-under zipper tab. Refold in half and secure all the layers of the zipper tab to the zipper with pins. Repeat with the second zipper tab and the other end of the trimmed zipper. Edgestitch along the zipper tab fold as shown. Trim the zipper tab sides even with the long edge of the zipper. The zipper assembly measures approximately 1 in. by 17 in. **12**

INSTALL THE ZIPPER

Retrieve the 3½-in. by 17-in. zipper panel with batting and the 3½-in. by 17-in. faced lining.

Sew.

Batted top zipper panel

Zipper

Zipper panel lining

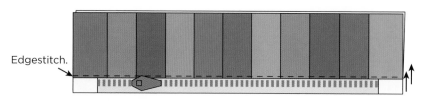

Edgestitch.

13

Place the upper zipper panel and a 3½-in. by 17-in. zipper panel lining right sides together. Along the lower edge of the zipper panel, insert the zipper between the layers, with the zipper and the zipper panel right sides together and with raw edges aligned. Secure the layers with pins or clips. Using a zipper foot, sew a ¼-in. seam. Finger-press firmly toward the panels, exposing the zipper, and edgestitch along the fold. **13**

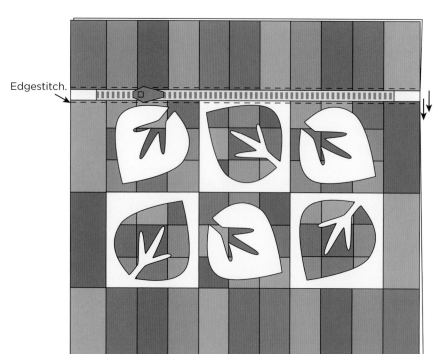

Edgestitch.

14

Use clips or pins to secure the outer raw edge of the zipper panel while pressing and edge-stitching along the fold at the zipper. The clips along the outer edge of the panel help to keep the hefty layers from shifting. The clips are especially nice for all kinds of bag construction because all the extra layers and heavier interfacing products can really do a number on your patchwork pins. The clips hold the layers firmly and help you keep your pins straight as . . . well . . . as a pin!

Sew.

Zipper panel

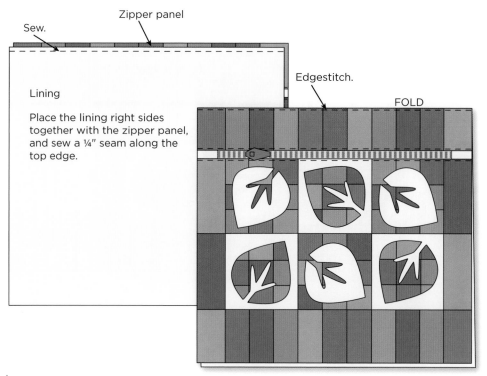

Lining

Place the lining right sides together with the zipper panel, and sew a ¼" seam along the top edge.

Edgestitch.

FOLD

15

Full size

16

Repeat the steps to sew the opposite zipper edge between the lower zipper panel and the 12½-in. by 17-in. faced lining. Using a zipper foot, sew a ¼-in. seam. Press and edgestitch as before. **14**

The zipper panel measures approximately 16¼ in. by 17 in. Pin-baste and quilt the top zipper panel section and the lower zipper panel section.

Measure 15½ in. from the bottom and trim all layers at the top edge of the panel. The zipper panel now measures 15½ in. by 17 in.

Place the remaining two 15½-in. by 17-in. lining rectangles, one faced and one with batting, wrong sides together with raw edges aligned. Pin-baste and quilt as desired. Place the zipper panel and the quilted lining right sides together with the raw edges aligned. Sew a ¼-in. seam along the top edge of the panel. Fold the panel in half, wrong sides together, so the seam runs along the turn of the fold. Edgestitch. **15**

Trace the curve **16** onto the corner of a piece of heavy paper and cut on the line to create a curved template. Stack both 15½-in. by 17-in. panel assemblies on your worksurface, with the folds at the top and the remaining three edges aligned.

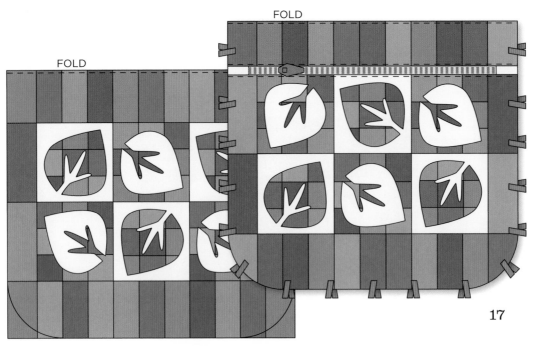

FOLD

FOLD

17

First fold →

Fold each side
toward the center.

Edgestitch →

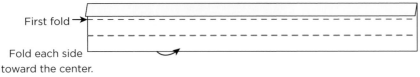

$^3/_8{}''$

8"

18

Position the paper template on a lower corner of the top panel. With a pencil, trace the curve onto the panel, and carefully trim all layers along the curved line. Repeat with the opposite lower panel corner. **17**

Pin or clip the panels together with the side and bottom raw edges aligned.

MAKE THE BUTTON LOOP AND BUTTON LOOP COVER

Fold the 1½-in. by 9-in. focus print strip in half lengthwise. Open the fold, fold each long edge to the center fold, and then refold on the center crease. Edgestitch along both folds; then trim the button loop to 8 in. long. **18**

Similarly, fold the 1½-in. by 2½-in. focus print strip in half lengthwise. Open the fold, and then fold each long edge to the center crease. Fold the assembly in half widthwise. Open the fold, and then fold each end toward the center crease. Press with a hot iron to set the folds and secure the layers temporarily with a pin. The button loop cover is ¾ in. by 1¼ in. **19**

First fold

Fold each side
toward the center.

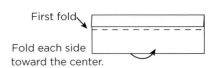

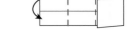

Button loop
cover, right
side

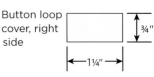

¾"

1¼"

19

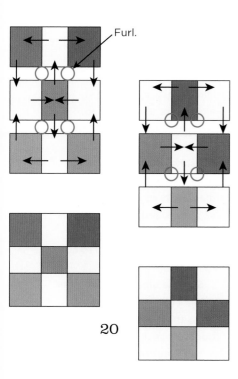

Furl.

20

Arrange and sew 4 purple and green (mix them up) $1\frac{1}{2}$-in. scrap squares and five $1\frac{1}{2}$-in. focus print squares into a basic 9-patch with scrap sides with furled seams. Repeat to make fifteen 9-patches that measure $3\frac{1}{2}$ in. square. **20**

Alternate and sew the thirty 9-patch blocks into a $3\frac{1}{2}$-in. by $90\frac{1}{2}$-in. strip; furl the 9-patch seams. Sew the ends together, and furl the seams to form a strap loop with a 90-in. circumference. Sew the three $4\frac{1}{2}$-in. width-of-fabric strips together end to end with diagonal seams, and press the connecting seams open. Trim the strip to $90\frac{1}{2}$ in. long, place the ends right sides together, and sew a $\frac{1}{4}$-in.

seam; furl the seams to form a 90-in. lining loop.

Place a 3-ft. to 4-ft. section of the lining on your worksurface, right side down. Let the rest of the lining hang off the table. Place a 4-in.-wide batting scrap on top of the 3-ft. to 4-ft. lining section; then place a similar size section of the 9-patch strap loop on top of the batting, right side up. Pin-baste the 3-ft. to 4-ft. section of the strap. Advance the strap layers on the worksurface and continue to layer and baste the strap one 3-ft. to 4-ft. section at a time until the entire strap loop is pin-basted. Quilt as desired. Trim the batting and lining fabric even with the long edges of the 9-patch strip.

Position the button loop cover on the main panel assembly, centered with the top edge of the button loop cover $\frac{3}{4}$ in. from the folded sack edge. Pin. Insert the button loop raw ends centered between the button loop cover and the right side of the main panel assembly. Pin, then edgestitch around the button loop cover perimeter to hold the button loop in place.

Sew a ceramic button on the zipper panel assembly, centered and $1\frac{1}{4}$ in. from the folded sack edge.

MAKE THE STRAP
Arrange and sew 5 purple and green (mix them) $1\frac{1}{2}$-in. scrap squares and four $1\frac{1}{2}$-in. focus print squares into a basic 9-patch with scrap corners and center with furled seams (see pp. 13–14). Repeat to make fifteen 9-patches that measure $3\frac{1}{2}$ in. square.

When connecting batting strips in the loop, prevent bumpy batting seams by placing a small cutting mat between the batting and the lining layer, then placing both ends of the batting strip on top of the mat. Make a diagonal cut through both batting layers, remove the short ends and the cutting mat, abut the two fresh-cut ends on the lining layer, and continue layering the strap.

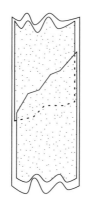

Overlap batting ends.

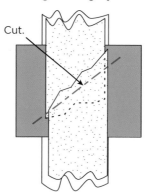

With a cutting mat under the batting, cut a straight diagonal line through batting layers.

Cut.

Abut fresh-cut batting ends and continue to baste the strap layers for quilting.

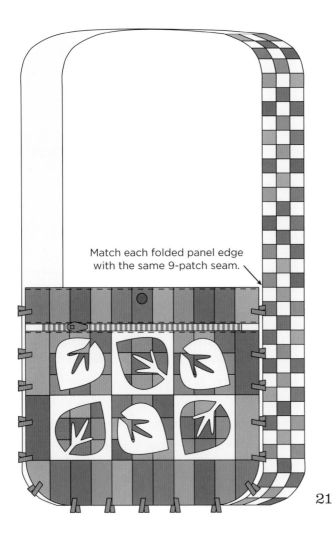

Match each folded panel edge
with the same 9-patch seam.

21

BIAS BINDING

Making bias binding is easy. Make a fresh cut to straighten both sides of the ½-yd. binding fabric. Cut off the selvages perpendicular to the sides. Fold one end diagonally to align two edges as shown, and then cut 2½-in. strips perpendicular to the fold. Refold as needed to cut more strips.

Sew the bias strips together using a diagonal seam and press the connecting seams open. Press the binding in half lengthwise wrong sides together. Make two bias binding strips, each approximately 100 in. long.

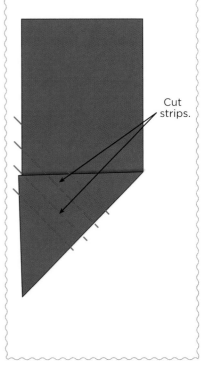

Cut strips.

FINISH THE SACK

Make 2 bias binding strips from the binding fabric (see the sidebar at right).

Place the strap and the zipper panel lining sides together and align one folded panel edge with a 9-patch seam in the strap. Starting in the strap, clip or pin the binding to the lining side of the strap with raw edges aligned. Continue securing the binding around the perimeter of the strap. At the panel, layer the zipper panel lining sides together between the binding and the strap.

Sew the binding using a ¼-in. seam. Connect the binding ends with a continuous seam as shown on pp. 211–212. Turn the folded edge of the binding to the pieced side of the strap, and hand-stitch it in place. **21**

Retrieve the main panel. Place the main panel lining sides together with the opposite strap edge. Align the panel rim edge with the opposite end of the 9-patch seam used to align the zipper panel. Repeat the process to secure the second binding strip around the perimeter of the remaining strap edge.

Bolster Pillow

FEATURING THE BASIC 9-PATCH

FINISHED SIZE: 16 in. long by 6 in. tall by 6 in. deep

PATTERN DIFFICULTY: Easy

Do you find making a bolster pillow intimidating? I think it's all about that circular piece of fabric at each end. Or maybe it's the zipper closure. However, when you break it down, a bolster is basically a rectangle. And sewing a circle is all about sewing a series of itty-bitty straight lines, also known as stitches, that make a circle.

To keep things super-simple in this bolster pillow, the scrappy main panel consists of vertical rows of 9-patch blocks with scrappy solid fabrics in between. Add a simple zipper closure, lots of pins for sewing the circular ends, and a purchased pillow form, and this project practically makes itself.

From your bins full of scrap fabrics, choose a few light-value and dark-value scraps—stick to a color theme or not. From your stash, pull out a fat eighth of something interesting for the pillow ends, and you're on your way to a quick and easy accessory for your home, porch, or garden.

SCRAPS NEEDED

Square Size	Description	Quantity Needed	Notes and Cutting Instructions
1½"	Dark-value scrap squares	66	• Cut from 2", 3½", or 5" scrap squares.
5"	Light-value scrap squares	17	From each of 12 squares, follow diagram **1** to cut: • One 3½" x 4½" rectangle. • Three 1½" squares. Follow diagram **2** to cut: • One 3½" x 3½" square. • Five 1½" x 1½" squares. From each of 2 squares, follow diagram **3** to cut: • One 2½" x 3½" rectangle. • Five 1½" x 1½" squares. From each of 2 squares, follow diagram **4** to cut: • One 1½" x 3½" rectangle. • Seven 1½" x 1½" squares; 2 squares will be unused.

Materials	Quantity Needed	Notes and Cutting Instructions
Focus print fabric	Fat eighth (9" x 21")	• Cut two 1" x 20½" strips. • Follow diagram **5** to trace and cut two 6½" circles onto the remaining fabric. • From the scraps, cut two 2" by 2½" zipper tab strips.
6" x 16" bolster pillow form		
22" zipper		
Binding fabric		
Backing fabric		

RECOMMENDED MATERIALS

Materials	Quantity Needed	Notes and Cutting Instructions
ScrapTherapy Middle Scrap Grid Interfacing	1 panel	

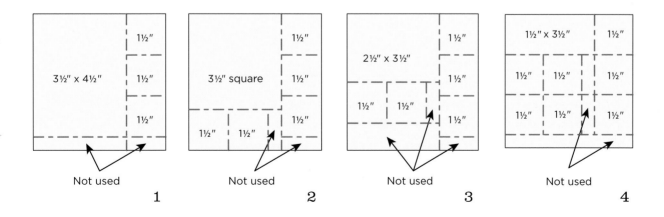

1
2
3
4

5

You can trace and cut the circles using the template. Alternatively, choose from a variety of cutting tools available to make circular cuts from fabric. Read the manufacturer's instructions carefully to make sure you include the seam allowance. The unfinished diameter of the cut circle should measure 6½ in.

Use the template to double-check your circles made with a circle-cutting tool. It's better to be safe than frustrated later if your fabric is either too large or too small for your pillow ends. Too large is easily fixed; too small, not so much.

The ScrapTherapy Middle Scrap Grid can be used to make the 9-patch blocks for this project. Follow the steps on pp. 22–25 for the furled 9-patch with interfacing. You'll need two full sections of one panel plus one-sixth of a panel section to make a total of thirteen 9-patch blocks. The partial blocks are sewn without interfacing.

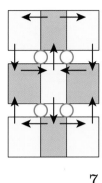

7

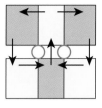

8

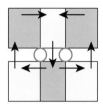

MAKE THE 9-PATCHES

Select five 1½-in. dark-value scrap squares and four 1½-in. light-value scrap squares. Arrange the 1½-in. squares into a 9-patch with dark-value corners and center and light-value sides. Sew them into a basic 9-patch as shown on pp. 10–11. **6**

Repeat to make eight 9-patch blocks that measure 3½ in. square.

Furl.

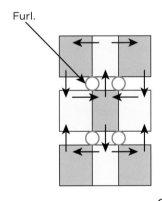

6

Since the small 9-patch block seams won't intersect with seams in adjacent blocks, the seam intersections may be furled or pressed without furling. I think I might be addicted to furling seams, so I prefer to furl when the opportunity presents itself to reduce bulk at the seam intersections, or when it makes sense for the rest of the quilt's construction. Furl or not, take your pick; for this step it's not critical.

Select four 1½-in. dark-value scrap squares and five 1½-in. light-value scrap squares. Arrange the 1½-in. squares into a 9-patch with light-value corners and center and dark-value sides. Sew into a basic 9-patch as shown on pp. 10–11. **7**

Repeat to make five 9-patch blocks that measure 3½ in. square.

Select three 1½-in. dark-value scrap squares and three 1½-in. light-value scrap squares. Arrange the 1½-in. squares into 2 rows of 3 squares as shown. Sew the scraps into rows, press the seams toward the dark-value scraps, and then sew the rows together. Furl the seams. **8**

Repeat the process with a second set of three 1½-in. dark-value scraps and three 1½-in. light-value scraps. Arrange the scraps into 2 rows and sew. Press the seams toward the light-value scraps. Sew the rows together. Furl the seams.

The 2 partial 9-patch blocks measure 2½ in. by 3½ in.

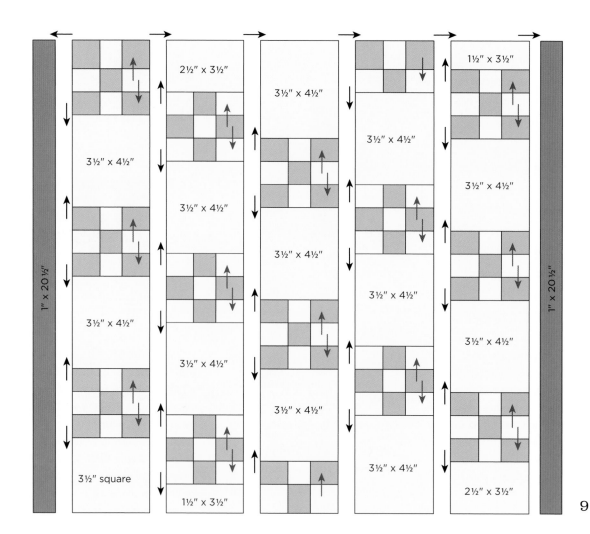

COMPLETE THE MAIN PILLOW PANEL

Arrange the 9-patch blocks, the partial 9-patch blocks, and the remaining light-value scraps into vertical rows as shown. **9** Note that the gray arrows represent seams pressed from a previous step. Sew the panel elements into rows, and press the seams as indicated.

Sew the rows together, and press the seams in one direction.

Sew a 1-in. by 20½-in. focus strip to each side of the panel.

The pillow panel measures 16½ in. by 20½ in. Set aside.

As the row seams are pressed, sections of each seam may resist the pressing direction because of the extra 9-patch seams along the row's edge. A hot iron, a puff or two of steam, and a bit of persistence should allow you to prevail over the layers of cotton and interfacing if you're using the Middle Scrap Grid Interfacing.

Of course, pressing stubborn seams open is an option for reducing bulk. Normally, I would not recommend pressing seams open. Seams pressed open—in any quilted project—may create a weaker seam and a shorter life for your project. This pillowcase won't be quilted, so the risk of quilting through—and severing—threads while stitching-in-the-ditch isn't a risk. It also will have a pillow form inside rather than batting, which might beard through pressed-open seams. It's your call!

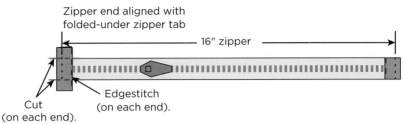

Zipper end aligned with
folded-under zipper tab

16″ zipper

Cut
(on each end).

Edgestitch
(on each end).

11

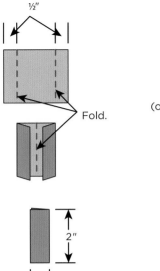

½″

Fold.

2″

¾″

10

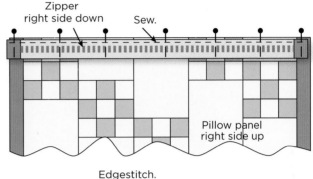

Zipper
right side down

Sew.

Pillow panel
right side up

Edgestitch.

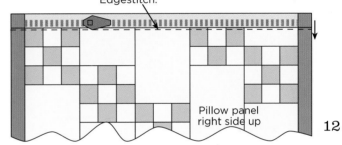

Pillow panel
right side up

12

PREPARE THE ZIPPER

Retrieve the zipper, move the zipper pull to the center, and trim each end of the zipper to make it 16 in. long.

> Warning! When you trim the zipper, you will very likely cut off all the stuff that keeps the zipper pull from sliding off either end. Keep the zipper pull safely in the center of the zipper until the fabric zipper tabs are installed and sewn.

Retrieve the 2-in. by 2½-in. focus print zipper tabs. Make a ½-in. fold, wrong sides together, on each short end of the 2-in. by 2½-in. zipper tab strip. Press.

Fold the zipper tab strip in half, wrong sides together. Press.

Repeat to make a second zipper tab that measures ¾ in. by 2 in. **10**

Open the zipper tab center fold and align one end of the zipper with the raw edge of the folded-under zipper tab. Refold in half and secure all the layers of the zipper tab to the zipper with pins. Repeat with the second zipper tab and the other end of the trimmed zipper. Edgestitch along the zipper tab fold as shown.

Trim the zipper tab sides even with the long edge of the zipper. The zipper assembly measures approximately 1 in. by 16½ in. **11**

INSTALL THE ZIPPER

Retrieve the pillow panel, and align the zipper right sides together with the end of the pillow panel. Secure with pins. Using a zipper foot, sew a ¼-in. seam.

> Begin sewing with the zipper halfway open. As you approach the zipper pull, stop sewing with the needle in the needle-down position, lift up the presser foot, and carefully move the zipper to the back of the needle, then continue sewing.

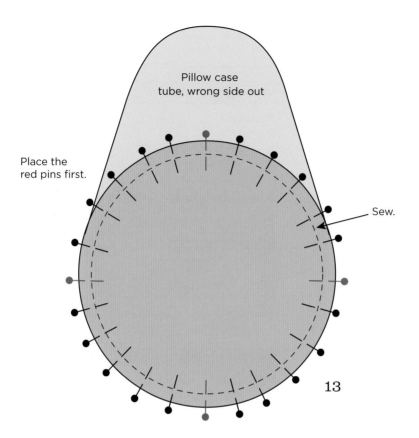

Pillow case
tube, wrong side out

Place the
red pins first.

Sew.

13

Finger-press the seam firmly toward the panel, and edgestitch along the fold. **12**

Align the remaining zipper edge along the opposite 16½-in. pillow panel end. Place the zipper edge and the panel right sides together, forming a tube. Pin to secure. Maneuver the panel under the presser foot with the zipper open. Sew the zipper to the panel with a ¼-in. seam. Finger-press the seam firmly toward the panel. Edgestitch along the fold as before.

COMPLETE THE PILLOW
Keep the pillowcase tube wrong side out. Fold the pillowcase tube opening in half twice to make a short crease to mark four quarters around the circumference.

Retrieve a 6½-in. focus print circle and fold it in half twice. Pinch the ends to mark four quarters around the circumference of the pillowcase end.

Place the pillowcase end right sides together with the pillowcase tube end. Align the quarter-circumference markings and secure the layers with pins. Ease in the edges of the pillowcase end to align with the pillowcase tube

edge and pin liberally around the circumference between the quarter marks. Sew with a ¼-in. seam. **13**

Important: Make sure the zipper is open. Then repeat the process to mark, pin, and sew the remaining focus print circle to the opposite end of the pillowcase tube.

Turn the pillowcase right side out, insert the pillow form, and close the zipper.

Beetle Mania

FEATURING THE BASIC 9-PATCH

FINISHED SIZE: 54 in. square
PATTERN DIFFICULTY: Easy

This project started as a simple floor quilt for baby playtime, but the easy basic 9-patch block assembly and bright scrap colors I chose wouldn't let me stop making blocks. When a quilt speaks to you, I've learned that you should probably listen. More blocks meant the floor quilt grew. While this project provides a healthy playspace for baby, it could nicely substitute for a beach or picnic blanket, or a throw, especially for a tween.

The bright scrap fabrics bring a hefty dose of whimsy and fun to the project. Add six low-volume fat quarters and a really snappy border print, and these beetles will warm your heart as you sew without adding to the scrap bin.

The easy, brightly colored ladybug appliqué blocks can be completed by hand—my sample was made with the back-basting method shown on pp. 205–206—or by machine, as described on pp. 206–207.

SCRAPS NEEDED

Square Size	Description	Quantity Needed	Notes and Cutting Instructions
1½″	Bright scrap squares	65	• Cut from 2″, 3½″, or 5″ squares.
3½″	Bright scrap squares	52	
5″	Scrap squares	16	• Following diagram **1** (on p. 136), from each of 12 squares, cut 2 matching 2½″ x 5″ rectangles for ladybug appliqués. Keep matching rectangles together. • Following diagram **1** (on p. 136), from each of the remaining 4 squares, cut a diagonal line ¼″ away from the diagonal.

FABRICS AND OTHER MATERIALS

Materials	Quantity Needed	Notes and Cutting Instructions
Low-volume print	6 fat quarters (each 18" x 21")	From each fat quarter, cut one 9½" x 21" strip and two 3½" x 21" strips. Subcut each 9½" x 21" strip into two 9½" squares. Mix up the 3½" x 21" strips, and then cut the following: • From 4 strips, cut five 3½" squares and two 1½" squares. • From 4 strips, cut four 3½" squares and six 1½" squares. • From 2 strips, cut four 3½" squares and five 1½" squares. • From 2 strips, cut four 3½" squares and five 1½" squares.
Black solid	⅓ yd.	
Border print	1 yd.	• Cut six 5" width-of-fabric strips.
Binding	½ yd.	• Cut six 2¼" width-of-fabric strips.
Backing	3½ yd.	
Batting	60" x 60"	

RECOMMENDED MATERIALS

Materials	Quantity Needed	Notes and Cutting Instructions
ScrapTherapy Middle Scrap Grid Interfacing	1 panel	• 2 sections of 1 panel and ⅙ of another panel will be used.
12"-wide paper-backed fusible web	1¼ yd.	

Be careful cutting! Cut the fat quarter strips along the fabric width-of-grain. If you cut along the length-of-grain, you'll need to recalculate the strip widths needed to achieve the number of squares required to complete the quilt.

Why not simply cut as many 3½-in. squares as possible from each strip, then move on and cut 1½-in. squares from the strips that are remaining? By splitting the different cut sizes between the strips, each fat quarter is represented evenly in the quilt blocks.

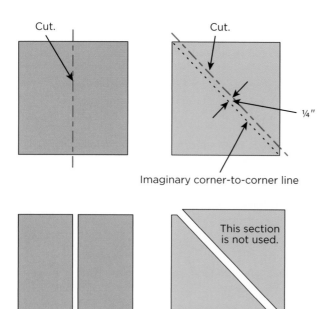

Cut.

Cut.

¼″

Imaginary corner-to-corner line

This section
is not used.

1

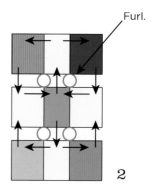

Furl.

2

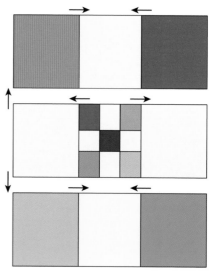

3

The ScrapTherapy Middle Scrap Grid Interfacing can be used to make the small 9-patch for the center of each pieced block. Follow the steps on pp. 10–11 for a basic 9-patch with interfacing. You'll need 2 full sections of a panel and one-sixth of a section for the thirteenth 9-patch block.

MAKE THE SMALL 9-PATCHES

Select five 1½-in. scrap squares and four 1½-in. low-volume/light-value squares cut from the fat quarters. Arrange the 1½-in. squares into a 9-patch with scrap corners and center and low-volume sides. Sew into a basic 9-patch as shown on pp. 10–11. **2**

Repeat to make 13 small 9-patches that measure 3½ in. square.

Since the small 9-patch block seams won't intersect with seams in adjacent blocks, the seam intersections may be furled or pressed without furling. I think I might be addicted to furling seams, so I prefer to furl when the opportunity presents itself to reduce bulk at the seam intersections, or when it makes sense for the rest of the quilt's construction. Furl or not, take your pick; for this step it's not critical.

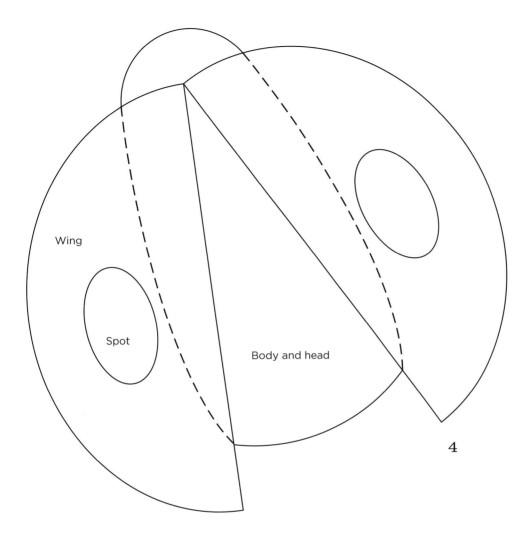

Wing

Spot

Body and head

4

Select four 3½-in. scrap squares, four 3½-in. low-volume/light-value squares cut from the fat quarters, and 1 small 9-patch. Arrange the 3½-in. squares and small 9-patch into a large 9-patch with scrap corners, low-volume sides, and small 9-patch center. Sew into a basic 9-patch as shown on pp. 10–11. Press the seams as shown. Note that the seam intersections are *not* furled for the large 9-patch. **3**

Repeat to make 13 large 9-patch blocks that measure 9½ in. square. Set aside.

For the large 9-patch blocks, the extra seams in the 9-patch center will resist being pressed toward the center of the block. When the appliqué blocks are complete, they'll be situated next to the 9-patches, so the seam direction at the outer edges of the block isn't critical; the internal seams will benefit from pressing to best advantage.

5

MAKE THE APPLIQUÉ BLOCKS

Trace 12 of the ladybug body/head shape and 24 each of the wing and spot shapes onto the paper side of the fusible web. Rough-cut around each shape. **4**

Fuse the body/head shapes and spot shapes to the wrong side of the black fabric. Fuse the wing shapes to the wrong side of the 2½-in. by 5-in. scraps in pairs. Keep matching scraps together throughout. Cut the shapes on the lines.

Arrange a body/head shape, 2 matching scrap wing shapes, and 2 spot shapes in layers centered on the right side of a 9½-in. fat quarter square as shown. Fuse. **5**

Secure the appliqué edges with a buttonhole, zigzag, or satin stitch using a thread color that matches the appliqué fabric.

Repeat to make 12 ladybug appliqué blocks that measure 9½ in. square.

Note that the ladybugs appear to face different directions in the quilt. Actually, each block is made with the same wonky-angle ladybug orientation. The bugs look like they are traveling in different directions because the appliqué blocks were rotated 90 degrees to the right, 90 degrees to the left, or 180 degrees to create playful buggy-ness. Does that bug you? *Wink!*

COMPLETE THE QUILT CENTER

Arrange the pieced blocks and appliqué blocks into 5 rows of 5 blocks, alternating the pieced and appliqué blocks as shown. **6** Sew the blocks into rows; press the block seams toward the appliqué blocks.

Sew the rows together and press the seams in one direction.

ADD THE BORDERS

Sew 3 of the 5-in. width-of-fabric border strips together end to end with a diagonal seam as shown on p. 205, and press the connecting seams open to make a 5-in. strip that is approximately 120 in. long. Sew the remaining 3 width-of-fabric strips together to make a second 120-in. border strip. From each strip, cut two 5-in. by 45½-in. borders.

Arrange the borders with the quilt center, and add the triangular scrap cornerstones as shown. Sew the cornerstones to each end of the top and bottom borders, and press the seams toward the border.

Sew the borders to the quilt center, sides first, then the top and bottom. Press the seam toward the border after each addition, as shown on the facing page.

QUILT AND BIND

Layer the backing, batting, and quilt top; baste. Quilt as desired.

Cut six 2¼-in. width-of-fabric strips for the binding. Sew the binding strips together end to end using a diagonal seam. Press the connecting seams open; then press the binding in half lengthwise, wrong sides together.

Trim the batting and backing even with the quilt top. With the raw edges aligned, sew the folded binding to the front of the quilt using a ¼-in. seam. Miter the binding at the corners.

I miter the binding at the corners even when the corner isn't a "standard" 90-degree angle. Check out the tips on pp. 210–211 for more details.

Turn the folded edge of the binding to the back of the quilt and hand-stitch it in place.

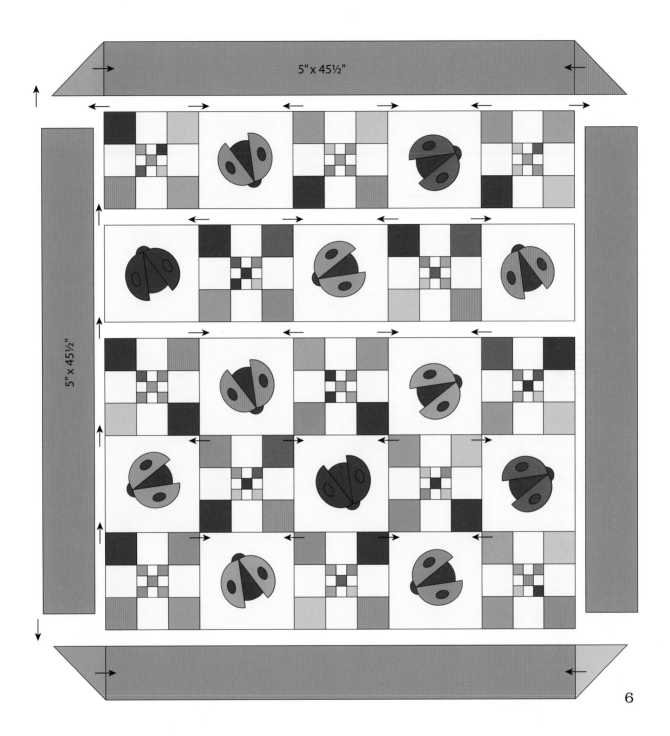

5" x 45½"

5" x 45½"

6

Citrus Coverlet

FEATURING THE ELEVATED 9-PATCH

FINISHED QUILT SIZE: **50 in. by 68 in.**
PATTERN DIFFICULTY: **Easy+**

I'm a puzzle freak! As a kid, one of my favorite cold-weather pastimes involved setting up a card table in the corner of the room with a box full of jigsaw puzzle pieces. The more complex the puzzle, the better! Searching for and finding the pieces that fit together to create pictures of far-off exotic places was the perfect way to spend a wintry weekend.

Sometimes I find a similar challenge with creating quilts. When the seams are pressed a certain way, and the blocks snap together like puzzle pieces, it feels a little like a throwback to those jigsaw puzzle days.

The "Citrus Coverlet" pulls together a variety of citrus-colored solid fabrics, 5-in. scrap squares in a variety of light-value prints (one for each 9-patch block), and some ScrapTherapy Little Scrap Grid Interfacing, if you choose to use it. The blocks are fairly easy to make; the challenge is in keeping the pattern consistent within each of the 140 blocks—it's easy to get one or more of the half-square triangles flipped in the wrong direction, breaking the secondary patterns the blocks make once they're assembled. The result is a cheerful throw to take the chill off those puzzle-building weekends.

SCRAPS NEEDED

Square Size	Description	Quantity Needed	Notes and Cutting Instructions
5″	Light-value print scrap squares	140	• Following diagram **1**, cut each square in half twice to make 4 matching 2½″ squares. On the back of each square, draw a diagonal line from corner to corner. Keep matched squares together.

Materials	Quantity Needed	Notes and Cutting Instructions
Solid citrus-colored fat eighths (9" x 21")	28	• Cut three 2½" x 21" strips from each fat eighth. From each of 2 strips, cut eight 2½" squares. From the remaining strip, cut four 2½" squares and five 2" squares. Separate the squares into 5 stacks that contain 4 matching 2½" squares and 1 matching 2" square.
Border and binding (solid or print) fabric	1 yd.	• Cut six 3" width-of-fabric strips. Set aside for the border. • Cut six 2¼" width-of-fabric strips for the binding.
Backing	3¼ yd.	• Seam horizontally.
Batting	56" x 74"	

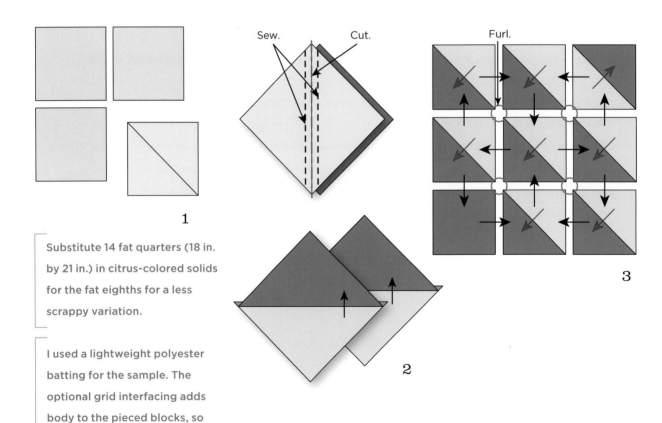

1

2

3

Sew. Cut. Furl.

Substitute 14 fat quarters (18 in. by 21 in.) in citrus-colored solids for the fat eighths for a less scrappy variation.

I used a lightweight polyester batting for the sample. The optional grid interfacing adds body to the pieced blocks, so the lighter batting seemed "just enough" to complete the project.

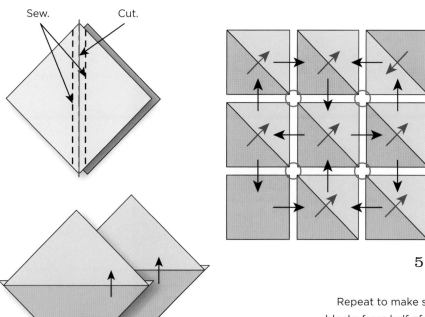

Sew.   Cut.

4

5

MAKE THE BLOCKS

Select 1 set of matching 2½-in. scrap squares and 1 stack of 4 matching 2½-in. and one 2-in. citrus squares. Place a 2½-in. scrap square and a 2½-in. citrus square right sides together with the scrap square on top. Sew a ¼-in. seam along both sides of the drawn line. Cut on the line, and press the seam toward the citrus fabric. Trim each of the half-square triangle (HST) units to 2 in. square. Repeat to make 8 HST units, with seams pressed toward the citrus fabric. **2**

Arrange the 8 HST units and the 2-in. citrus square into a 9-patch block as shown. Sew the squares into the basic 9-patch block with furled seams (see pp. 13–14). Be careful to press the row seams as indicated. The 9-patch block measures 5 in. square. **3**

To help show the pressing direction within the blocks, without crowding the illustrations with lots of arrows, the green blocks indicate blocks with HST units pressed toward the citrus-themed fabrics, and the orange blocks represent blocks with HST units pressed toward the scrap fabrics, which are consistently represented by gray. In reality, your quilt will have lots of citrus colors and lots of different light-value scraps.

Repeat to make seventy 9-patch blocks from half of the sets of scrap squares and citrus stacks.

Select 1 set of matching 2½-in. scrap squares and 1 stack of 4 matching 2½-in. and one 2-in. citrus squares. Place a 2½-in. scrap square and a 2½-in. citrus square right sides together with the scrap square on top. Sew a ¼-in. seam along both sides of the drawn line. Cut on the line and press the seam toward the scrap fabric. Trim each of the HST units to 2 in. square. Repeat to make 8 HST units, and press seams toward the scrap fabric. **4**

Arrange the 8 HST units and the 2-in. citrus square into a 9-patch block as shown. Sew the squares into the basic 9-patch block with furled seams (see p. 13). Be careful to press the row seams as indicated, the same as the first block. The only difference is the HST pressing direction. The 9-patch block measures 5 in. square. **5**

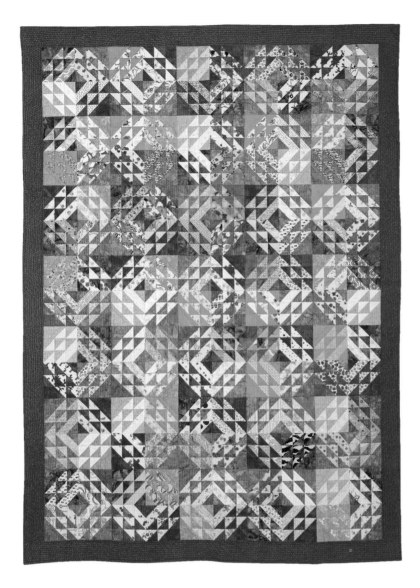

Sew the blocks into rows, and furl the seam intersection within the connecting seams. Sew the rows together, and furl the seam intersections in the connecting seams. The quilt center measures 45½ in. by 63½ in. **6**

MAKE THE BORDERS

Sew all six 3-in. width-of-fabric border strips together end to end with a diagonal seam as shown on p. 205, and press the connecting seams open to make a strip 3 in. by approximately 240 in. long.

Cut two 3-in. by 63½-in. side borders and two 3-in. by 50½-in. top/bottom borders. Sew the borders to the quilt, sewing the sides first, and then the top and bottom. Press the seam toward the border after each addition. **6**

QUILT AND BIND

Layer the backing, batting, and quilt top; baste. Quilt as desired.

Sew the binding strips together end to end using a diagonal seam. Press the connecting seams open; then press the binding in half lengthwise, wrong sides together.

Trim the batting and backing even with the quilt top. With the raw edges aligned, sew the folded binding to the front of the quilt using a ¼-in. seam. Miter the binding at the corners.

Turn the folded edge of the binding to the back of the quilt and hand-stitch it in place.

Notice that the row seams and 9-patch seams are pressed the same for each variation of the block. The only difference is the HST unit seam direction. The furled seam intersection is important for the seams to nest in the final quilt top construction.

Repeat to make seventy 9-patch blocks from the remaining half of the sets of scrap squares and citrus stacks.

Arrange the blocks into 14 rows of 10 blocks each. Alternate the blocks with HST seams pressed toward the citrus fabric with the blocks with HST seams pressed toward the scrap fabric. Pay close attention to the rotation of the blocks within the rows.

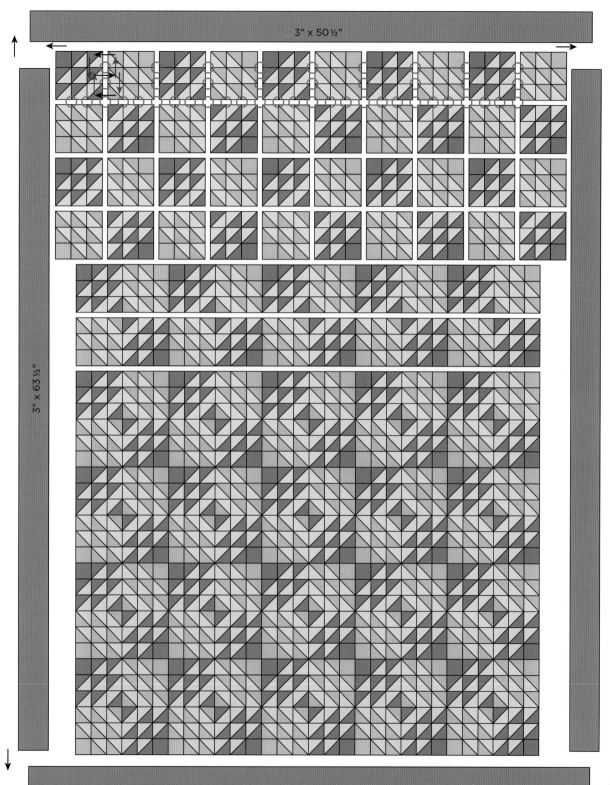

3" x 50 ½"

3" x 63 ½"

6

USING THE 9-PATCH INTERFACING

The 9-patch blocks for this project can benefit from the ScrapTherapy Little Scrap Grid Interfacing.

Trim extra interfacing. Prepare sections of the grid to make six 9-patch blocks at a time. Since the blocks involve pieced elements, arrange and fuse the HST units carefully on the interfacing so the HST units are centered and square within the dotted and dashed lines on the grid. Arrange the two block variations in the same orientation on the interfacing, and sew and press all blocks

the same. Sew the 6 vertical seams first (marked with the red arrows). Snip the interfacing at the 4 crosshairs, then press and sew each seam identified by the green arrows. Review the detailed instructions for the basic 9-patch furled with interfacing on pp. 22–25.

Separate the blocks into 2 stacks, one with HST seams pressed toward the scrap fabric and one with HST seams pressed toward the citrus fabric, and arrange the blocks into the quilt layout as described on p. 144.

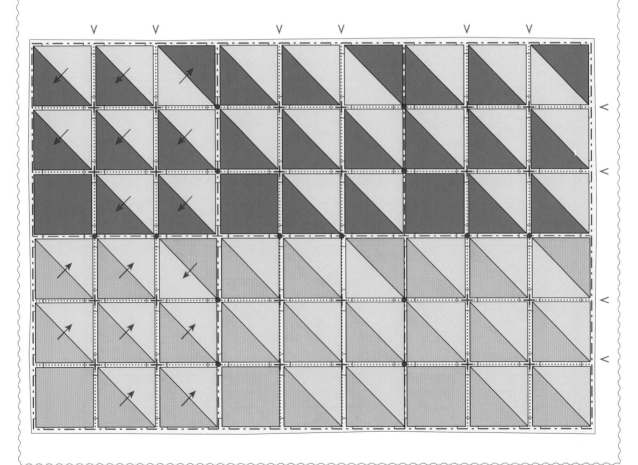

Elsa's Prayer Quilt

FEATURING THE TRANSFORMED AND ELEVATED 9-PATCH

FINISHED SIZE: 43 in. by 57 in. (prayer/lap); 41 in. by 41 in. (baby)
PATTERN DIFFICULTY: Intermediate

The inspiration for this project came from *Frozen*, the popular animated feature film from Disney. Early in the storyline, the two sisters, Anna and Elsa, are separated by a massive door that features decorative wooden carvings and paintings. One evening, my husband was flipping through channels (as husbands are known to do), and he landed on this movie. When that scene came on, I saw a potential quilt based on those carvings and paintings.

The scrappy star and tulip shapes in this quilt were inspired by the decorative paintings on that door. I paired them with aqua-colored yardage for my own take on *Frozen*. The leftovers from the stitch-and-flip elements that create the star blocks in the quilt's center are repurposed in the ring of tulip shapes in the pieced border.

At first glance, this quilt might seem out of place in a book featuring 9-patch projects. Where's the 9-patch, after all? The modified 4-patch star points made from scraps in a single main color are the 9-patch block corners. The tiny accent scrap square in the center of the block is the 9-patch center, and the skinny sashing elements are the 9-patch sides. The technique to make the 4-patch corners is similar to the technique used to make "Pomegranate Rose Table Topper" on p. 79.

The size of this quilt is well suited to a prayer quilt—typically a lap-size quilt given to someone convalescing from a serious illness. If your quilt is destined to be a prayer quilt for someone special, let your thoughts wander to all things wonderful as you select your scraps and sew them together so the quilt's recipient will be wrapped in your good thoughts and be comforted. Because of the pieced border elements, the math to downsize the quilt gets tricky, so I've included some additional instructions to make a baby quilt (p. 159) while keeping true to the pattern.

Square Size	Description	Quantity Needed	Notes and Cutting Instructions
2″	Accent color scrap squares	6	• Trim each square to $1\frac{1}{2}$″ square for block centers.
$3\frac{1}{2}$″	Main color scrap squares	96	
$3\frac{1}{2}$″	Accent color scrap squares	24	• Following diagram **1**, cut each scrap square into four $1\frac{1}{4}$″ squares. Draw a diagonal line from corner to corner on the back of each. Keep matched squares together.

FABRICS AND OTHER MATERIALS FOR THE PRAYER QUILT

Materials	Quantity Needed	Notes and Cutting Instructions
Background solid or print	$2\frac{3}{4}$ yd.	• Cut seven $3\frac{1}{2}$″ width-of-fabric strips; subcut into seventy-two $3\frac{1}{2}$″ squares. Following diagram **2**, on the back of 48 squares, draw two diagonal lines, one from corner to corner and the other parallel to the first and $\frac{1}{2}$″ away. • Cut three 2″ width-of-fabric strips; subcut into twelve 2″ x 10″ strips. Following diagram **3**, on the right side of each strip, draw a line in the center along the length of the strip. • Cut five 2″ width-of-fabric strips; subcut into ninety-six 2″ squares. Following diagram **4**, on the back of half of the squares, draw a diagonal line from corner to corner. • Cut four $1\frac{1}{2}$″ width-of-fabric strips; subcut into twenty-four $1\frac{1}{2}$″ x $6\frac{1}{2}$″ strips for the blocks. • Cut three $1\frac{1}{2}$″ width-of-fabric strips; subcut into twenty-four $1\frac{1}{2}$″ x $3\frac{1}{2}$″ strips for the pieced border. • Cut three $2\frac{1}{2}$″ width-of-fabric strips; subcut into two $2\frac{1}{2}$″ x $28\frac{1}{2}$″ horizontal sashing strips and three $2\frac{1}{2}$″ x $13\frac{1}{2}$″ vertical sashing strips. • Cut three $2\frac{1}{2}$″ width-of-fabric strips, and set aside for the side inner borders. • Cut two 2″ width-of-fabric strips; subcut into two 2″ x $32\frac{1}{2}$″ top and bottom inner borders. • Cut six 3″ width-of-fabric strips, and set aside for the outer borders.
Binding	$\frac{1}{2}$ yd.	• Cut six $2\frac{1}{4}$″ width-of-fabric strips for the binding.
Backing	3 yd.	• Seam horizontally.
Batting	49″ x 63″	

Square Size	Description	Quantity Needed	Notes and Cutting Instructions
2"	Accent color scrap squares	4	Trim each square to 1½" square for block centers.
3½"	Main color scrap squares	68	
3½"	Accent color scrap squares	16	Following diagram **1**, cut each scrap square into four 1¼" squares. Draw a diagonal line from corner to corner on the back of each. Keep matched squares together.

FABRICS AND OTHER MATERIALS FOR THE BABY QUILT

Materials	Quantity Needed	Notes and Cutting Instructions
Background print	2 yd.	• Cut five 3½" width-of-fabric strips; subcut into forty-eight 3½" squares. Following diagram **2**, on the back of 32 squares, draw two diagonal lines, one from corner to corner and the other parallel to the first and ½" away. • Cut two 2" width-of-fabric strips; subcut into eight 2" x 10" strips. Following diagram **3**, on the right side of each strip, draw a line in the center along the length of the strip. • Cut four 2" width-of-fabric strips; subcut into sixty-four 2" squares. Following diagram **4**, on the back of half of the squares, draw a diagonal line from corner to corner. • Cut three 1½" width-of-fabric strips; subcut into sixteen 1½" x 6½" strips for the blocks. • Cut two 1½" width-of-fabric strips; subcut into twelve 1½" x 3½" strips for the pieced border. • Cut two 1½" width-of-fabric strips; subcut into one 1½" x 27½" horizontal sashing strip and two 1½" x 13½" vertical sashing strips. • Cut four 2" width-of-fabric strips; subcut into two 2" x 27½" inner side borders and two 2" x 36½" top and bottom inner borders. From strip remainders, cut four 2" x 3½" strips for the top and bottom pieced borders. • Cut five 3" width-of-fabric strips, and set aside for the outer borders.
Binding	³⁄₈ yd.	• Cut five 2¼" width-of-fabric strips for the binding.
Backing	2⅔ yd.	
Batting	47" x 47"	

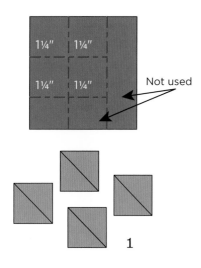

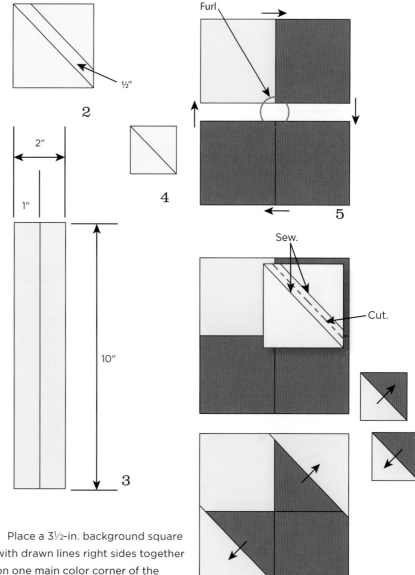

MAKE THE BLOCKS

With lots of stitching, cutting, and pressing along the bias fabric grain, there is very little margin for error and lots of potential for blocks that may be just shy of their expected size. Try to maintain a consistent scant ¼-in. seam allowance as you sew the 4-patches, the stitch-and-flip units, and the sashing elements in these next few steps.

Select a 3½-in. background square and three 3½-in. main color scrap squares and arrange them into a 4-patch. Sew the squares into 2 rows, and press as shown. Sew the rows together and furl the seam as shown on pp. 13–14. **5**

Place a 3½-in. background square with drawn lines right sides together on one main color corner of the 4-patch unit. **6** Sew on both lines, cut apart between the lines, and press the seam on the 4-patch unit toward the corner. Press the half-square triangle (HST) toward the scrap fabric and trim to 2 in. square.

Similarly, place a 3½-in. background square with drawn lines right sides together on the opposite main color corner of the 4-patch unit as shown. Sew on both lines, cut apart

between the lines, and press the seam on the 4-patch unit toward the corner. Press 1 HST toward the background fabric and 1 HST toward the scrap fabric, and trim to 2 in. square. **6**

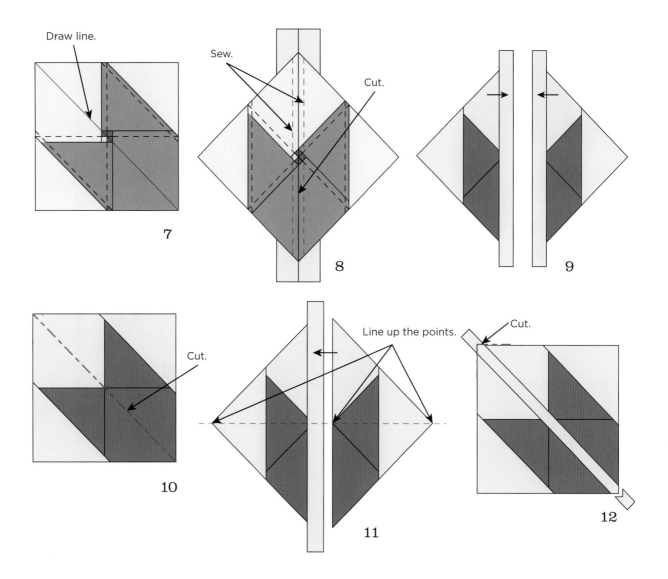

Draw line.

Sew.

Cut.

7

8

9

Cut.

10

Line up the points.

Cut.

11

12

For the prayer quilt, repeat to make twenty-four 4-patch blocks that measure 6½ in. square and forty-eight 2-in. HST units, half with seams pressed toward the scrap fabric and half with seams pressed toward the background fabric. For the baby quilt, repeat to make sixteen 4-patch blocks that measure 6½ in. square and thirty-two 2-in. HST units, half with seams pressed toward the scrap fabric and half with

seams pressed toward the background fabric.

Draw a diagonal line from corner to corner on the back of half of the 4-patch blocks. Draw the line parallel to the 2 stitch-and-flip seams. Set aside the remaining 4-patch blocks. **7**

Place a 2-in. by 10-in. background strip right side up on your work-surface. Place a 4-patch block on the strip right side down, centered roughly on the strip with drawn lines

aligned. Pin liberally to secure the layers along the fabric bias. Sew ¼ in. away from both sides of the line. **8**

After both seams are sewn, cut on the line, and press the seam toward the sashing strip. Repeat with each 4-patch block and marked strip to make a total of 24 sashed half blocks for the prayer quilt and 16 sashed half blocks for the baby quilt. Do not trim the sashed ends. Keep similar sashed half blocks together. **9**

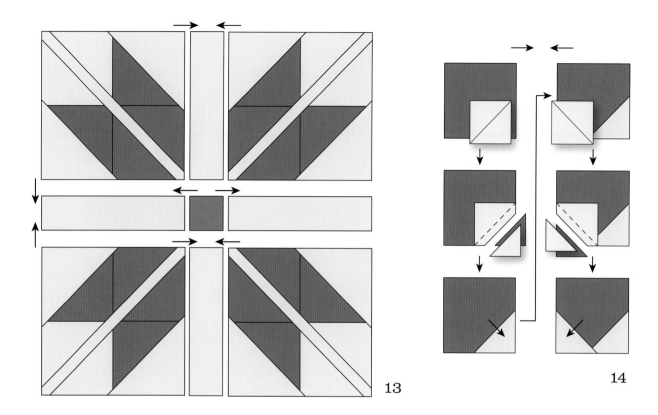

13

14

Retrieve the remaining 4-patch blocks, and cut them along the diagonal as shown. Cut through the center of the block and along the diagonal that is parallel to the stitch-and-flip seams. Keep similar half blocks together. **10**

Select a sashed half block and its "opposite" half block, and place them right sides together, aligning the sashing edge with the bias-cut block edge. Be sure the 4-patch center seam intersection and the block points are lined up to form a straight line perpendicular to the seam. Pin liberally before sewing a scant ¼-in. seam. Press the seam toward the sashing. **11**

With a square ruler that is at least 6½ in. square, trim the sashing ends so the block is 6½ in. square. Repeat to make twenty-four 6½-in. sashed 4-patches for the prayer quilt and sixteen 6½-in. sashed 4-patches for the baby quilt. **12**

Select 4 sashed 4-patches, four 1½-in. by 6½-in. background strips, and one 1½-in. scrap square, and arrange them into a 9-patch as shown. Sew the units into 3 rows, press the seams toward the 1½-in. strip, and then sew the rows together and press the seams toward the center. Repeat to make 6 blocks that measure 13½ in. square for the prayer quilt and 4 blocks that measure 13½ in. square for the baby

quilt. Set the blocks aside while you make the pieced border elements. **13**

MAKE THE TULIP BORDER UNITS

Select a 3½-in. main color scrap square and a marked 2-in. background square and place right sides together, aligned at one corner of the larger scrap as shown. Sew on the line, trim the extra fabric, and press toward the corner. Add a second 2-in. background square as shown. Sew on the line, trim the extra fabric, and press toward the corner. Repeat to make 24 lower tulip units for the prayer quilt and 16 lower tulip units for the baby quilt. Set aside. **14**

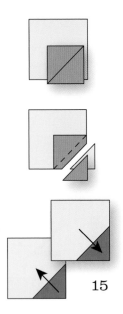

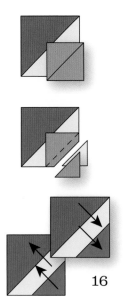

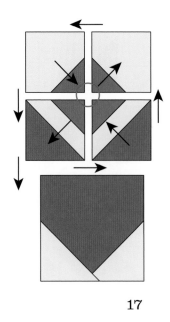

15

16

17

Select one set of 4 matching 1¼-in. accent squares. Place one 1¼-in. accent square on a 2-in. background square right sides together with the accent scrap on top and corners aligned as shown. Sew on the line. Trim the extra fabric ¼ in. away from the seam. Repeat to make a second 2-in. background square with the sewn, trimmed, and pressed 1¼-in. accent square. Press the seam toward the scrap on one unit and toward the background unit on the second unit. Keep similar units together. **15**

Select 2 HST units set aside earlier, one pressed toward the scrap and one pressed toward the background fabric. Align a 1¼-in. accent square right sides together with the corner of each selected HST unit as shown. Sew, trim, and press, using the existing HST seam to determine the pressing direction for the accent fabric seam. **16**

Arrange the 4 units with matching accent fabrics as shown at the top of the illustration, then sew the units into a 4-patch, and furl the seams as described on pp. 13–14. Sew the 4-patch to a lower tulip unit. Press the seam toward the lower tulip unit. Repeat to make 24 tulip border units that measure 3½ in. by 6½ in. for the prayer quilt and 16 tulip border units that measure 3½ in. by 6½ in. for the baby quilt. **17**

ASSEMBLE THE QUILT
PRAYER QUILT
Arrange 6 blocks, three 2½-in. by 13½-in. vertical sashing strips, and two 2½-in. by 28½-in. horizontal sashing strips into the quilt top as shown. **18** Sew the blocks and vertical sashing strips into rows, and sew the rows to the horizontal sashing strips. Press the seams toward the sashing strips after each addition.

Sew three 2½-in. width-of-fabric strips together end to end to make a side border strip that is approximately 2½ in. by 120 in., then subcut two 2½-in. by 43½-in. side inner borders.

Sew the 2½-in. by 43½-in. side inner borders to the quilt; then sew the 2-in. by 32½-in. top and bottom inner borders to the quilt. Press the seams toward the border after each addition. **18**

3" x 43½"

2½" x 32½"

2½" x 13½"

2½" x 28½"

2½" x 43½"

3" x 52½"

2½" x 28½"

Leave approximately 9" unsewn

18

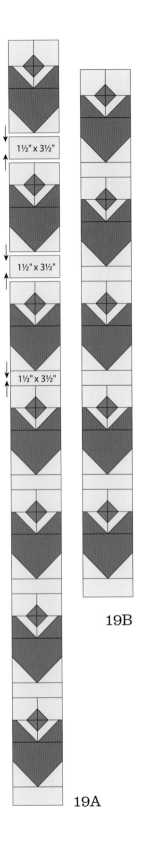

19B

19A

Select and sew 7 tulip border units and seven 1½-in. by 3½-in. background strips as shown to make a side pieced border that measures 3½ in. by 49½ in. **19A** Start with a tulip border unit and end with a 1½-in. by 3½-in. background strip. Repeat to make a second side pieced border.

Select and sew 5 pieced border units and five 1½-in. by 3½-in. background strips as shown to make a top and a bottom pieced border that measures 3½ in. by 35½ in. Start with a tulip border unit and end with a 1½-in. by 3½-in. background strip sewn to the bottom of a tulip border unit. **19B**

"Hold up! The borders are longer than the quilt top! I've done something wrong!" Actually, to make the math work on the pieced borders, the borders are longer than the quilt top *on purpose*. As you sew the first side border to the lap quilt, align the top edge of the border with the top edge of the quilt and sew. You'll soon notice some of the border is hanging off the end. That's as it should be. Stop sewing before you get all the way to the bottom edge; then sew the remaining three sides as you normally would. Finish up the partial seam, and the quilt is back on track.

Sew the pieced borders to the quilt, starting with the left side border in the upper left corner of the quilt. Pin the border in place and sew, leaving the last 9 in. of the border unsewn, as indicated by the red dotted line on illustration **18**. Press the partial seam toward the inner border. Sew the top border next, then the right side, and then the bottom. Finally, sew the left side partial seam. Press the seam toward the inner border after each addition.

Be mindful of the position and rotation of the pieced border elements as you sew them into borders and as you sew them to the quilt.

Sew three 3-in. width-of-fabric strips together end to end to make a side outer border strip that is approximately 3 in. by 120 in. Press the connecting seams open. Subcut two 3-in. by 52½-in. side outer borders. Sew three 3-in. width-of-fabric strips together end to end to make a top/bottom outer border strip that is approximately 3 in. by 120 in. Press the connecting seams open. Cut two 3-in. by 43½-in. top/bottom outer borders.

Sew the 3-in. by 52½-in. side outer borders to the quilt, and press the seam toward the outer border. Sew the 3-in. by 43½-in. top/bottom borders to the quilt, and press the seam toward the outer border. The quilt measures 43½ in. by 57½ in.

BABY QUILT

Arrange 4 blocks, two 1½-in. by 13½-in. vertical sashing strips, and one 1½-in. by 27½-in. horizontal sashing strip into the quilt top as shown on p. 161. Sew the blocks and vertical sashing strips into rows; then sew the rows to the horizontal sashing strips. Press the seams toward the sashing strips after each addition.

Select and sew 4 pieced border units and three 1½-in. by 3½-in. background strips as shown on p. 161 to make a side pieced border that measures 3½ in. by 27½ in. Press the seams toward the 1½-in. by 3½-in. background strips as you make the border. Repeat to make 4 pieced borders.

Sew the 2-in. by 27½-in. side inner borders to the quilt; then sew the 3½-in. by 27½-in. side pieced borders to the quilt. Press the seams toward the borders.

Sew the 2-in. by 36½-in. top and bottom inner borders to the quilt. Press the seams toward the border after each addition.

Sew a 2-in. by 3½-in. background strip to each end of each remaining pieced border, then sew a 3½-in. main color scrap to each end of each border. Press the seams toward the background strip. Make two 3½-in. by 36½-in. top and bottom pieced borders.

Sew the top and bottom pieced borders to the quilt. Press the seam toward the inner border after each addition.

> Be mindful of the position of the pieced border elements.

Trim two 3-in. width-of-fabric strips into two 3-in. by 36½-in. side outer borders. Sew the remaining three 3-in. width-of-fabric strips end to end to make a top/bottom outer border strip that is approximately 3 in. by 120 in. Subcut two 3-in. by 41½-in. side outer borders.

Sew the 3-in. by 36½-in. side outer borders to the quilt, and press the seam toward the outer border. Sew the 3-in. by 41½-in. top and bottom outer borders to the quilt, and press the seam toward the outer border. The quilt measures 41½ in. by 41½ in. **20**

QUILT AND BIND

Layer the backing, batting, and quilt top; baste. Quilt as desired.

Refer to the charts on pp. 149–150 for the number of strips cut for the prayer and baby quilts. Sew the binding strips together end to end using a diagonal seam. Press the connecting seams open; then press the binding in half lengthwise, wrong sides together.

Trim the batting and backing even with the quilt top. With the raw edges aligned, sew the folded binding to the front of the quilt using a ¼-in. seam. Miter the binding at the corners.

Turn the folded edge of the binding to the back of the quilt and hand-stitch it in place.

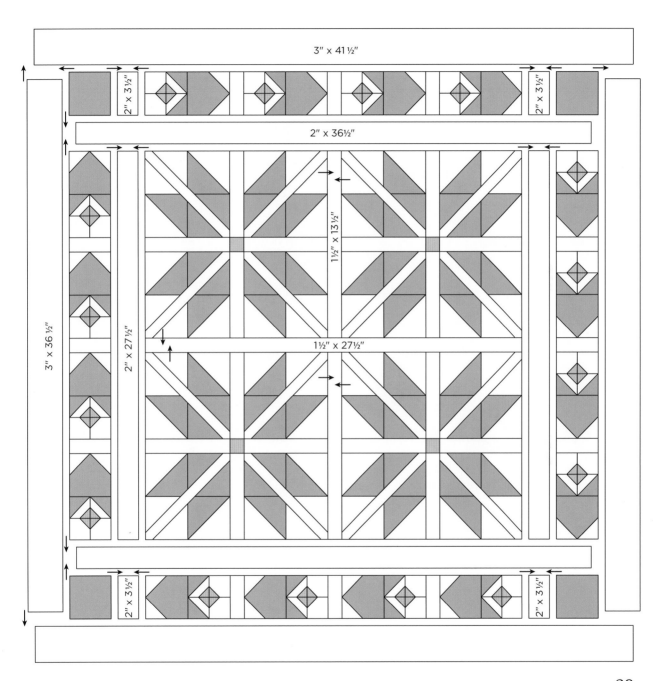

3" x 41½"

2" x 3½"

2" x 3½"

2" x 36½"

1½" x 13½"

3" x 36½"

2" x 27½"

1½" x 27½"

2" x 3½"

2" x 3½"

20

elsa's prayer quilt   **161**

Sneaky Peek Project Pouches

FEATURING THE 9-PATCH TRANSFORMED

FINISHED SIZE: 10 in. square (small pouch); 14 in. square (large pouch)
PATTERN DIFFICULTY: Intermediate

Maybe I shouldn't admit to this, but sometimes I have more than one quilty project started at a time. Okay, on second thought, I confess, I have lots of quilty projects at various stages of completion. I try to stick with one project and work on it diligently until it's complete. But you know how it goes—life gets in the way, holidays come and go, or something new and different grabs your eye.

I do make an effort to come back to everything I start, but staying organized can be tricky.

These zippered project pouches—in two sizes—will keep your in-progress quilty projects organized. The vinyl window protects the project or blocks and provides at-a-glance organization. And the best part: You can make as many as you want (or need) from your scraps and some stash fabrics.

Interfacing products in different weights give the pouch stability and stiffness for sturdy vertical or horizontal storage.

SCRAPS NEEDED FOR SMALL POUCH

Square Size	Description	Quantity Needed	Notes and Cutting Instructions
1½"	Dark-value scrap squares	120	• Cut from 2", 3½", or 5" scrap squares.
1½"	Light-value scrap squares	96	• Cut from 2", 3½", or 5" scrap squares.

Materials	Quantity Needed	Notes and Cutting Instructions
Solid-reading print fabric	1 fat quarter	• Cut one 12½" x 21" strip; subcut into one 12½" back lining square and two 3" x 10½" front lining strips. • Cut two 2" x 3½" zipper tab strips.
Single-sided fusible stiff interfacing	12½" square	• Fuse to the wrong side of the 12½" back lining square. • I use Face-It Firm by Lazy Girl Designs.
3" x 10½" single-sided fusible light woven interfacing	2	• Fuse to the 3" x 10½" front lining strips. • I use Face-It Soft by Lazy Girl Designs.
Single-sided fusible batting scraps	12" square, 10" x 10½" rectangle	• I use Dream Fusion by Quilters Dream.
12-gauge clear vinyl	5¾" x 10½"	
Binding fabric	¼ yd.	• Cut two 2½" width-of-fabric strips for the binding.
18" zipper	1	

RECOMMENDED MATERIALS FOR SMALL POUCH

Materials	Quantity Needed	Notes and Cutting Instructions
ScrapTherapy Middle Scrap Grid Interfacing	1 panel	
Clover Wonder Clips		

Square Size	Description	Quantity Needed	Notes and Cutting Instructions
2″	Dark-value scrap squares	120	
2″	Light-value scrap squares	96	

FABRICS AND OTHER MATERIALS FOR LARGE POUCH

Materials	Quantity Needed	Notes and Cutting Instructions
Solid-reading print fabric	½ yd.	• Cut one 16½″ x 42″ strip; subcut into one 16½″ back lining square and two 4″ x 14½″ front lining strips. • Cut two 2″ x 3½″ zipper tab strips.
Single-sided fusible stiff interfacing	16½″ square	• Fuse to the wrong side of the 16½″ back lining square. • I use Face-It Firm by Lazy Girl Design.
4″ x 14½″ single-sided fusible light woven interfacing	2	• Fuse to the wrong side of the 4″ x 14½″ front lining strips. • I use Face-It Soft by Lazy Girl Designs.
Single-sided fusible batting scraps	16″ square, 12″ x 14″ rectangle	• I use Dream Fusion by Quilters Dream.
12-gauge clear vinyl	7¾″ x 14½″	
Binding fabric	¼ yd.	• Cut two 2½″ width-of-fabric strips for the binding.
18″ zipper	1	

RECOMMENDED MATERIALS FOR LARGE POUCH

Materials	Quantity Needed	Notes and Cutting Instructions
ScrapTherapy Little Scrap Grid Interfacing	2 panels	
Clover Wonder Clips		

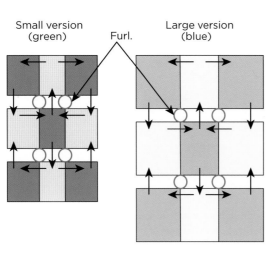

Small version (green) Furl. Large version (blue)

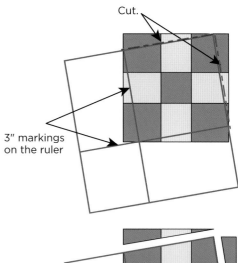

Cut.

3" markings on the ruler

1

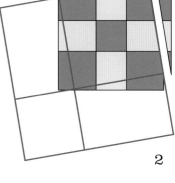

2

MAKE THE 9-PATCHES
SMALL POUCH
Select five 1½-in. dark-value scrap squares and four 1½-in. light-value scrap squares. Arrange the 1½-in. squares into a 9-patch block with dark-value corners and center and light-value sides. Sew into a basic furled 9-patch as shown on pp. 10–11. **1**

Repeat to make twenty-four 9-patch blocks that measure 3½ in. square.

LARGE POUCH
Select five 2-in. dark-value scrap squares and four 2-in. light-value scrap squares. Arrange the 2-in. squares into a 9-patch block with dark-value corners and center and light-value sides. Sew into a basic furled 9-patch as shown on pp. 10–11. **1**

Repeat to make twenty-four 9-patch blocks that measure 5 in. square.

> Using the 9-patch interfacing products for these projects is especially nice because it adds a little bit of extra body and stability to the pouch fabric that you wouldn't get from sewing the scraps without it. It's like having a built-in bonus body treatment! Hmm, that feels kinda like a day at the spa!

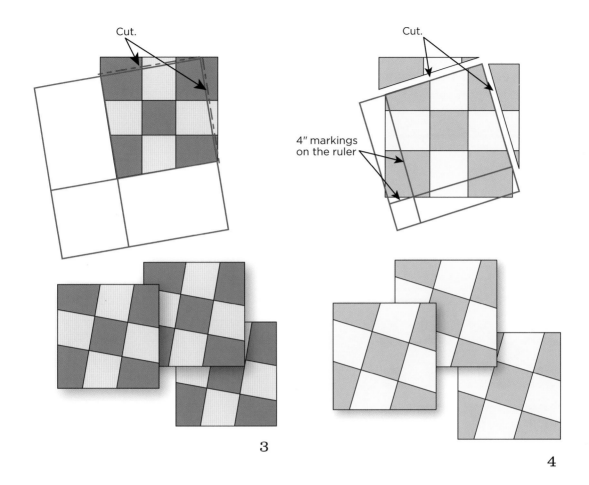

Cut.

Cut.

4" markings
on the ruler

3

4

While I tend to keep my iron set on high heat, some facing products, like Face-It Soft and Face-It Firm, react better when the iron is dialed down a notch or two.

TRIM THE 9-PATCHES
SMALL POUCH

Place a 9-patch block on your cutting mat. Position a small square ruler on top of the 9-patch, and rotate the ruler so the 3-in. markings each intersect with the block edges. Trim the first two sides of the block. **2**

Rotate the block 180 degrees and align the block's cut edges with the 3-in. markings on the ruler. Trim the remaining two sides of the block. **3**

LARGE POUCH

Follow the same steps for the 3-in. 9-patch blocks used in the small pouch to make twenty-four 4-in. 9-patch blocks for the large pouch: Place the block on the cutting mat, align a square ruler so the 4-in. markings intersect with the block edges, and trim the four sides. **4**

PIECE THE BACK PANEL

The small and large pouches are pieced together in the same way. Arrange the blocks into 6 rows of 4 blocks each. Sew the blocks into rows. Press the row seams alternately as shown **5** and set 2 rows aside for the front panels.

Sew the remaining 4 rows together to make the back panel. Furl the seams at the block intersections. The pieced back panel for the small pouch measures 10½ in. square. The pieced back panel for the large pouch measures 14½ in. square.

If you rotate the ruler and trim your 9-patch the "wrong" way, don't worry. In fact, left-handed quilters may find it easier to rotate the ruler in the opposite direction. Just trim them all the same, and you'll be in excellent shape.

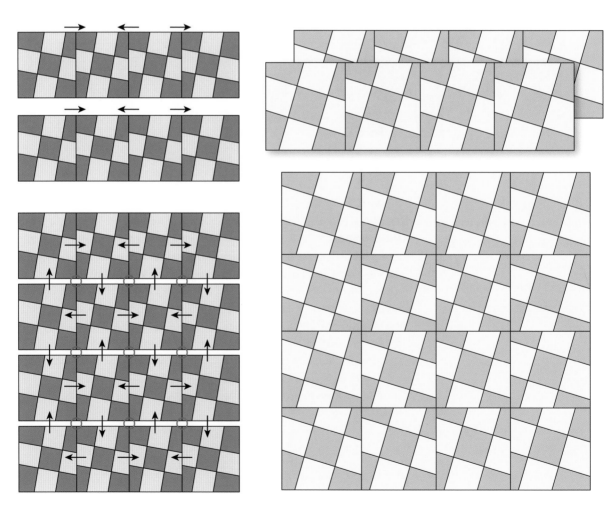

5

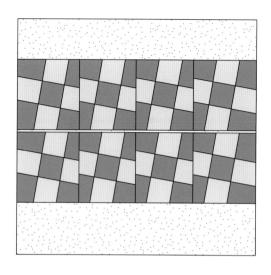

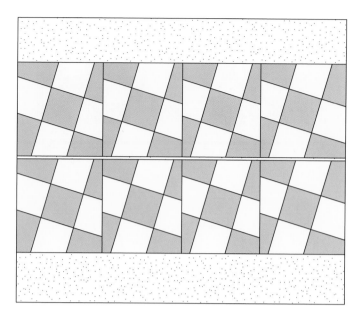

COMPLETE THE BACK PANEL

Center and fuse the 12-in. batting square for the small pouch or 16-in. batting square for the large pouch to the wrong side of the back panel. Be careful not to touch the iron to the fusible side of the batting. Layer the 10½-in. (small pouch) or 14½-in. (large pouch) faced back lining panel and the pieced back panel wrong sides together, with the pieced back panel on top. Pin-baste. Quilt as desired.

> Because of the extra layers of interfacing, consider using a walking foot and some straight-line quilting to quilt the back panel. Or use a free-motion/ darning foot with an easy, generic free-motion pattern. In either case, a fresh, extra-sharp jeans needle will help the sewing machine conquer the heavier-than-usual material thickness.

> If you aren't using fusible batting, layer the lining, batting square, and back panel. Pin-baste and quilt.

Trim the batting and backing even with the main panel. Set aside.

COMPLETE THE FRONT PANEL

SMALL POUCH

Center and align one long edge of both 3-in. by 10½-in. front panels on the 10-in. by 10½-in. batting scrap. Fuse. Be careful not to touch the iron to the fusible side of the batting. **6**

> If you aren't using single-sided fusible batting, pin-baste the front panel and batting layers together.

Quilt the two-layer sandwich as desired. Cut between the two panels and trim the batting even with the panel edges.

Select one 3-in. by 10½-in. quilted panel for the bottom panel and one for the zipper panel. Set the bottom panel aside.

Stack the zipper panel and one of the 3-in. by 10½-in. front lining panels on the cutting mat, raw edges aligned. Cut both layers in half lengthwise to make two 1½-in. by 10½-in. linings and two 1½-in. by 10½-in. zipper panels—a top zipper panel and a bottom zipper panel. Set aside. **7**

LARGE POUCH

Center and align one long edge of both 4-in. by 14½-in. front panels on the 12-in. by 14½-in. batting scrap. Fuse. Be careful not to touch the iron to the fusible side of the batting. **6**

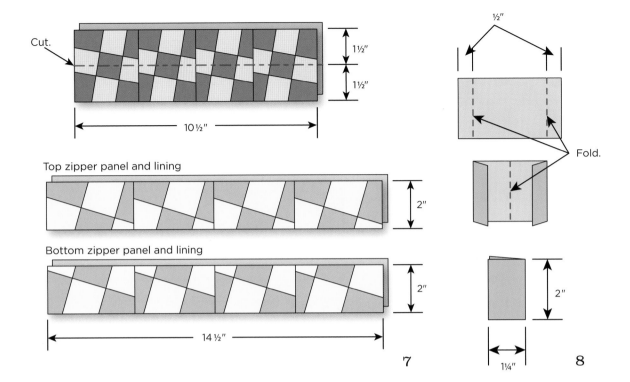

Cut.

1½"

1½"

10½"

Top zipper panel and lining

2"

Bottom zipper panel and lining

2"

14½"

7

½"

Fold.

2"

1¼"

8

Quilt the two-layer sandwich as desired. Cut between the two panels and trim the batting even with the panel edges.

Select one 4-in. by 14½-in. quilted panel for the bottom panel and one for the zipper panel. Set the bottom panel aside.

Stack the zipper panel and one of the 4-in. by 14½-in. front lining panels on the cutting mat, raw edges aligned. Cut both layers in half lengthwise to make two 2-in. by 14½-in. linings and two 2-in. by 14½-in. zipper panels—a top zipper panel and a bottom zipper panel. Set aside. **7**

PREPARE THE ZIPPER

Retrieve the zipper, move the zipper pull to the center, and trim each end of the zipper to make it 9 in. long for the small pouch and 13 in. long for the large pouch.

Warning! When you trim the zipper, you will very likely cut off all the stuff that keeps the zipper pull from sliding off either end. Keep the zipper pull safely in the center of the zipper until the fabric zipper tabs are sewn.

Zipper tabs are made the same for both sizes. Retrieve the 2-in. by 3½-in. lining fabric zipper tab strips. Make a ½-in. fold, wrong sides together, on each short end of the zipper tab strip. Press.

Fold the zipper tab strip in half, wrong sides together. Press.

Repeat to make a second zipper tab that measures 1¼ in. by 2 in. **8**

Open the zipper tab center fold and align one end of the zipper with the raw edge of the folded-under zipper tab. Refold in half and secure all the layers of the zipper tab to the zipper with pins. Repeat with the second zipper tab and the other end of the trimmed zipper. Edgestitch along the zipper tab fold as shown. **9**

Small pouch

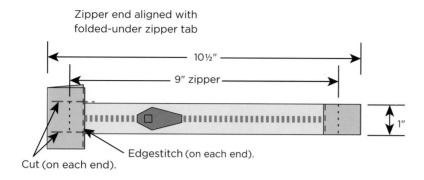

Zipper end aligned with
folded-under zipper tab

10½"

9" zipper

1"

Edgestitch (on each end).

Cut (on each end).

Large pouch

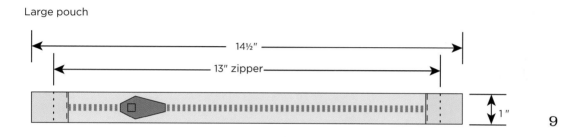

14½"

13" zipper

1"

9

Trim the zipper tab sides even with the long edge of the zipper. The zipper assembly measures approximately 1 in. by 10½ in. for the small pouch and 1 in. by 14½ in. for the large pouch.

INSTALL THE ZIPPER

SMALL POUCH

Retrieve the 1½-in. by 10½-in. top and bottom zipper panels and the 1½-in. by 10½-in. top and bottom zipper panel lining strips.

Place the top zipper panel and a zipper panel lining right sides together. Along the lower edge of the zipper panel, insert the zipper between the layers with the zipper and the zipper panel right sides together and with raw edges aligned. Secure the layers with pins

or clips. Using a zipper foot, sew a ¼-in. seam. Finger-press firmly toward the panels, and edgestitch along the fold. **10**

> Use clips or pins to secure the outer raw edge of the zipper panel while pressing and edgestitching along the fold at the zipper.

Repeat the steps to sew the opposite zipper edge between the lower zipper panel and the remaining zipper lining. Sew a ¼-in. seam. Press and edgestitch as before.

With pinking shears, pink the very bottom edge of the zipper assembly to minimize fraying. The zipper

assembly measures 3 in. by 10½ in. Set aside. **11**

LARGE POUCH

Retrieve the 2-in. by 14½-in. top and bottom zipper panels and the 2-in. by 14½-in. top and bottom zipper panel lining strips.

Place the top zipper panel and a zipper panel lining right sides together. Along the lower edge of the zipper panel, insert the zipper between the layers with the zipper and the zipper panel right sides together and with raw edges aligned. Secure the layers with pins or clips. Using a zipper foot, sew a ¼-in. seam. Finger-press firmly toward the panels, and edgestitch along the fold. **10**

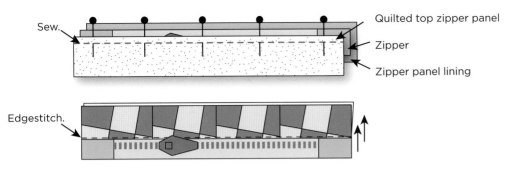

Sew.

Quilted top zipper panel

Zipper

Zipper panel lining

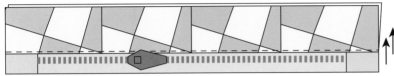

Edgestitch.

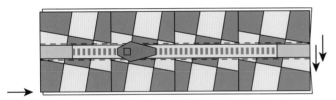

10

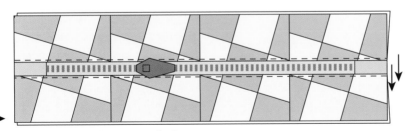

Pink all layers along the lower panel edge.

Pink all layers along the lower panel edge.

11

A double-fold binding brings all parts together to complete this pouch. However, with the stiff interfacing and vinyl in the front and back panels, creating a continuous binding using traditional binding techniques could be tricky. On p. 175 you'll find the steps to close the binding loop before it's applied to the pouch. Through the construction of either size pouch, accurate piecing and trimming are important to guarantee a "seamless" finish.

Repeat the steps to sew the opposite zipper edge between the lower zipper panel and the remaining zipper lining. Sew a 1/4-in. seam. Press and edgestitch as before.

With pinking shears, pink the very bottom edge of the zipper assembly to minimize fraying. The zipper assembly measures 4 in. by 14 1/2 in. Set aside. **11**

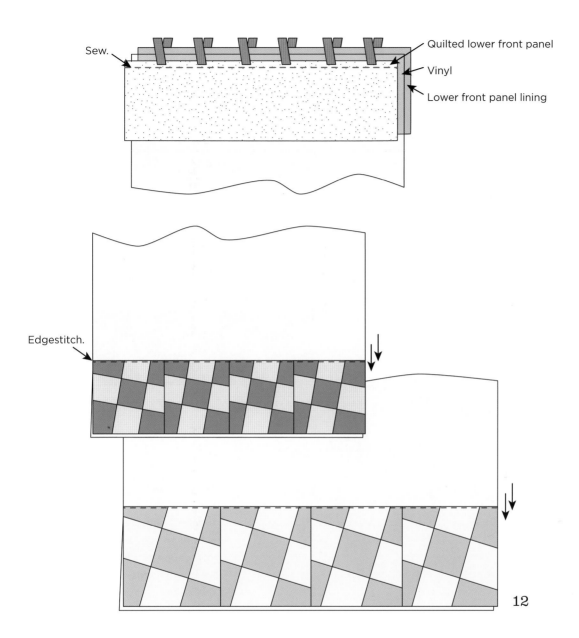

Sew.

Quilted lower front panel

Vinyl

Lower front panel lining

Edgestitch.

12

INSTALL THE VINYL
SMALL POUCH
Place the top edge of the 3-in. by 10½-in. lower front panel and the 3-in. by 10½-in. lining right sides together. Insert the vinyl between the layers with raw edges aligned.

Secure with clips. Using a walking foot, sew the vinyl between the lower front panel with a ¼-in. seam. Firmly finger-press the fold on either side of the vinyl toward the panels. Edgestitch at the fold. **12**

To avoid leaving pin holes in the vinyl, use Wonder Clips to secure the layers instead of pins.

Be careful not to touch the hot iron to the vinyl—it will melt!

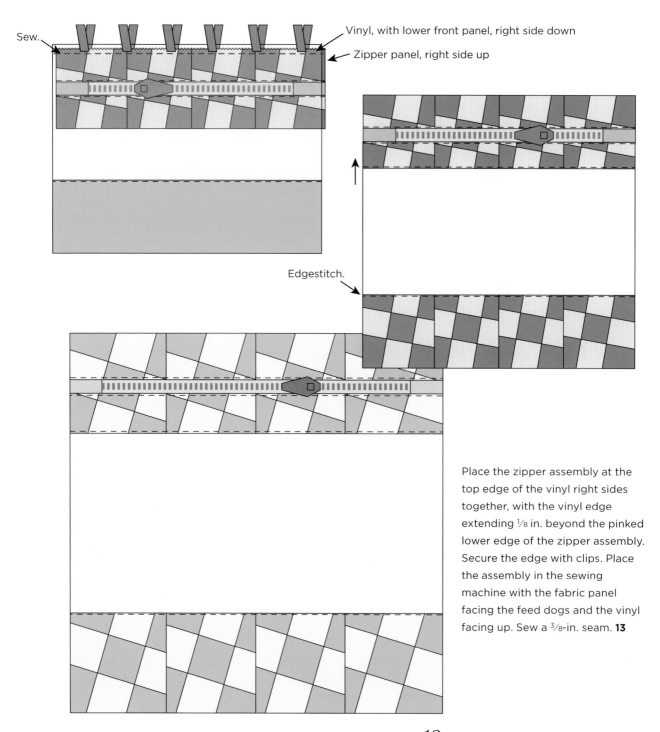

Sew.

Vinyl, with lower front panel, right side down

Zipper panel, right side up

Edgestitch.

Place the zipper assembly at the top edge of the vinyl right sides together, with the vinyl edge extending 1/8 in. beyond the pinked lower edge of the zipper assembly. Secure the edge with clips. Place the assembly in the sewing machine with the fabric panel facing the feed dogs and the vinyl facing up. Sew a 3/8-in. seam. **13**

13

Sewing vinyl can be a very sticky business because a metal foot can stick to the vinyl. Instead, try using a plastic foot. If you don't have a plastic foot, place a piece of tissue paper between the vinyl and the foot. My favorite nonstick alternative is to temporarily place a small piece of blue painter's tape on the bottom of the metal foot without interfering with the needle. One small narrow piece of tape on either side, like little blue anti-stick skis, will keep the vinyl moving right along.

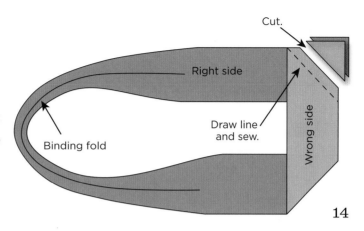

Firmly finger-press the seam toward the zipper assembly. With the fabric facing the feed dogs and the vinyl facing up, edgestitch along the fold. The front assembly measures $10\frac{1}{2}$ in. square.

LARGE POUCH

Place the top edge of the 4-in. by $14\frac{1}{2}$-in. lower front panel and the 4-in. by $14\frac{1}{2}$-in. lining right sides together. Insert the vinyl between the layers, with raw edges aligned. Secure with clips. Using a walking foot, sew the vinyl between the lower front panel with a $\frac{1}{4}$-in. seam. Firmly finger-press the fold on either side of the vinyl toward the panels. Edgestitch at the fold. **12**

Place the zipper assembly at the top edge of the vinyl right sides together, with the vinyl edge extending $\frac{1}{8}$ in. beyond the pinked lower edge of the zipper assembly.

Secure the edge with clips. Place the assembly in the sewing machine with the fabric panel facing the feed dogs and the vinyl facing up. Sew a $\frac{3}{8}$-in. seam. **13**

See the tip above for how to prevent a metal presser foot from sticking to the vinyl.

Firmly finger-press the seam toward the zipper assembly. With the fabric facing the feed dogs and the vinyl facing up, edgestitch along the fold. The front assembly measures $14\frac{1}{2}$ in. square.

BIND

Layer the back panel right side down and the front assembly right side up with raw edges aligned. Sew the binding strips together end to end using a diagonal seam as described on p. 205.

Trim the $2\frac{1}{2}$-in. binding strip to $44\frac{1}{2}$ in. long for the small pouch and $60\frac{1}{2}$ in. long for the large pouch. Press the binding strip in half lengthwise, wrong sides together.

Unfold one end of the binding and lay it flat on your worksurface, right side up. Unfold the opposite end of the binding strip and align it perpendicular to the opposite end of the strip, forming a loop. The wrong side of the strip will be facing up. Be careful not to twist the strip. Draw a diagonal line from corner to corner where the strips intersect. **14**

Pin to secure the layers and sew on the line. Trim $\frac{1}{4}$ in. away from the seam. Press the connecting seam open; then refold the binding strip. Secure the binding to the front of the pouch edge with a $\frac{1}{4}$-in. seam. Start in the middle of one side and sew one side at a time, just as you would for the binding on a large quilt. Miter the binding at the corners.

Turn the folded edge of the binding to the back of the pouch and hand-stitch it in place.

Argyle Dreams

FEATURING THE BASIC 9-PATCH AND NESTED 9-PATCH

FINISHED QUILT SIZE: **63 in. by 81 in.**
PATTERN DIFFICULTY: **Intermediate+**

Sometimes I make a quilt for the challenge, never expecting that it might become something others might like to make, too. This quilt made its public debut at the Vermont Quilt Festival in 2015. It was hanging high above the main entry hallway, not at eye level. Even so, several people approached me and asked about the pattern.

I have to confess, the quilt was inspired by a precut stack of 10-in. squares from a fabric line by my designer friend Carolyn Friedlander. The light-value background scraps and crazy scrappy border make a big impact in this quilt. Choose six fat quarters, each representing one of six distinctly different solid-reading colors for the zigs and the zags in the quilt, then go to town filling in the light-value background pieces from your scrap bins. Make sure the scrappy background fabrics contrast sharply in value from your fat quarter selections. There are too many seams in this quilt for the pieced diagonal lines to be lost in a sea of blended low-contrast background and fat quarter fabrics.

For this quilt, the ScrapTherapy Mini Scrap Grid Interfacing can be a huge time-saver and helps to ensure accuracy in the construction of the miniature 9-patch blocks. However, you don't need the grid to create this striking scrappy quilt.

SCRAPS NEEDED

Square Size	Description	Quantity Needed	Notes and Cutting Instructions
2″	Light-value scrap squares	640	• Cut 320 squares twice to make a total of 1,280 1″ squares.
5″	Light-value scrap squares	105	• Used for background.
1″	Scrap squares (for the scrappy middle border option; see p. 186)	1,476	• Cut from the leftover fat quarters and 2″, 3½″, and 5″ fabrics that coordinate with the fat quarters.

Materials	Quantity Needed	Notes and Cutting Instructions
Distinctly different solid-reading fabrics	6 fat quarters	• Label each fat quarter A through F. • From colors A and F fat quarters, cut five 1″ x 20″ strips; subcut into eighty-eight 1″ squares. • From colors B, C, D, and E fat quarters, cut seven 1″ x 20″ strips; subcut into one hundred thirty-one 1″ squares. • Reserve the extra fabric for the scrappy middle border.
Solid-reading print fabric	1½ yd.	• Cut seven 1¼″ width-of-fabric strips for the inner borders. • Cut eight 5″ width-of-fabric strips for the outer borders.
Binding	²/₃ yd.	• Cut eight 2¼″ width-of-fabric strips for the binding.
Backing	4¾ yd.	
Batting	68″ x 86″	
Contrasting fabric (for the yardage middle border option; see p. 187)	½ yd.	• Cut eight 2″ width-of-fabric strips for the non-scrappy version of the middle borders.

RECOMMENDED MATERIALS

Materials	Quantity Needed	Notes and Cutting Instructions
ScrapTherapy Mini Scrap Grid Interfacing	8 panels	• For the quilt center.
ScrapTherapy Mini Scrap Grid Interfacing	3 panels	• For the mini scrap version of the middle border.

The pattern elements made from the fat quarters are labeled with the first six letters of the alphabet, A through F, reading on the quilt from left to right. It will be helpful to label your fat quarter fabric selections similarly.

Don't get overwhelmed by cutting all the tiny scraps at once! Cut incrementally as fat quarter pieces or scrap pieces are needed.

MAKE THE MINI BLOCKS

The diagonal stripe pattern in the quilt is achieved with mini basic 9-patch blocks made from 1-in. squares, as shown on pp. 10–11. Furling the 9-patch seams will reduce bulk. Follow the charts on pp. 179–180 to make mini 9-patch blocks that measure 2 in. square in the quantities shown. The fat quarter fabric is identified by letter within each block. Follow the graphics carefully. Use a variety of light-value 1-in. scrap squares for the background of each mini block.

MINI BLOCKS

Block	1-in. Squares	Quantity
	3 A 6 background	24
	3 A 6 background	2
	3 A 2 B 4 background	2
	2 A 3 B 4 background	2
	3 B 6 background	34
	3 B 6 background	3

Block	1-in. Squares	Quantity
	3 B 2 C 4 background	2
	2 B 3 C 4 background	2
	3 C 6 background	34
	3 C 6 background	3
	3 C 2 D 4 background	2
	2 C 3 D 4 background	2

Block	1-in. Squares	Quantity
	3 D 6 background	34
	3 D 6 background	3
	3 D 2 E 4 background	2
	2 D 3 E 4 background	2
	3 E 6 background	34
	3 E 6 background	3

Block	1-in. Squares	Quantity
	3 E 2 F 4 background	2
	2 E 3 F 4 background	2
	3 F 6 background	24
	3 F 6 background	2

Consider placing mini blocks in resealable bags by color to stay organized. The "Sneaky Peek Project Pouch" on p. 162 can be put to good use for this project, especially once the miniature 9-patch blocks start becoming the larger 9-patch blocks. It gets confusing to handle stacks of miniature 9-patch blocks in six different colorways, so once you make all the blocks from one fat quarter color, refer to the charts on pp. 181–185 to make the larger blocks requiring the mini blocks in that color.

MAKE THE LARGE BLOCKS

The large 9-patch blocks are made with mini 9-patches and 2-in. background squares. Follow the charts on pp. 10–11 to make basic 9-patch blocks that measure 5 in. square as shown on p. 13. Furling the 9-patch seams as for the furled 9-patch blocks is suggested and will reduce bulk. However, the seams that are pressed toward mini 9-patch blocks may need a bit of coaxing with a light mist of water or puff of steam. The fat quarter fabric is identified by letter within each block illustration. Follow the graphics and quantities carefully. Be sure to use a variety of light-value scrap 2-in. background squares in each large 9-patch block. Each large 9-patch block measures 5 in. square.

LARGE BLOCKS

Block	2-in. Squares/Blocks	Quantity
	3 A mini blocks 6 background	4
	3 A mini blocks 6 background	2
	2 A mini blocks 2 B mini blocks 1 A/B mini block 4 background	2
	2 A mini blocks 2 B mini blocks 1 B/A mini block 4 background	2

Block	2-in. Squares/Blocks	Quantity	Block
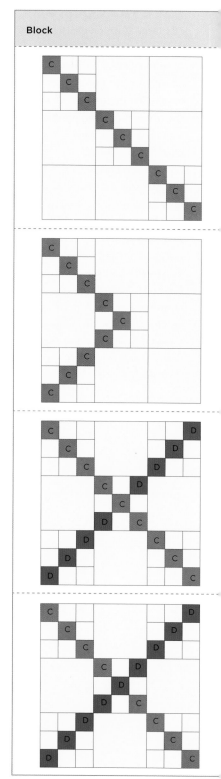	3 B mini blocks 6 background	4	
	3 B mini blocks 6 background	3	
	2 B mini blocks 2 C mini blocks 1 B/C mini block 4 background	2	
	2 B mini blocks 2 C mini blocks 1 C/B mini block 4 background	2	

2-in. Squares/Blocks	Quantity	Block	2-in. Squares/Blocks	Quantity
3 C mini blocks 6 background	4	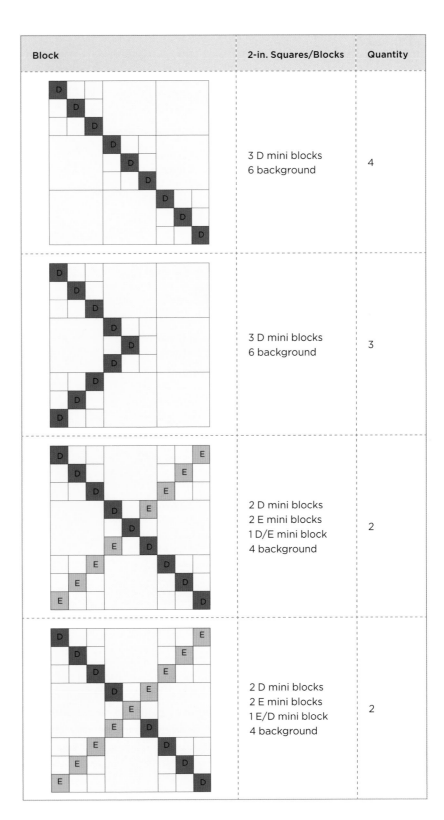	3 D mini blocks 6 background	4
3 C mini blocks 6 background	3		3 D mini blocks 6 background	3
2 C mini blocks 2 D mini blocks 1 C/D mini block 4 background	2		2 D mini blocks 2 E mini blocks 1 D/E mini block 4 background	2
2 C mini blocks 2 D mini blocks 1 D/C mini block 4 background	2		2 D mini blocks 2 E mini blocks 1 E/D mini block 4 background	2

Block	2-in. Squares/Blocks	Quantity	Block
	3 E mini blocks 6 background	4	
	3 E mini blocks 6 background	3	
	2 E mini blocks 2 F mini blocks 1 E/F mini block 4 background	2	

Arrange 5-in. background squares and large 9-patch blocks into 15 rows of 11 blocks and squares as shown on p. 188. Be careful with the block orientation, especially where pieced diagonal stripes intersect.

Sew the blocks into rows; press the seams alternately in each row. Sew the rows and press the seams to best advantage. The quilt center measures 50 in. by 68 in.

2-in. Squares/Blocks	Quantity
2 E mini blocks 2 F mini blocks 1 F/E mini block 4 background	2
3 F mini blocks 6 background	4
3 F mini blocks 6 background	2

Both sides of each row seam have alternating blocks with lots of pieced mini 9-patch elements. Some parts of the seam will press easily at your request, while other sections of the same seam may resist pressing. One option is to press the row seams open. Personally, I'm not a fan of pressing such long seams open because it increases the potential for batting to migrate through the seam over time. Pressing the seams to "best advantage" means evaluating each row seam and deciding on the pressing direction based on the path of least resistance across the entire seam. A light mist of water or a puff of steam from the iron might coax a stubborn seam into submission.

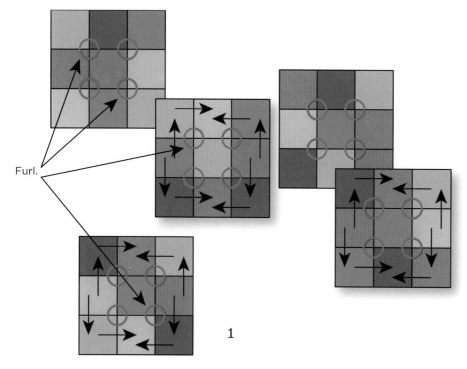

Furl.

1

MAKE THE INNER BORDERS

Sew 2 of the seven 1¼-in. inner border strips together end to end with a diagonal seam as shown on p. 205, and press the connecting seams open to make a 1¼-in. strip approximately 80 in. long. Sew 2 more strips together to make a second 80-in. border strip. Trim each strip to 1¼ in. by 68 in. for the side inner borders. Sew the remaining 3 strips together end to end with a diagonal seam, and press the seams open to make a 1¼-in. strip approximately 120 in. long. Cut two 1¼-in. by 51½-in. top and bottom borders from the 120-in. strip.

Sew the inner borders to the quilt, sides first, then top and bottom. Press the seams toward the inner border after each addition. The quilt top measures 51½ in. by 69½ in.

MAKE THE MIDDLE BORDERS

SCRAPPY OPTION

Cut the leftover fat quarter fabric into 1-in. by 20-in. strips. Fat quarters A and F should each yield at least twelve 1-in. by 20-in. strips. Fat quarters B, C, D, and E should each yield at least ten 1-in. by 20-in. strips. Cut each strip into twenty 1-in. squares for a total of nine hundred sixty 1-in. squares of the 1,476 squares needed for the middle border. Cut the remaining 516 squares from a combination of coordinating 2-in., 3½-in., and 5-in. squares from your scrap bins. For more information on cutting the ScrapTherapy-size scraps into smaller squares, review the information on p. 9.

From the varied 1-in. scrap squares, sew one hundred sixty-four

2-in. blended, furled 9-patch blocks following the steps on pp. 13–14. **1**

Sew forty-six 2-in. blended 9-patches in a row to make a 2-in. by 69½-in. scrappy side middle border. Rotate the blocks 90 degrees as they are sewn next to each other so the block seams nest; then press and furl the block seams to reduce bulk. Make 2 scrappy middle borders. **2**

Similarly, sew 36 blended 9-patches in a row to make a 2-in. by 54½-in. scrappy top middle border. Rotate the blocks, furl, and press as the blocks are sewn together. Make a second 2-in. by 54½-in. middle border with the remaining 36 blended 9-patches for the bottom of the quilt.

If you're using the Mini Scrap Grid Interfacing for the border 9-patch piecing, look for tips in the sidebar on p. 190.

Sew the scrappy middle borders to the quilt, sides first, then top and bottom. Press the seams toward the inner border after each addition. The quilt top measures 54½ in. by 72½ in.

Furl.

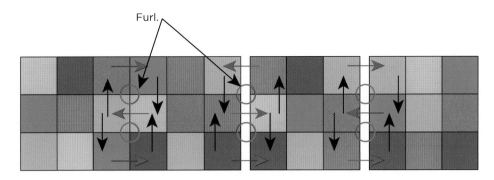

2

The scrappy middle border adds a dramatic finish to this quilt. And it's a great way to use up the rest of the fat quarter leftovers from the diagonal stripes along with some more coordinating scrap squares. But with the end in sight, no one will fault you for jumping to the yardage option for the middle border. Slap that border on and get to the finish line!

YARDAGE OPTION
Sew 2 of the eight 2-in. middle border strips together end to end with a diagonal seam as shown on p. 205, and press the connecting seams open to make a 2-in. strip approximately 80 in. long. Make four 2-in. by 80-in. middle border strips. Trim 2 of the strips to 2 in. by 69½ in. for the side middle borders, and trim the remaining 2 strips to 2 in. by 54½ in. for the top and bottom middle borders.

Sew the middle borders to the quilt, sides first, then top and bottom. Press the seams toward the middle border after each addition. The quilt top now measures 54½ in. by 72½ in.

MAKE THE OUTER BORDERS
Sew 2 of the eight 5-in. outer border strips together end to end with a diagonal seam as shown on p. 205, and press the connecting seams open to make a 5-in. strip approximately 80 in. long. Make four 5-in. by 80-in. outer border strips. Trim 2 of the strips to 5 in. by 72½ in. for the side outer borders, and trim the remaining 2 strips to 2 in. by 63½ in. for the top and bottom outer borders. **3**

Sew the outer borders to the quilt, sides first, then top and bottom. Press the seams toward the outer border after each addition. The quilt top measures 63½ in. by 81½ in.

QUILT AND BIND
Layer the backing, batting, and quilt top; baste. Quilt as desired.

Sew the binding strips together end to end using a diagonal seam. Press the connecting seams open; then press the binding in half lengthwise, wrong sides together.

Trim the batting and backing even with the quilt top. With the raw edges aligned, sew the folded binding to the front of the quilt using a ¼-in. seam. Miter the binding at the corners.

Turn the folded edge of the binding to the back of the quilt and hand-stitch it in place.

argyle dreams **187**

5"x 63½"

1¼" x 51½"

5" x 72½"

1¼" x 68"

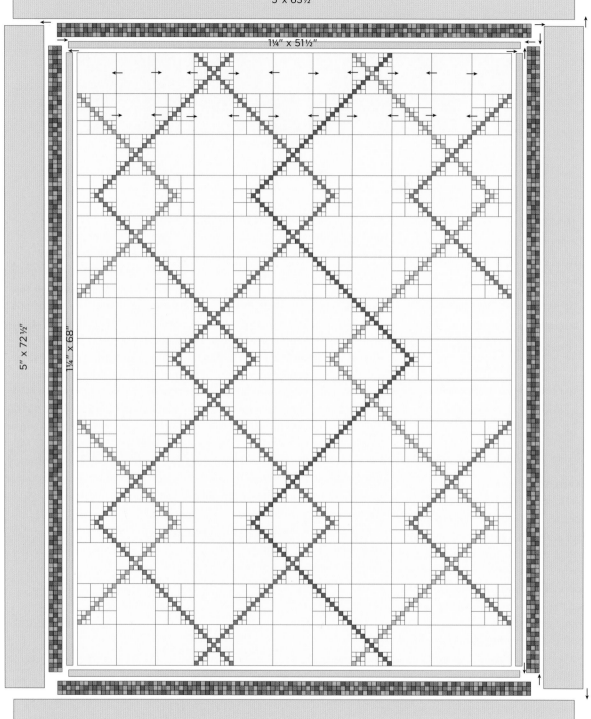

3

USING THE 9-PATCH INTERFACING

The ScrapTherapy Mini Scrap Grid Interfacing can be used to make the miniature 9-patch blocks for the quilt center and the blended miniature 9-patch blocks for the optional scrappy middle border. Follow the steps on pp. 18–24 to make furled 9-patch blocks with interfacing. Follow the charts on pp. 179–180 carefully as you arrange the scraps and 1-in. squares cut from fat quarters on the grid in the correct quantities and configuration.

Use the same process to make the blended miniature 9-patch blocks for the border. There is no need to keep track of colors in any of the 9-patch positions—just fill up the grid, then fold, sew, snip, and fold and sew again using the printed lines.

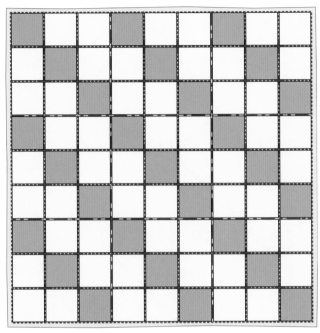

Sample quilt center grid layout

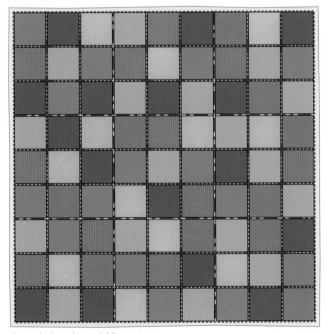

Sample border grid layout

Laptop Sleeve

FEATURING THE ELEVATED 9-PATCH

FINISHED SIZE: 11 in. by 18 in.

PATTERN DIFFICULTY: Intermediate

I travel quite a bit, and I like to bring my laptop with me to stay on top of all things online when a smaller mobile device just won't do. However, when I have to pack a big briefcase, I find more stuff that I simply "have" to bring to use up the space, even though I'm not likely to use it all.

This little case solves it all. It's just the right size to carry a 17-in. (or smaller) laptop and sturdy enough to protect it. It even has a handy zipper pouch for power cord and mouse storage.

The main player fabric for this laptop sleeve might surprise you. The intended technology contents called for something business-y on the exterior. The red and white scrappy accents encircling the case lend an air of subdued playfulness. But crack open either zipper and let the fun begin with a cheerful cherry print that inspired the whole thing. After all, technology shouldn't just be about work, right?

With all the layers of linings and exteriors, it's important to stay organized. If you are, you'll find this laptop sleeve goes together nicely.

SCRAPS NEEDED

Square Size	Description	Quantity Needed	Notes and Cutting Instructions
1½"	White scrap squares	18	• Cut from 2", 3½", or 5" scrap squares.
1½"	Black scrap squares	72	• Cut from 2", 3½", or 5" scrap squares.
3½"	Black scrap squares	9	
3½"	White scrap squares	9	• Following diagram **1** (on p. 194), draw a diagonal line from corner to corner on the back of each square for the QST units.

Materials	Quantity Needed	Notes and Cutting Instructions
Black print	1/2 yd.	• Cut one 5¼" width-of-fabric strip. • Cut one 2¼" width-of-fabric strip. • Cut one 2" width-of-fabric strip; subcut into four 2" x 3½" zipper tab strips.
White print	3/4 yd.	• Cut two 11½" width-of-fabric strips; subcut into four 11½" x 18½" lining rectangles. Fuse 3 lining rectangles with one 11½" x 18½" Face-It Soft rectangle (see below). Fuse one lining rectangle with one 11½" x 18½" Face-It Firm rectangle (see below).
Black solid	1/4 yd.	• Cut one 5" width-of-fabric strip; subcut into two 5" x 12½" rectangles. Fuse one 5" x 12½" Face-It Soft rectangle to the wrong side of each black solid rectangle (see below).
Red accent print	1/8 yd.	• Cut two 1¼" width-of-fabric strips.
Face-It Firm interfacing by Lazy Girl Designs	1 yd. (20" wide)	• Cut one 11½" x 18½" rectangle, two 6" x 18½" rectangles, and two 3" x 18½" rectangles.
Face-It Soft interfacing by Lazy Girl Designs	1 1/2 yd. (20" wide)	• Cut three 11½" x 18½" rectangles and two 5" x 12½" rectangles.
Single-sided fusible batting scraps		• Cut three 11½" x 18½" rectangles and two 3" x 4" rectangles; I used Dream Fusion by Quilters Dream.
22" zipper	2	• I used striped zippers by StudioKat Designs.

Materials	Quantity Needed	Notes and Cutting Instructions
ScrapTherapy Middle Scrap Grid Interfacing	1/2 panel	
Clover Wonder Clips		

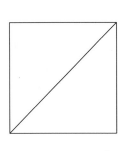

1

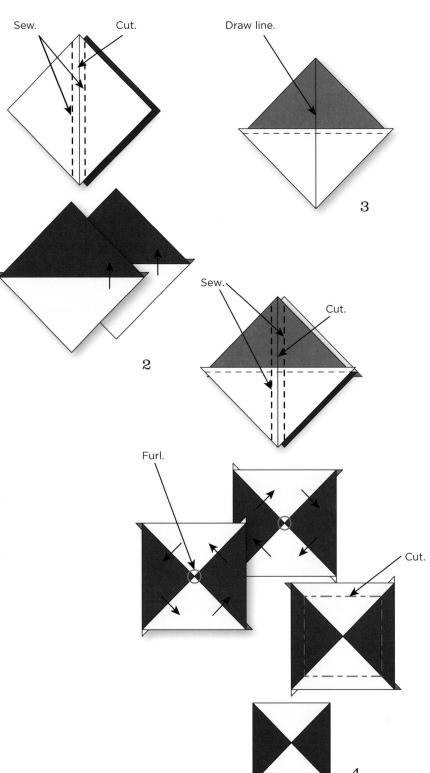

MAKE THE 9-PATCHES
QUARTER-SQUARE TRIANGLES

Place a 3$\frac{1}{2}$-in. marked white scrap square right sides together with a 3$\frac{1}{2}$-in. black scrap square with the white square on top. Sew a $\frac{1}{4}$-in. seam on both sides of the drawn line and cut apart on the line to make 2 half-square triangle (HST) units. Press the seam toward the black triangle on both units. Repeat with the remaining 3$\frac{1}{2}$-in. white and black scrap squares to make 18 HST units. **2**

On the back of 9 HST units, draw a diagonal line from corner to corner perpendicular to the existing seam. **3**

Place a marked HST unit right sides together with a second HST unit. Mix them up! Sew a $\frac{1}{4}$-in. seam on both sides of the drawn line and cut apart on the line to make 2 quarter-square triangle (QST) units. Furl the seams as shown on pp. 13–14, and trim each unit to 1$\frac{1}{2}$ in. square, centering the seam intersection. Repeat with the remaining white/black scrap HST units to make 18 QST units. **4**

USING THE 9-PATCH INTERFACING

The ScrapTherapy Middle Scrap Grid Interfacing is a perfect companion to make the 9-patch blocks for this project, even with the pieced elements within the 9-patch blocks. Follow the steps on pp. 22–25 for the furled 9-patch with interfacing, but be sure to review the following information carefully to make sure all the 9-patch seams intersect nicely. You'll need 2 sections of six 9-patches, or half of a panel, to make the twelve 9-patches needed for the accent pieces that make this project pop.

The interfacing is particularly helpful for the pieced 9-patches in this bag because it adds extra body and stability without adding additional interfacing products to the pieced elements of the external panels.

Prepare each grid section as shown on p. 18 by removing any excess interfacing around the grid edge.

Arrange the scraps to form 6 similar blocks on the first grid segment as shown on the upper left. **S1** Sew the shorter vertical seams identified with a red arrow first. Then snip, fold, nest, and oppose seams—making note of the seam-pressing direction used—and sew the horizontal seams identified with green arrows. Cut the 9-patch blocks apart and furl as shown on pp. 22–25.

Arrange the scraps on the second grid segment as shown on the lower left. **S2** Sew, snip, press, and sew as above, following the opposite pressing configuration you used to nest and oppose the seams from the first grid section, before sewing the longer horizontal rows. Cut the blocks apart and furl the seams as before.

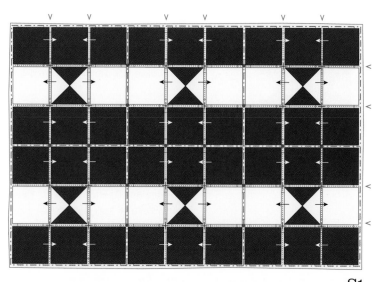

S1

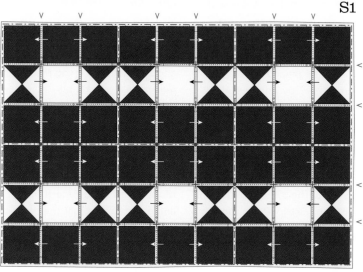

S2

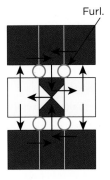

5

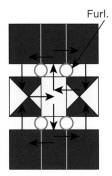

6

Select six 1½-in. black scraps, two 1½-in. white scraps, and a 1½-in. QST unit, and arrange them into a 9-patch block as shown. **5** Sew the scrap elements into rows; then sew the rows together. Press the seams as indicated.

Repeat to make six 9-patch blocks with a pieced center that measure 3½ in. square.

Select six 1½-in. black scraps, one 1½-in. white scrap, and two 1½-in. QST units, and arrange them into a 9-patch block as shown. **6** Sew the scrap elements into rows; then sew the rows together. Press the seams as indicated.

Repeat to make six 9-patch blocks with 2 pieced sides that measure 3½ in. square.

COMPLETE THE PIECED 9-PATCH ACCENT STRIP

Select, arrange, and sew three 3½-in. square 9-patch blocks with a pieced center and three 3½-in. square 9-patch blocks with 2 pieced sides as shown. **7** Furl the connecting seams. The pieced accent strip measures 3½ in. by 18½ in. Make 2 and set aside.

PREPARE THE QUILTED PANELS

Strip-piece a 1¼-in. red width-of-fabric strip to the 5¼-in. black print width-of-fabric strip. Press the seam toward the red fabric. Subcut the strip into two 6-in. by 18½-in. upper panels. **8**

Fuse a 6-in. by 18½-in. Face-It Firm rectangle to the wrong side of each upper panel.

Similarly, strip-piece a 1¼-in. red width-of-fabric strip to the 2¼-in. black print width-of-fabric strip. Press the seam toward the black print. Subcut the strip into two 3-in. by 18½-in. lower panels. **8**

Fuse a 3-in. by 18½-in. Face-It Firm rectangle to the wrong side of each lower panel.

Sew a pieced accent strip in between an upper panel and a lower panel. Press the seams toward the upper and lower panels. Make 2. Each external panel measures 11½ in. by 18½ in. **9**

Fuse an 11½-in. by 18½-in. fusible batting rectangle to the wrong side of each external panel. Quilt each panel (with batting only, not backing) as desired.

Place an 11½-in. by 18½-in. faced (with Face-It Soft) lining piece on your cutting mat, right side up. Place one quilted 11½-in. by 18½-in. external panel on top of the lining fabric, right side up with all sides aligned. Measure and cut both layers 8 in. from the bottom edge. Set aside all 4 pieces—an upper zipper panel and upper zipper lining that each measures 3½ in. by 18½ in. and a lower zipper panel and lower zipper lining that each measures 8 in. by 18½ in.—for the zipper assembly. **10**

Fuse an 11½-in. by 18½-in. fusible batting rectangle to the wrong side of the faced (with Face-It Firm) lining rectangle. Quilt the three-layer panel (lining, facing, batting) as desired to make the middle lining panel. Set aside for the final assembly.

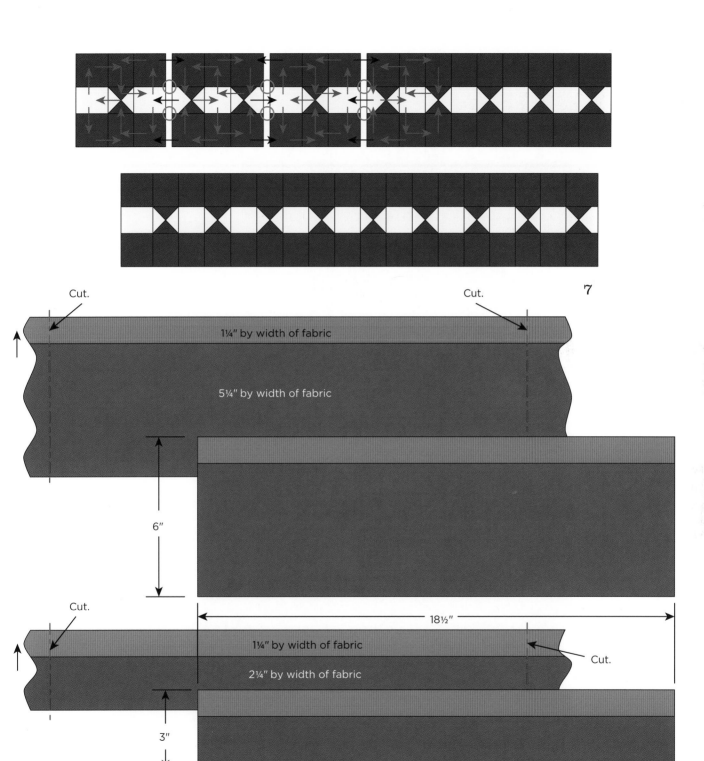

7

Cut.   Cut.

1¼" by width of fabric

5¼" by width of fabric

6"

Cut.   Cut.

18½"

1¼" by width of fabric

2¼" by width of fabric

3"

8

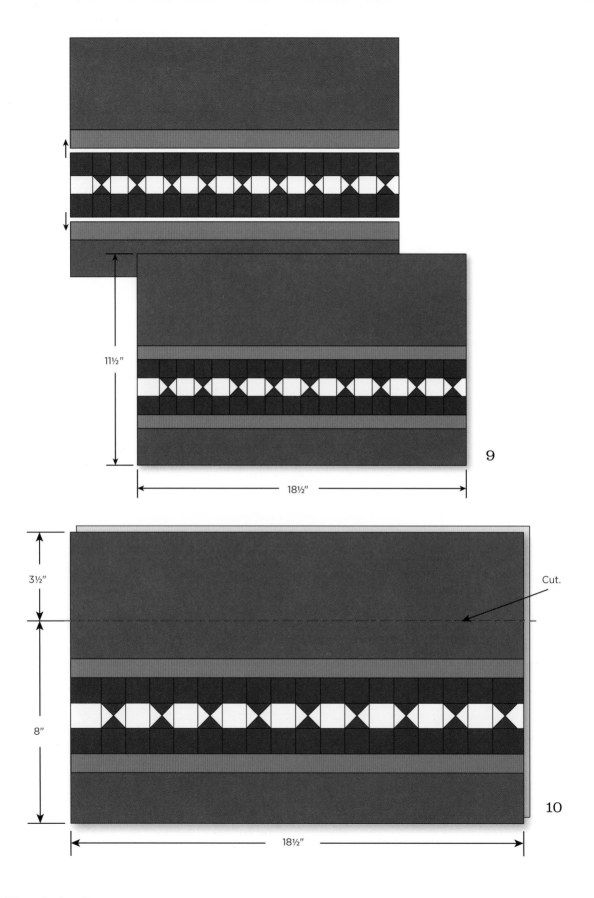

9

11½"

18½"

3½"

Cut.

8"

18½"

10

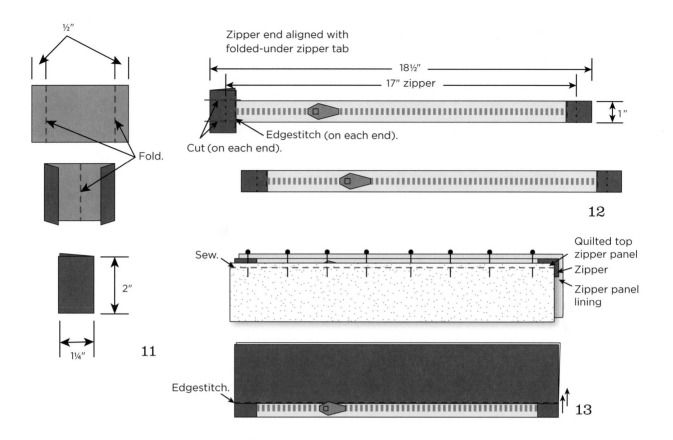

Zipper end aligned with folded-under zipper tab

18½"

17" zipper

½"

1"

Fold.

Edgestitch (on each end).

Cut (on each end).

12

Sew.

Quilted top zipper panel

Zipper

Zipper panel lining

2"

1¼"

11

Edgestitch.

13

PREPARE THE ZIPPER

Retrieve the zipper, move the zipper pull to the center, and trim each end of the zipper to make it 17 in. long.

Warning! When you trim the zipper, you will very likely cut off all the stuff that keeps the zipper pull from sliding off either end. Keep the zipper pull safely in the center of the zipper until the fabric zipper tabs are sewn.

Retrieve the 2-in. by 3½-in. zipper tab strips. Make a ½-in. fold, wrong sides together, on each short end

of the 2-in. by 3½-in. zipper tab strip. Press.

Fold the zipper tab strip in half, wrong sides together. Press.

Repeat to make 4 zipper tabs that measure 1¼ in. by 2 in. **11**

Open the zipper tab center fold and align one end of the zipper with the raw edge of the folded-under zipper tab. Refold in half and secure all the layers of the zipper tab to the zipper with pins. Repeat with the second zipper tab and the other end of the trimmed zipper. Edgestitch along the zipper tab fold as shown. Trim the zipper tab sides even with the long edge of the zipper. The zipper assembly measures approximately 1 in. by 18½ in. Make 2. **12**

INSTALL THE ZIPPERS

INSTALL THE FRONT ZIPPER

Retrieve the 3½-in. by 18½-in. upper zipper panel and lining.

Position the two zippers in the laptop sleeve so they both open and close in the same direction.

Place the upper zipper panel and upper zipper lining right sides together. Along the lower edge of the zipper panel, insert the zipper between the layers, with the zipper and the upper zipper panel right sides together and raw edges aligned. Secure the layers with pins or clips. Using a zipper foot, sew a

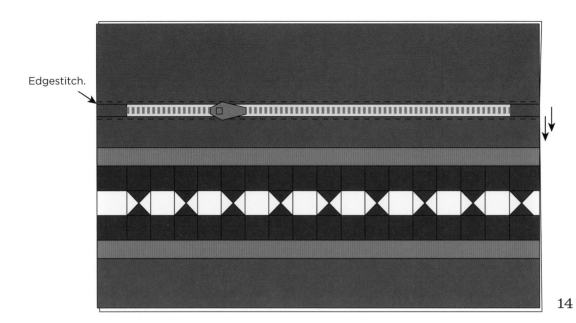

Edgestitch.

14

¼-in. seam. Finger-press firmly toward the panels, and edgestitch along the fold. **13**

> Use clips or pins to secure the outer raw edge of the zipper panel while pressing and edge-stitching along the fold at the zipper. The clips along the outer edge of the panel help to keep the hefty layers from shifting. The clips are especially nice for all kinds of bag construction because the extra layers and heavier interfacing products can really do a number on your patchwork pins. The clips hold the layers firmly and help you keep your pins straight as—well—as a pin!

Repeat these steps to sew the 8-in. by 18½-in. lower zipper panel and lining to the opposite zipper edge. Using a zipper foot, sew a ¼-in. seam. Press and edgestitch as before.

Trim the top edge of the zippered panel if needed so it measures 11½ in. by 18½ in. **14**

MAKE AND INSTALL THE HANDLES

Center two 3-in. by 4-in. batting squares on the faced side of a 5-in. by 12½-in. solid black rectangle, then position each batting rectangle 1 in. toward the outer edge of the solid black rectangle so the batting rectangles overlap 3 in. in the center, as shown in the top drawing. **15** Fold the long edges over the batting; then fold again, so the folded edges meet at the center. Pin to secure the layers.

On each end, make two diagonal folds so the raw edges meet in the center, then fold the end over the raw edges and edgestitch along the fold. Repeat with both ends of each handle.

Remove the pins and fold the handle in half lengthwise, then edgestitch along the fold, starting and stopping 2 in. from each end with a backstitch. The ends will flare out and have a squared end. **15** The handle measures approximately 11 in. long. Make 2 handles.

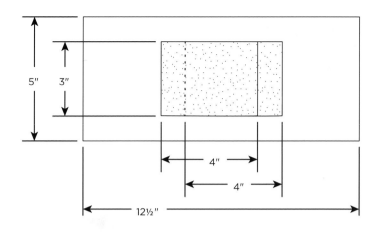

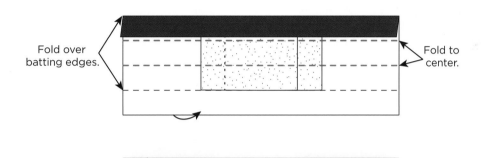

Fold over batting edges.

Fold to center.

Fold corners diagonally to center.

Edgestitch along both end folds.

Fold point toward center.

Fold center in half lengthwise.

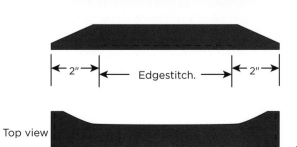

2"

Edgestitch.

2"

Top view

15

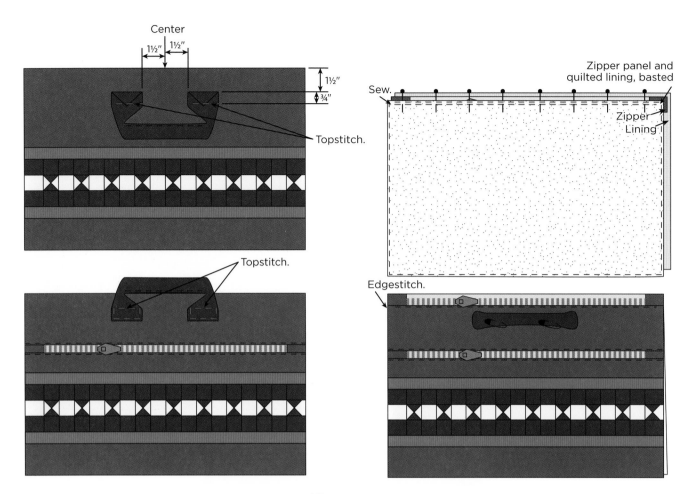

16

17

Retrieve the zipper panel and the 11½-in. by 18½-in. quilted back panel. At the top edge of each panel, measure 9¼ in. from the end to find the center. Pin each handle end, with the right side of the handle facing the right side of the panel, so the inside handle edge is 1½ in. from the top edge of the panel and 1½ in. from the center. Topstitch ¾ in. from the handle fold.

Fold the handle over itself and topstitch a ⅜-in. by 1¼-in. rectangle to secure the handle layers as shown. Repeat to install a handle on each panel. **16**

INSTALL THE TOP ZIPPER

To get the handles out of the way for the next steps, securely pin them temporarily to the interior of each panel.

Retrieve the 11½-in. by 18½-in. quilted lining and the zipper panel and place them lining sides together with all raw edges aligned. Baste around the perimeter within the ¼-in. seam allowance to make the zippered pouch panel.

Place the basted zippered pouch panel and a faced 11½-in. by 18½-in. lining piece right sides together with

the top edges aligned. Insert the zipper between the layers, with the zipper and the zippered pouch panel right sides together and with edges aligned. Secure the layers with pins or clips. Using a zipper foot, sew a ¼-in. seam, starting and stopping ½ in. from each end with a backstitch. Finger-press firmly toward the panels, and edgestitch along the fold, starting and stopping ½ in. from the ends with a backstitch. **17**

Repeat the steps above to sew the opposite zipper edge between the exterior and the remaining faced

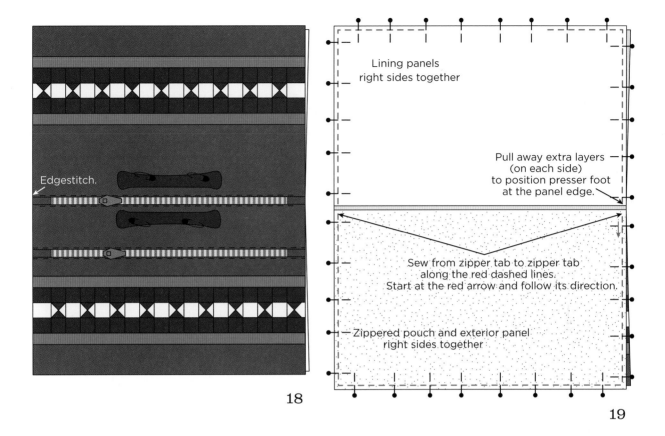

18

19

lining panel. Sew a 1/4-in. seam. Stop and start 1/2 in. away from the ends with a backstitch. Finger-press toward the panels, and edgestitch 1/2 in. away from the ends with a backstitch. **18**

These seams can be difficult because of all the bulk at the zipper tab. Carefully pull away the extra layers before inserting the layers under the presser foot. A 1/4-in. foot will be easier to use than a wider foot like an open-toe or walking foot.

COMPLETE THE LAPTOP SLEEVE

Open the zipper.

Fold the bag assembly so that both lining panels are on one side, the exterior and zippered pouch panels are on the other side, and the zipper is in the middle. Place the two exterior panels right sides together with the raw edges aligned. Pin or clip to secure around all exterior panel edges.

Starting at the top folded edge of one end of the zipper tab, sew a 1/4-in. seam along the three sides. Stop at the corner with the sewing machine needle in the needle-down position, lift the presser foot, pivot the bag assembly, and continue sewing. Finish at the zipper tab on the opposite end of the zipper.

Repeat the process with the lining panels. Align, secure with pins or clips, and sew a 1/4-in. seam, leaving an 8-in. opening in the center of the bottom edge of the lining for turning. **19**

Turn the bag right side out through the opening in the lining. Close the opening by hand or machine and position the lining inside the pouch.

APPENDIX I: QUILTMAKING BASICS

I've made a few assumptions in the process of preparing the quilt patterns and instructions for this book. Perhaps you've made a few quilts and already have a good grasp of the basics of quilt construction. In that light, you may view this section as a collection of hints that might be of interest as you create the projects specific to this book.

Many quilters know that almost every quilting technique can be done differently with the same or similar results. For example, some quilters would rather cut fabric into mathematically correct sizes before sewing, for, let's say, half-square triangle units. Some prefer to sew pieces slightly larger than needed, then trim after sewing and pressing. Some might argue that only one way is correct. Some may say that one way is better than the other. And they'd all be right, depending on the circumstances!

My advice: As a hobbyist, find the technique that makes the most sense for you. The more you quilt, the more you'll generate some favorite best practices.

So in the following pages of basic quilting tips, I'm not going to say that my way is the best way. I prefer to think that my way is, well, my way.

FABRIC

If you have fabric, thread, and batting, you have pretty much everything you need to make a quilt.

By and large, the quilts in this book are designed for cotton quilting fabrics. Can other fabrics work? Sure. But for the purposes of this book, I'd recommend 100 percent quilting-quality cotton. Use the best stuff you can afford. When you purchase high-quality quilting fabrics for your quilts, it stands to reason that you'll have that same quality in your scrap fabrics.

THREAD

Along with the fabric, I like to use 100 percent cotton thread, for the basic reason that cotton thread will age at the same rate as the cotton fabric used to make the quilt. Other options include polyester, rayon, and cotton/poly blends.

BATTING

Cotton batting, too, right? Well . . . I cannot tell a lie. My favorite batting is 100 percent washable wool. Why? It doesn't retain folds like cotton batting does. It's lighter and fluffier than cotton batting, so quilting patterns seem more dramatic. It's a dream to quilt by hand or machine. On a bed, it transitions easily from season to season, and it really is washable and dryable on light settings.

For a project that I know might get a lot of use and get washed a lot, I'll use cotton—usually an 80/20 cotton/poly blend.

ACCURACY

Accuracy in a pieced quilt top always comes down to three things: cutting, piecing, and pressing. Throughout the instructions in this collection, I have tried to provide unfinished sizes of in-process elements, so you can check to make sure your sewing is staying on track. If something is off, check that the pieces are cut accurately, that seams are not too big or too small, and that the pressing didn't create a stretched-out shape or extra folds near the seam allowance.

SEWING MACHINE

For your hobby, invest in the best sewing machine you can afford. Visit several dealers and test-drive a variety of models. When you are shopping for a new sewing machine, be sure to ask about servicing. Whether you sew a little or a lot, your machine will need regular maintenance. Your relationship with the service department at your dealer can make a huge difference in the enjoyment of your hobby.

Features to look for in a quilting machine:

- even, straight stitches, with balanced, adjustable tension
- a $\frac{1}{4}$-in. foot
- needle-up, needle-down capability
- adjustable needle position so you can move the needle to the left or to the right
- decorative stitch options, particularly zigzag and buttonhole stitches for use in machine appliqué
- if you're going to do your own quilting, an attachable or integrated walking foot and a free-motion darning foot, plus the ability to drop the feed dogs for free-motion quilting
- a large throat
- hand controls that override the foot pedal for free-motion quilting

CONNECTING STRIPS FOR BORDERS, BINDING, BAG HANDLES, AND OTHER APPLICATIONS

When connecting cross-grain strips end to end, I prefer to use a diagonal seam. A diagonal seam is stronger and less noticeable than a straight one. An exception: When connecting seams for a cross-grain border using striped fabric, I try to match the stripes using a vertical seam.

TO SEW A DIAGONAL SEAM

1. Align cut strips, right sides together, with ends perpendicular.
2. With a pencil, draw a line across the diagonal intersection.
3. Pin to secure, and sew directly on the line.
4. Trim the ends $\frac{1}{4}$ in. away from the seam.
5. Trim the point extensions.

6. Press the seams open. This is one of the few times I press seams open.

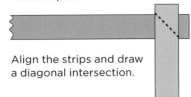

Align the strips and draw a diagonal intersection.

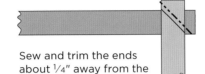

Sew and trim the ends about $\frac{1}{4}$" away from the line of stitching.

APPLIQUÉ

Beginner quilters often shy away from appliqué quilts. They're so beautiful and have so many pieces, and beginners think they must be complicated. But like anything else in quilting and in life, once you break down the steps and find the method and technique that suits you, it's all really pretty easy and can be very satisfying.

With so many appliqué methods to choose from, it's sometimes difficult to decide which to use. Because I really enjoy handwork, I often choose hand appliqué and the back-basting method when the shapes are simple with only a few deep curves or points, like Beetle Mania on p. 133. Often, I'll choose machine appliqué using fusible web if the shapes are more complex. If I want to secure appliqué pieces to the quilt after it is quilted, I'll either choose machine appliqué using fusible web or machine appliqué using fusible interfacing.

HAND APPLIQUÉ

If I had to pick only one, back basting would be my favorite method. It's extremely accurate and very relaxing to do. Once you draw the motif on the back of the background fabric, no further prep is required for the fabric used for the appliqué shapes. So this method lends itself very nicely to travel or a summer day relaxing comfortably in a favorite Adirondack chair.

1. Trace the appliqué shape in reverse onto the back of the base fabric. **A**

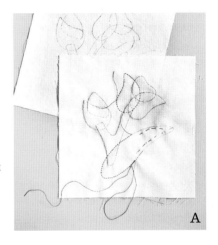

2. Cut the appliqué fabric piece slightly larger than the appliqué shape.
3. Pin the shape to the right side of the fabric, right side up, so that the appliqué fabric covers the lines plus at least a $\frac{1}{8}$-in. seam allowance, preferably a little more. Hold the fabrics to a light source to be sure all lines plus seam allowances are adequately planned.
4. From the wrong side of the background fabric, pin-baste roughly around the shape using appliqué pins.

5. From the wrong side of the background fabric, using a heavy thread (like YLI Hand Quilting Thread) in a high-contrast color, a thicker needle (I use a size 7 sharp), and a thimble if you wear one, sew a tight running stitch (about 10 stitches to the inch) directly on the line to secure the appliqué shape to the block. Don't knot the thread at the beginning or end of the running stitch, and stitch all the way around the shape.

6. From the front, trim the appliqué fabric about 1/8 in. from the running stitch. Leave the running stitch in place for at least an hour or overnight. **B**

7. Working from the front, and using an appliqué needle (size 8 or 9 sharp), a very fine cotton thread (50 or 60 weight) in a color that matches the appliqué, and a thimble if you wear one, pull out a few of the running stitches. Bend the appliqué seam allowance under, and secure the fold to the background fabric with short appliqué stitches that just catch the fold of the shape. **C** The heavier needle and thread will have left a perfora-

tion in the appliqué fabric that will allow the seam allowance to turn under exactly where you want it. And the running stitch will also have left marks in the base fabric so you can just barely see the outline of the shape.

8. Proceed around the appliqué shape, pulling out the running stitches about 1/2 in. ahead of where you are securing the appliqué.

9. Continue adding the appliqué pieces, one layer at a time, until the block is complete. **D**

MACHINE APPLIQUÉ USING FUSIBLE INTERFACING

Fusible web is a paper-backed, heat-sensitive adhesive. For fusible appliqué, you want the light, sew-through variety. Be careful—some fusible web shouldn't be used for machine sewing. The adhesive on the heavier fusibles will gum up your sewing machine. Your quilt shop should be able to help you get the right stuff.

Fusible appliqué is my method of choice when I'm under tight time constraints to finish a project. It's also great for complex shapes with

seams that won't turn under nicely. But some brands of fusible web can make your appliqué shape stiff. To avoid this, follow this little trick.

1. Using a permanent Pigma® pen, trace the appliqué shape in *reverse* onto the paper side of the fusible web.

2. Roughly trim the paper around the shape, and cut a slit in the center of the shape. Then cut away the center of the shape, about 1/4 in. away from the appliqué line.

3. With a hot iron, fuse the roughly trimmed shape to the wrong side of the appliqué fabric.

4. Trim the appliqué shape on the traced line. **E**

5. Place the appliqué shape on the background fabric and the fusible web on the appliqué facing the right side of the background fabric, arranging the shape as directed in the pattern. Remove the paper, and fuse the appliqué shape onto the background with a hot steam iron.

6. Sew around the appliqué shape with a zigzag, satin, or blanket

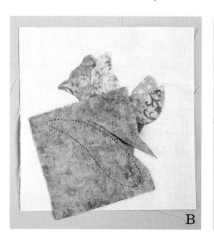
B

C

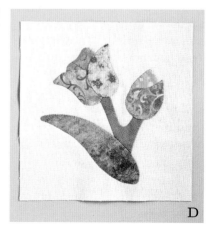
D

stitch using thread that matches the appliqué shape or thread that contrasts with the shape, depending on the look you want. Be sure to use an open-toe foot for any of these stitches.

7. For a motif that has multiple shapes, you can fuse, then stitch each shape into place or fuse all the shapes, then stitch around the entire motif.

E

ADDING BORDERS

Most of the quilt projects in this book include recommended border instructions. Some of the smaller quilts, like "Elsa's Prayer Quilt" on p. 147, could be upsized simply with an additional border of a coordinating print fabric.

To add a border to a quilt, some suggest that you measure the quilt top in three places and then average the numbers and cut your border to size—a perfectly valid theory. I prefer to skip the math and the rulers and measure the border for larger quilts using the quilt itself as the measuring device. Here's how:

1. If you're adding side borders first, take the quilt and fold it in half, so top and bottom edges are aligned.
2. Lay the folded quilt flat on a large worksurface.
3. Find a vertical seam somewhere in the center of the quilt. This will be a line-up guide for the border measurement.
4. Fold the side border, which has been roughly cut a little larger than the suggested border measurement from the pattern, in half.
5. Lay the folded border on the folded quilt, with the folds aligned and with a border edge aligned with a center vertical seam on the quilt.
6. Hold the fold in place on top of the quilt with one hand, and gently smooth the border across the quilt with the other hand, so there's no extra slack in the border fabric. Be careful not to stretch the border.
7. Cut the border even with the raw edge of the quilt. **F**
8. Repeat with the second border.
9. Open the quilt and place it right side up on your worksurface.
10. Unfold a side border, and place it along the side edge of the quilt with right sides together.
11. Pin one trimmed border strip to the quilt. Pin the ends first.
12. Then pin the center and ease the fabric in between until the entire border is pinned in place. Use lots of pins (about one pin at least every 2 in.), and remove them as needed to reposition and ease out any lumpy or stretchy spots. **G**

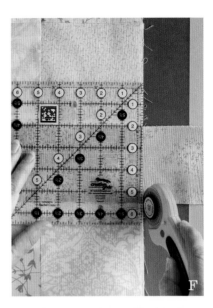

F

G

13. Move the pinned quilt to the sewing machine and sew, using a ¼-in. seam allowance to attach the border. Press the border seam following the pattern recommendation.
14. Repeat for the remaining side border and the top and bottom borders.

FIXING MISTAKES

Ta-da! It's finally done. You've been up late for the last three nights with the end in sight. Your scraps have been obliterated, or at least one or two stacks have been purged from the bins, and they are now part of your newest quilt creation.

You stand back. And there it is—a mistake! A block is sewn upside down, the color is way off, something is definitely wrong. And it's ever so obvious. Disappointed, you put the project away for a few hours and turn to another distraction. After a while, you come back to it, and there it is . . . again. This time, it's all you see and it's bugging you.

One perfectly fine solution to a mistake is to leave it alone. It's there and it's part of the quilt. If that won't work for you, here's how to make things better.

TO FIX A PIECING MISTAKE IN A COMPLETED QUILT TOP

1. Locate and mark the mistake. **H**
2. Turn the quilt wrong side up. With a seam ripper, pull out all four seams connecting the misplaced block or block element, plus at least 1 in. of the seams on adjoining sides, following the original row and block piecing configuration. This will create a square- or rectangular-shaped hole in the quilt, with adjoining seams unsewn. **I**
3. Replace or adjust the mistake in its proper position, and, with right sides together, pin one side of the corrected block into place. Sew using a $1/4$-in. seam allowance. Pull the extra quilt material out of the way; it will be awkward, but workable.
4. Sew the opposite parallel seam in place in a similar manner, using pins as needed.

5. Sew the remaining two perpendicular seams, pinning and nesting the seam intersections as necessary.
6. Press the repaired seams, first from the back, then from the front of the quilt top. **J**

APPENDIX II: QUILTING 101

MACHINE QUILTING

Once the quilt is basted, take a step back and decide on a quilting plan. When I quilt, I like to create texture. I typically start with some in-the-ditch quilting around borders or blocks. Then I spread the quilt out again and take another look before filling in with free-motion quilting. Look for secondary patterns within the play between light and dark. Decide what areas will be quilted lightly so they remain puffy and what areas will be more densely stitched to flatten them.

Consider thread color. Some quilters like to use variegated thread, while others like to create contrast. I prefer quilting with a solid-color cotton thread that blends with the main color scheme of the quilt. Truth be known, my most commonly used thread color for quilting is natural.

Position the sewing machine 2 ft. to 3 ft. from the edge of your sewing table, so some of the quilt's bulk and weight is supported on the table. Target a block or section of the quilt and remove a handful of safety pins to free up an area between 8 in. and 12 in. square. Stuff the quilt into the machine with the unpinned area under the foot. Use your fingers to form a pair of parentheses on either side of the needle and gently press outward with the palm of your hand. Gloves with rubber fingertips or palms help you maintain control on the quilt as you gently guide the quilt to create the quilting pattern.

You may jump from one block to the next, removing the pins as you go. Unlike hand quilting, as long as you were meticulous with layering the quilt sandwich and ultra-zealous with pin basting, you don't have to quilt from the center outward, as is commonly suggested. I often move from one spot to another!

STRAIGHT-LINE QUILTING USING A WALKING FOOT

- Use straight lines to define the spaces and set the stage for free-motion fill stitching.
- Find end-to-end and diagonal paths for quilting lines.
- Look beyond the blocks and create secondary patterns not necessarily obvious from the piecing alone.
- Your entire quilt may be quilted using the walking foot and straight-line quilting.

FREE-MOTION QUILTING

- If you're a novice at free-motion quilting, start with a medium-size meandering line. Practice on a small sandwich and strive for smooth lines and gentle transitions from curve to curve. Imagine you're drawing back country roads or Mickey Mouse hands as you move the fabric.
- As your meandering improves, try other patterns, or just doodle. Swirlies, bishop's fan, leaves, and feathers are some of my favorite filler patterns.

Some quilters wonder why they struggle with free-motion quilting. Here's my theory: Often the advice to the aspiring quilter is to draw the desired design on a piece of paper, which will make you feel more comfortable when you quilt it on the sewing machine. I don't agree with this. Think about it; when you draw, the paper stays in one place

GENERAL QUILTING TIPS

- Refer to the batting package for the recommended distance between quilting lines.
- Change to a darning foot and drop or cover your feed dogs. Consult your machine instruction book for details on inactivating the feed dogs.
- Quilting gloves with rubber fingertips and/or palms are helpful for holding and moving the quilt as you stitch.

and you move the pencil around with your hand. When you make the free-motion stitches with the sewing machine, the "pencil" is the needle, and it stays in one place, moving up and down making stitches. The quilt moves underneath the needle. No wonder it feels so awkward! In my mind, the best way to learn free-motion quilting is to practice: jump in and do it. Let go. Relax. Remember to breathe!

ADDING BINDING

MITERED BINDING CORNERS (90 DEGREES)

1. Pin or clip the binding to one side of the quilt, with raw edges aligned. Attach it with a ¼-in. seam, stopping the stitching ¼ in. before the corner with the needle in the needle-down position. Pivot the quilt under the presser foot 45 degrees, and sew off the edge; cut the threads. **A**

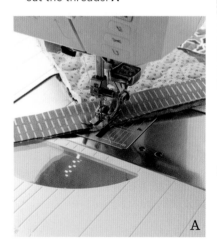

A

2. Place the quilt on a worksurface, with the sewn binding on the right and the unbound side of the quilt on the bottom. Fold the unsewn binding to the right at a 45-degree

YOU WIN!

Here's my rule of thumb for machine quilting: You and the quilt are gonna duke it out. And *you* are gonna win! Be bold! It's a pile of cotton and fluff, after all, and it squishes!

It's hard to imagine being able to stuff an entire quilt under the sewing machine arm, and you don't have to. You have to stuff only half of the quilt in there, and only while you're quilting the exact center of the quilt. Quilt one side of the project, then turn the quilt and work on the other side. As you quilt, you remove pins, and the quilt gets lighter in weight and easier to maneuver.

I've tried rolling up the quilt and throwing it over my shoulder to support it—that just didn't work for me. I prefer to loosely fold the quilt, almost like an accordion fold, and gently ease the quilt into place for quilting. I find this squishing and repositioning process allows me to move around more freely.

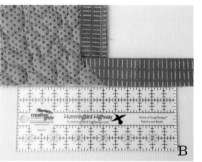

B

C

angle so the raw edge of the binding makes a straight line with the lower raw edge of the quilt. **B**

3. Fold the binding a second time so that the folded edge of the binding is aligned with the right edge of the quilt and the raw edge of the binding is aligned with the bottom edge of the quilt. Pin or clip to secure the binding in place along the lower edge of the quilt. **C**

4. Sew a ¼-in. seam to stitch the binding to the quilt. Repeat the

same mitering process at each corner.

MITERED BINDING CORNERS (GREATER THAN 90 DEGREES)

This technique also works to secure the binding to a quilt with an angle that is greater than 90 degrees.

1. Sew the binding to the right side of the quilt as before, but stop about 1 in. before the corner with the needle in the needle-down

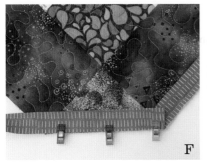

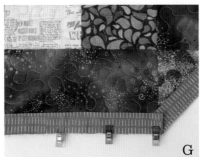

half of that is 1⅛ in.) Make two lines on the binding, each 1⅛ in. away from the fold. This calculation works for any width of double-fold binding.

3. Fold the quilt onto itself, and pin the quilt layers, creating some slack to allow you to work easily with the binding ends. **I**

4. Bring the binding end from the left above the quilt onto the work-surface and open the fold. Place the binding right side up so you can see the marking line.

position. With the quilt still in place in the machine, fold the binding toward the right, forming a straight line along the raw edge of the binding and the bottom edge of the quilt. Finger-press the binding. **D**

2. Mark the fold with a pencil. **E**

3. Continue sewing the binding along the right side of the quilt to the drawn line. Pivot the quilt under the presser foot as before and sew on the line off the edge of the quilt; cut the thread. Refold the binding to the right along the diagonal seam, then fold the binding back onto itself, with the fold at the corner and the raw edge of the binding aligned with the bottom edge of the quilt. Pin or clip to secure the layers. **F**

4. Repeat the same mitering process at each greater-than-90-degree corner. **G**

JOINING BINDING ENDS

As with many methods and techniques in quilting, several options achieve the same result. Here's how I join binding ends for a continuous binding closure.

1. After trimming the batting and backing even with the quilt top, start along one edge and sew the binding to the quilt edges, leaving about 24 in. of the binding unsewn: 12 in. at the beginning and 12 in. at the end. Place the unbound section of the quilt flat on your worksurface. Lay the binding ends evenly along the raw edge of the quilt and fold the binding back on itself so the folds meet and "kiss." **H**

2. Make two marks on the top binding layer one-half the width of the binding from the fold. (I usually cut my binding strips 2¼ in., so

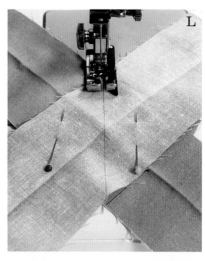

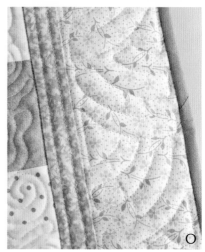

5. Open the crease, and fold the right binding end, wrong sides together, at the marking line.

6. Align the fold from the right binding with the edge of the left binding. At the same time, align the marking on the left binding with the edge of the right binding. **J**

7. Open the right binding fold, and draw a line parallel to the quilt top, from edge to edge, as shown. Secure the binding with pins on both sides of the drawn line. **K**

8. Sew on the line. **L**

9. Trim about ¼ in. away from the seam (unpin the quilt to test it first, if you like). **M**

10. Pin and sew the remaining binding to the quilt edge. **N** Notice that it's almost continuous. **O**

If you have a basket of binding end pieces from quilts past, a scrap quilt is the perfect opportunity to use them up. Connect leftover binding strips end to end, and attach the binding to the quilt like any other double-fold binding.

HAND-SEWN BINDING CORNERS

Once I've secured the binding all the way around the quilt, I like to sew the folded binding edge to the back of the quilt by hand. You can sew it by machine, but this finishing touch is one of my favorite parts of quiltmaking—almost like personal time with old friends before you are parted from them.

1. Find a comfortable chair with good lighting.
2. Place the quilt on your lap with the backing facing up.
3. Thread a needle and knot the end. Insert the thread where it will be hidden by the binding once sewn.
4. Turn the binding fold from the front to the back so it's ready to sew, and secure the fold in place with pins or clips. Secure about 18 in. of binding ahead of where you are working with pins or binding clips. Remove and advance the clips as you sew.
5. The binding stitch is similar to the appliqué stitch. Come up from the quilt, and grab just a few threads of the binding fold.
6. Insert the needle into the quilt backing, just barely behind the spot where the needle exited the binding fold.
7. Travel about ⅛ in. through the batting layer of the quilt, and come up through the backing and grab the binding fold. Keep repeating until you approach a corner.

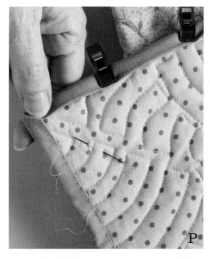

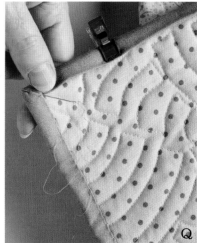

8. About 2 in. or 3 in. before the corner, park your needle in the quilt, and fold the binding from the adjacent (left) side of the quilt and tuck it underneath the binding fold to the right. **P**
9. Continue sewing to the corner intersection, then travel along the diagonal fold toward the outermost corner of the quilt and up through the fold in the binding. **Q**

10. Take one stitch through all the quilt layers to the front of the quilt, and secure the mitered fold on the front. Then pull the needle back through all layers and return to sewing the binding along the side to the next corner. **R**
11. These extra steps at the corner will keep the corners crisp over time and reduce the bulk at the corner. Notice that the binding thicknesses on the front and back oppose each other. **S**

GLOSSARY

APPLIQUÉ BLOCK
A quilt element that incorporates fabric shapes sewn onto a background fabric. Appliqué may be done by hand or by machine using a variety of techniques.

APPLIQUÉ PRESSING SHEET
A heat-inert synthetic liner placed between the iron and the fabric as a barrier; heat will pass through the liner, but fusible glue will not adhere to the sheet.

BACK BASTING
A type of hand-appliqué technique. The arrangement of appliqué shapes is drawn on the back of the main block fabric; then the pieces are placed on the front of the block in layers and basted from the back. The shapes are trimmed, and seams turned under and sewn to the background fabric from the front to complete the block.

BACKSTITCH
A backward stitch or a stitch on top of an existing stitch to keep the thread from getting loose.

BASTE
An extra-long stitch by hand or machine to hold fabrics in place for the next step in the process, such as piecing, quilting, or appliqué.

BIAS
Fabric cut on an angle, as opposed to straight of grain. Fabric cut along the bias is more stretchy than fabric cut along the lengthwise or crosswise grain. Also, the 45-degree line on an acrylic quilter's ruler.

BLANKET STITCH
A decorative stitch made by hand or machine commonly used along the edge of an appliqué shape.

CHAIN PIECING
An efficient method for sewing block elements by machine. Sew two pieces of fabric together, make a few stitches in between, and then sew the next two pieces of fabric together. The result can be a long "chain" of sewn units connected by threads in between units.

CORNERSTONE, CORNER-STONE BLOCK
A square of fabric placed between sashing strips. The square can be one piece of fabric or made from several pieces sewn into a small block used as a cornerstone.

DARNING FOOT
A sewing machine attachment used for free-motion quilting. The darning foot is often used with the sewing machine feed dogs in the lowered position, allowing fabric to move freely under the foot to make curved quilting designs.

DECORATIVE STITCH
A machine or hand stitch that is wider and more involved than basic utility stitches, such as the straight stitch.

DIRECTIONAL PRINT FABRIC
A fabric print with design elements that face one or two ways. Depending on how the fabric is placed in a project, some elements may appear upside down.

DOUBLE BACKSTITCH
A short anchoring stitch, with a repeat of a stitch on top of itself, in a series of running stitches.

DOUBLE-FOLD BINDING
A method of covering the raw edges of the finished quilt sandwich whereby a long strip of fabric is folded in half, attached to the quilt from the front with raw edges aligned, and folded and sewn to the back of the quilt, typically by hand.

DUAL FEED
An integrated sewing machine feed device available on some sewing machine models that allows several layers of fabric to advance through the sewing machine with equal pressure from the top and bottom of the fabric. The dual feed operates similarly to a walking foot.

EDGESTITCH
Sewing through a few fabric layers along the extreme rim of the piece, often to keep a folded edge compressed.

ELONGATED 9-PATCH

A 9-patch block with a square center and corners and rectangular sides.

FAT QUARTER

A quantity of fabric representing 1/2 yd. of fabric that has then been cut in half along the lengthwise grain. A fat quarter is usually 18 in. by 21 in.

FINISHED SIZE

The width and length of a block unit, block, or quilt section that excludes seam allowances.

FLANGE

An accent for a border or binding, usually made from a narrow strip of fabric folded in half lengthwise, then inserted, raw edges aligned, between two fabrics seamed together. Also a flattened border around the outer edge of a pillow.

FLYING GEESE

A block element made from one quarter-square triangle and two half-square triangles. The resulting unit is a triangle within a rectangle that resembles the V-shaped formation made by migrating geese.

4-PATCH OR 4-PATCH BLOCK

A classic quilt block pattern that is made by sewing four fabric squares of the same size into two rows of two squares each.

FREE-MOTION QUILTING

A quilting technique using a darning foot with the sewing machine feed dogs dropped below the bed. The quilt sandwich is moved under the sewing machine needle using smooth, curvy strokes to create curved stitching patterns.

FURLING

A seam-pressing method where four seams meet. The center of the seam allowance is opened, allowing the remaining four seams to be pressed to one side, rotating around the center in a clockwise or counterclockwise direction.

FUSIBLE INTERFACING

A lightweight fabric similar to a stabilizer that has heat-sensitive glue. The interfacing may be printed with shapes for appliqué or piecing or may be unprinted. The interfacing may also be made with woven or nonwoven fabric.

FUSIBLE WEB

A heat-sensitive fabric adhesive that usually comes with a paper backing on one or both sides. Used for techniques like appliqué to adhere two pieces of fabric together without adding any additional fabric like interfacing.

HALF-SQUARE TRIANGLE

The right isosceles triangle that results from cutting a square in half diagonally.

HALF-SQUARE TRIANGLE UNIT

The resulting square unit made from sewing two half-square triangles together.

IN-THE-DITCH

Straight-line sewing to topstitch or quilt directly along the seamline.

LENGTH OF GRAIN

The direction along the selvage as fabric comes off the bolt. Also called lengthwise grain.

9-PATCH OR 9-PATCH BLOCK

A classic quilt block pattern that is made by sewing nine fabric squares into three rows of three blocks each.

9-PATCH CENTER

The fabric element in the middle of a 9-patch block.

9-PATCH CORNER

The fabric element in each of the four outer corners of a 9-patch block.

9-PATCH SIDE

The fabric element in the middle of each outer edge of a 9-patch block.

ON-POINT SET

Blocks that have been arranged into a quilt in diagonal rows using setting triangles along the edge of the quilt or quilt center.

PIECED BLOCK

A section of a quilt made entirely from fabric that has been cut into geometric shapes sewn together using 1/4-in. seams. A quilt is usually made with several blocks sewn together in rows.

PINWHEEL OR PINWHEEL BLOCK

A classic quilt block pattern that is made by sewing four half-square triangle units so the triangle points meet in the center and the colors alternate within the units. The block resembles a child's pinwheel toy.

POSTAGE STAMP
A quilt or section of a quilt made entirely by piecing squares that are the same size but not necessarily the same color or value.

PRAIRIE POINTS
A finishing technique that incorporates squares that are folded in half twice. The raw edge of the folded triangle is incorporated in the seam, creating a jagged-edge appearance on the finished quilt. Prairie points may also be incorporated as a border embellishment.

QUARTER-SQUARE TRIANGLE
The resulting right isosceles triangles from cutting a square in half along both diagonals.

QUARTER-SQUARE TRIANGLE UNIT
The resulting square unit made from sewing four quarter-square triangles together.

RUNNING STITCH
Equally spaced stitches made by rocking a threaded needle from front to back through one or more fabric layers. May be decorative as for quilting or embroidery or functional as for joining fabric pieces or making ruffles.

SASHING
Rectangular strips commonly placed between blocks in a quilt.

SATIN STITCH
A decorative stitch made by hand or machine commonly used along the edge of an appliqué shape. Also a zigzag stitch with a narrow stitch length.

SEAM ALLOWANCE
The area between the stitching line and the raw edge of the fabric when two pieces are sewn together. Seam allowances are typically pressed to one side or pressed open to create a flat finished product.

SETTING TRIANGLE
Half-square and quarter-square triangles that complete the straight edges of a quilt when the blocks are set and sewn on-point or in rows that are at a 45-degree angle. Typically quarter-square triangles are used along the sides and half-square triangles on the corners. The triangles keep the less-stretchy straight of grain along the outside or border edge of the quilt.

STRAIGHT SET
Blocks that have been arranged into a quilt in horizontal and vertical rows.

STRIP PIECING
A time-saving piecing technique of sewing two width-of-fabric strips together, which are then typically cross-cut into smaller sizes.

TACK STITCH OR BAR TACK STITCH
A satin or zigzag stitch with no stitch length. It can be used at the edge of a seam opening to keep the seam from opening farther.

TOPSTITCH
Sewing through a few fabric layers, often to hold a fold compressed or to keep fabric from curling with use.

UNFINISHED SIZE
The width and length of a block unit, block, or quilt section that includes seam allowances, often provided at various checkpoints in a pattern to make sure piecing and seam allowances are accurate.

VALUE
The relative intensity or absence of color.

WALKING OR EVEN-FEED FOOT
A sewing machine attachment that works in conjunction with the feed dogs to advance the fabric from the top and bottom. Used for straight-line quilting or sewing through multiple layers of fabric.

WIDTH-OF-FABRIC OR WIDTH-OF-GRAIN
The crosswise, selvage-to-selvage direction as the fabric comes off the bolt. Quilting cotton fabrics are typically between 40 in. and 42 in. wide off the bolt.

ZIGZAG STITCH
A decorative stitch made by hand or machine commonly used along the edge of an appliqué shape. A zigzag stitch is also used to reinforce a raw fabric edge.

RESOURCES

Visit these websites for additional information about products or events mentioned in this book.

SCRAPTHERAPY
For Mini, Middle, and Little Scrap Grid Interfacing products, the latest tutorials and ScrapTherapy patterns, and to subscribe to "Good Migrations" eNews
www.hummingbird-highway.com

CLOVER NEEDLECRAFT
Wonder Clips, sewing notions
www.clover-usa.com

CREATIVE GRIDS
Rulers
www.creativegridsusa.com

HOBBS BONDED FIBERS
Batting
www.hobbsbatting.com

IRIS
6-quart modular boxes
www.irisusainc.com

LAZY GIRL DESIGNS
Face-It Soft and Face-It Firm interfacing products
www.lazygirldesigns.com

OLFA
Rotary cutters and mats
www.olfa.com/quilt-and-craft/

QUILT WITH MARCI BAKER
Qtools Cutting Edge
www.quiltwithmarcibaker.com

QUILTERS DREAM
Dream Fusion fusible batting
www.quiltersdreambatting.com

QUILTSMART, INC.
ZigZapps! Circles and other printed fusible interfacing products
www.quiltsmart.com

RELIABLE CORPORATION
Velocity Iron
www.reliablecorporation.com

STUDIOKAT DESIGNS
Novelty zippers for bags and apparel
www.studiokatdesigns.com

YLI
Hand Quilting Thread
www.ylicorp.com

METRIC EQUIVALENTS

One inch equals approximately 2.54 centimeters.

To convert inches to centimeters, multiply the figure in inches by 2.54 and round off to the nearest half centimeter, or use the chart below, in which figures are rounded off (1 centimeter equals 10 millimeters).

1/8 in. = 3 mm	4 in. = 10 cm	16 in. = 40.5 cm
1/4 in. = 6 mm	5 in. = 12.5 cm	18 in. = 45.5 cm
3/8 in. = 1 cm	6 in. = 15 cm	20 in. = 51 cm
1/2 in. = 1.3 cm	7 in. = 18 cm	21 in. = 53.5 cm
5/8 in. = 1.5 cm	8 in. = 20.5 cm	22 in. = 56 cm
3/4 in. = 2 cm	9 in. = 23 cm	24 in. = 61 cm
7/8 in. = 2.2 cm	10 in. = 25.5 cm	25 in. = 63.5 cm
1 in. = 2.5 cm	12 in. = 30.5 cm	36 in. = 92 cm
2 in. = 5 cm	14 in. = 35.5 cm	45 in. = 114.5 cm
3 in. = 7.5 cm	15 in. = 38 cm	60 in. = 152 cm

INDEX

A

Accuracy, 37–38, 204
Appliqué, 205–7
  appliqué block, 214
  hand appliqué, 205–6
  machine appliqué, 206–7
Appliqué pressing sheet, 19, 214

B

Back basting, 214
Backing, 39
Backstitch, 214
  double backstitch, 214
Bag, pouch, and sleeve projects
  Cross-Body Market Sack, 11, 27, 40,
    110–24
  Laptop Sleeve, 26, 27, 191–203
  Sneaky Peek Project Pouch, 162–75,
    180
Bar tack stitch, 216
Basic 9-patch and projects, 4
  Argyle Dreams, 5, 11, 25, 32, 176–90
  Beetle Mania, 11, 16, 27, 133–39, 205
  Bolster Pillow, 125–32
  Cross-Body Market Sack, 11, 27, 40,
    110–24
  Daisy Fresh Runner, 11, 62–68
  Mix 'n' Match Mug Mats, 92–99
Baste
  back basting, 214
  definition and technique, 214
  layering and basting, 39–40
  pin-basting, 39–40
Batting
  connecting strips and avoiding
    bumpy seams, 123
  pressing seams open and migration
    of, 14, 185
  types to buy, 204
Bias, 214
Bias binding, 40, 124
Binding
  connecting strips for, 205
  cross-grain binding, 40, 205
  double-fold binding, 172, 214
  end pieces, idea for using, 212
  hand-sewn corners, 213
  joining binding ends, 211–12
  mitering corners, 40, 138, 210–11
  preparing quilt for, 40
  techniques for adding, 210–11
Blanket stitch, 214

Blended 9-patch blocks, 11–12, 63,
  65–67, 72, 84, 186, 190
Borders
  connecting strips for, 205
  pieced borders, 66
  postage stamp, 65, 67
  tips for adding, 207
  using borders or sashing to upsize
    a block, 9

C

Chain piecing, 37, 214
Circles and circle-cutting tool, 128
Color
  choosing for projects, 5
  light-colored markings on dark
    blocks, 103
  "muddy" blocks, selecting colors to
    avoid, 69
  pressing configurations and
    decisions, 12–14
  small scraps, color selection for, 9,
    82
  sorting by value, 33–34
  strip-piecing technique, 15
  theme for a quilt and choosing,
    34–36
  traditional 9-patch variations, 10–12
  value, 5, 9, 10–12, 33–34, 216
Cornerstone/cornerstone block, 214
Cross-grain binding, 40, 205
Cutting mat, 31

D

Darning foot, 40, 169, 209, 214
Decorative stitch, 214
Diagonal seams, 40, 205
Dot design, 11
Double backstitch, 214
Double-fold binding, 172, 214
Dual feed, 214

E

Edgestitch, 214
Elevated 9-patch and projects, 4, 7
  Citrus Coverlet, 26, 27, 140–46
  Elsa's Prayer Quilt, 2, 147–61
  Laptop Sleeve, 26, 27, 191–203
  Mix 'n' Match Mug Mats, 92–99
  Moody Blue, 44–53
Elongated (rectangular) 9-patch, 10,
  215
Even-feed (walking) foot, 40, 169,
  209, 216

F

Fabric
  directional print fabric, 214
  fat quarters, 30, 215
  length-of-grain, 215
  print fabrics tips, 9, 34
  storage of, 30
  storage of fabric themes, 35
  types to buy, 204
  width-of-fabric/width-of-grain, 216
  yardage and instructions for
    projects, 5
  See also Color; Scrap fabric and
    squares
Fat quarters, 30, 215
Feed dogs, 209
Flange, 215
Flying geese, 25, 72–73, 215
4-patch/4-patch block
  design of, 215
  furling seams of, 13, 50
  scraps for making, 3–4
  starting out as first quilt block, 3
Free-motion quilting, 40, 169, 209–10,
  215
Furling
  definition and technique, 13–14, 215
  4-patch units, 13, 50
  "innies" and "outies," 13–14, 21–22, 23
  interfacing and, 23–24
  9-patch units, 13–14, 23–24, 27
  purpose of and when to use, 25,
    129, 136
Fusible interfacing and web, 37, 215

G

Gadgets and tools, 31, 36–37
Grid interfacing. *See* 9-patch grid
  interfacing

H

Half-square triangle, 38, 215
Hand quilting, 40
Hidden 9-patch and project, 5, 7
  Fiesta! 25, 32, 69–78

I

"Innies" and "outies," 13–14, 21–22, 23
Interfacing
  fusible interfacing and web, 37, 215
  iron temperature for, 167
  printed circle interfacing, 59
  See also 9-patch grid interfacing

In-the-ditch quilting, 14, 130, 209, 215
Irish chain design, 11, 63
Iron
   cleaning sole plate, 19
   temperature of for interfacing, 214
   using pressing sheet with, 19, 214

L

Labels, 40–41
Layering and basting, 39–40
Length-of-grain/lengthwise grain, 215
Line and diagonal line design, 11
Little Scrap Grid Interfacing
   development and purpose of, 17–18
   instructions for using, 25–27
   phrase for staying on track to skip
      every third set of lines, 26
   size of blocks made with, 18, 25
   use in projects, 85, 94, 99, 114, 146

M

Machine quilting, 39–40, 209–10
Middle Scrap Grid Interfacing
   development and purpose of, 17–18
   instructions for using, 25–27
   phrase for staying on track to skip
      every third set of lines, 26
   size of blocks made with, 18, 25
   use in projects, 67, 78, 94, 99, 114,
      129, 195
Mini Scrap Grid Interfacing
   development and purpose of, 17–18
   instructions for using, 18–25
   size of blocks made with, 18
   use in projects, 67, 186, 190
Mistakes, tips for fixing, 208
Mitering corners, 40, 138, 210–11

N

Nested 9-patch and projects, 4, 7
   Argyle Dreams, 5, 11, 25, 32, 176–90
   Button Collection Pillow, 25, 54–61
   Daisy Fresh Runner, 11, 62–68
9-patch/9-patch block
   design of, 3, 7, 215
   options for using and designs that
      use, 3
   parts and pieces, 7–8, 215
   rectangular (elongated) elements,
      10, 215
   scraps for making, 3–4
   strip-piecing technique, 15, 216
   test block, 36
   traditional variations, 10–12

trimming block elements, 38
truing up finished blocks, 37–38
9-patch center, 7–8, 215
9-patch corner, 7–8, 215
9-patch grid interfacing
   body and stability from, 4, 166
   development and purpose of, 4,
      17–18
   interfacing seams and, 23–24
   phrase for staying on track to skip
      every third set of lines, 26
   repositioning scraps on, 19, 26
   size of blocks made with, 18, 25
   See also Little Scrap Grid
      Interfacing; Middle Scrap Grid
      Interfacing; Mini Scrap Grid
      Interfacing
9-patch side, 7–8, 215

O

On-point set, 215
Os and Xs design, 11
Outies and innies, 13–14, 21–22, 23

P

Photos of quilt and label, 41
Piecing
   accuracy of, 37–38, 204
   adjustments with seam allowance,
      37–38, 66
   chain piecing, 37, 214
   pieced block, 215
   pieced borders, 66
   strip-piecing technique, 15, 216
Pillow projects
   Bolster Pillow, 125–32
   Button Collection Pillow, 25, 54–61
Pin-basting, 39–40
Pinwheel/pinwheel block, 215
Postage stamp quilt or section, 11–12,
   63, 65–67, 101, 216
Pouch and sleeve projects
   Laptop Sleeve, 26, 27, 191–203
   Sneaky Peek Project Pouch, 162–75,
      180
Prairie points, 89–90, 216
Pressing
   to best advantage, 185
   directions and configurations, 5,
      12–14, 21–22, 23
   seams, pressing open, 14, 130, 185
   stubborn seams, 130

troubleshooting finished blocks,
   37–38
   See also Furling
Pressing sheet, 19, 214

Q

Qtools Cutting Edge and Sewing
   Edge, 31
Quarter-square triangles and units,
   216
Quilting
   in-the-ditch, 14, 130, 209, 215
   free-motion quilting, 40, 169,
      209–10, 215
   machine quilting, 209–10
   squishing and folding quilt under
      sewing machine arm, 210
   thread color choices, 209
   tied quilts, 40
Quilt projects
   Argyle Dreams, 5, 11, 25, 32, 176–90
   Beetle Mania, 11, 16, 27, 133–39, 205
   Citrus Coverlet, 26, 27, 140–46
   Elsa's Prayer Quilt, 2, 147–61
   Fiesta! 25, 32, 69–78
   Moody Blue, 44–53
   Split the Check Quilt, 100–109
Quilts
   labels for, 40–41
   photos of, 41
   techniques and methods for
      making, choosing what makes
      sense, 37, 204
   theme for a scrap quilt, 34–36

R

Rectangular (elongated) 9-patch, 10,
   215
Rotary cutter and blade, 31
Rotating cutting mat, 31
Ruler
   palming the ruler, 33
   trimming tools, 36, 38
   type to buy, 31
   vinyl strips for marking cutting line,
      31, 32
Running stitch, 216

S

Sandwiching, 39
Sashing, 216
   using borders or sashing to upsize
      a block, 9

Satin stitch, 216
Scrap fabric and squares
    cutting squares and tips for cutting,
        30–33
    definition of scrap fabric, 30
    number of squares made from a
        scrap, 9
    sizes of squares, 3–4, 31–32
    small scraps, color selection for, 9,
        82
    sorting, 33–34
    storage of, 31, 32
    theme for a quilt, 34–36
    unused scrap fabrics and
        development of patterns,
        29–30
Seam allowance
    consistency and accuracy of, 9, 37,
        38, 204
    definition and size of, 5, 37, 216
    pieced border or block adjustments
        with, 37–38, 66
Seams
    accuracy of, 37, 38, 204
    connecting batting strips and
        avoiding bumpy seams, 123
    diagonal seams, 40, 205
    pressing directions and
        configurations, 5, 12–14, 21–22,
        23
    pressing open, 14, 130, 185
    pressing stubborn, 130
    pressing to best advantage, 185
    snipping through thread at, 21, 23,
        27
    test seam, 38
    troubleshooting finished blocks,
        37–38
    See also Furling
Setting triangles, 216
Sewing machine
    buying tip and features to look for,
        204–5
    dual feed, 40, 214
    maintenance of, 204
    squishing and folding quilt under
        sewing machine arm, 210

Sewing machine attachments
    darning foot, 40, 169, 209, 214
    walking/even-feed food, 40, 169,
        209, 216
Size of scraps and blocks
    chart of 9-patch sizes and size of
        squares to create them, 8, 9
    finished size, 8–9, 215
    grid interfacing sizes, 18
    number of scrap squares made
        from a scrap, 9
    rectangular 9-patch block
        elements, 10
    unfinished size, 8–9, 216
    using borders or sashing to upsize
        a block, 9
Sleeve project. See Pouch and sleeve
    projects
Storage bins, 31, 32
Straight set, 216
Strip-piecing technique, 15, 216

T
Table runner and mat projects
    Daisy Fresh Runner, 11, 62–68
    Mix 'n' Match Mug Mats, 92–99
    Pomegranate Rose Table Topper,
        79–91
Tack stitch, 216
Test block, 36
Theme for a scrap quilt, 34–36
Thread, 204
Tied quilts, 40
Tools and gadgets, 31, 36–37
Topstitch, 216
Transformed 9-patch and projects,
    4, 7
    Elsa's Prayer Quilt, 2, 147–61
    Mix 'n' Match Mug Mats, 92–99
    Pomegranate Rose Table Topper,
        79–91
    Sneaky Peek Project Pouch, 162–75,
        180
    Split the Check Quilt, 100–109
Trimming block elements, 38
Trimming tools, 36, 38
Truing up finished blocks, 37–38

V
Value, color, 216
Vinyl, 173–75

W
Walking foot, 40, 169, 209, 216
Width-of-fabric/width-of-grain, 216

X
Xs and Os design, 11

Z
Zigzag stitch, 216
Zippers
    clips or pins to secure edges, 120,
        171, 174, 200, 202–3
    preparing and installing for a bag,
        pouch, and sleeve projects,
        119–21, 170–72, 199–200
    preparing and installing for a pillow,
        131–32
    trimming to length, 119, 131, 170, 199